BOOKS ABOUT AFRICA
AVAILABLE FROM WAVELAND PRESS, INC.

THE BARABAIG
East African Cattle-herders
George J. Klima

CASTING OUT ANGER
Religion among the Taita of Kenya
Grace Gredys Harris

CHILDREN OF THEIR FATHERS
Growing up among the Ngoni of Malawi
Margaret Read

THE DINKA OF THE SUDAN
Francis Mading Deng

GOOD COMPANY
A Study of Nyakyusa Age-villages
Monica Wilson

ITINERANT TOWNSMEN
Friendship and Social Order in Urban Uganda
David Jacobson

KAFR EL-ELOW
Continuity and Change in an Egyptian Community
Second Edition
Hani Fakhouri

THE KAGURU
A Matrilineal People of East Africa
T.O. Beidelman

AFRICA AND AFRICANS

Third Edition

Paul Bohannan
Professor Emeritus, University of Southern California

Philip Curtin
The Johns Hopkins University

Prospect Heights, Illinois

For information about this book, write or call:

Waveland Press, Inc.
P.O. Box 400
Prospect Heights, Illinois 60070
(312) 634-0081

The line illustrations for this book were prepared by the
Graphic Arts Division of The American Museum of Natural
History.

A few passages from *African History,* by Philip D. Curtin,
published by the Service Center for Teachers of History of
the American Historical Association in 1964, are reprinted
with the kind permission of the American Historical Association.

ISBN   0-88133-347-6

Printed in the United States of America

7   6   5   4   3   2

CONTENTS

LIST OF MAPS

Part One

AFRICAN BACKGROUND

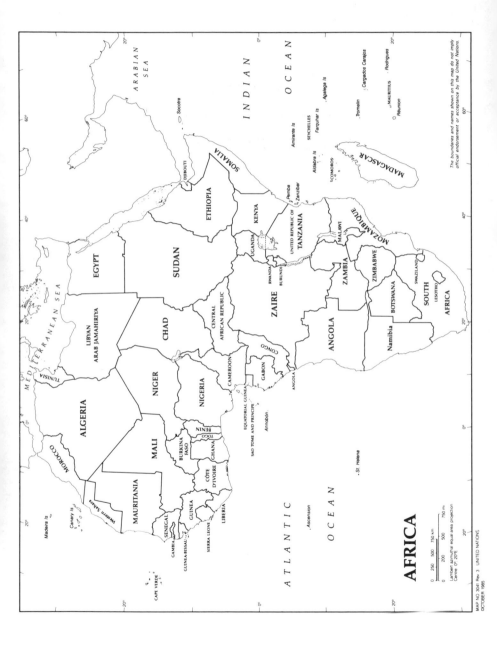

Figure 1. Africa in 1985.

Chapter One

THE MYTH AND THE FACT

FOR EUROPEANS AND NORTH AMERICANS, AFRICA has been seen for centuries through a web of myth so pervasive and so glib that understanding has to come through two stages. First, the myth itself has to be studied so that it can be stripped away to expose the reality hidden behind it. In the sense of the old aphorism, "It's not what we don't know that's dangerous, it's what we do know that's not true." Only then can we undertake the second state: seeing what is in fact there.

Africa has a curious place in the world-outlook of the Western people. It was known as the "Dark Continent," but the darkness was our own ignorance. Europeans learned about Africa late. They knew a great deal about the geography of most other parts of the world before explorers began the systematic penetration of Africa in the nineteenth century. During the colonial era—for tropical Africa, roughly 1880 to 1960—Europeans who went to govern Africa or do business there learned a great deal more than they had ever known before. This new familiarity percolated down to the rest of the population as well. British and French school children learned about their great missionaries like David Livingstone or Cardinal Lavigérie, their military leaders like Kitchener or Archinard.

3

But Americans were spared this sense of familiarity with "colonial history"—the history of Europeans in Africa. Few Americans went to Africa. Until the 1950s, American diplomats went only to the few independent countries like Liberia or Ethiopia. Elsewhere the United States had only a few consulates, attached to their embassies in the European capitals; the State Department dealt with Africa as a minor aspect of European affairs.

By the late 1950s, that all began to change rapidly. In America, the post-war concern with what was to be the "third world," came to include Africa as well as Asia and Latin America. African Studies Programs emerged at several universities. The politics, economics, and history of the continent joined the study of African culture, already begun by anthropologists. In North American universities before the mid-1950s, African history was taught only as a part of "Negro history" in a few pre-dominantly-black colleges. By the mid-1980s, African history had become a recognized part of historical knowledge. African art and African culture are prominent in American museums. The continuing importance of the African heritage in shaping American popular music from jazz to rock came to be recognized as never before. Along with the civil rights movement and the imminent independence of most of tropical Africa, Afro-Americans began to be interested in their African heritage. Hundreds of Afro-Americans went to Africa each year as tourists to see for themselves the land of their ancestors.

But, in spite of the new and more systematic search for knowledge about Africa, the old myths lived on and new myths joined them. Part of the problem comes from the way the news media report African affairs. A newspaper editor, or the editor of a TV news program, has to make difficult choices. Information flows in from all over the world. Only so much can be printed or aired. From the American perspective, the important foreign news comes from Western Europe and Japan, from China and the Soviet Union, with an occasional crisis drawing periodic concern to other areas—to Southeast Asia in the 1960s, to both Central America the Middle East in the early 1980s, or to the festering struggle over apartheid in South Africa from the mid-1970s onward. The rest of Africa makes the news only when an especially troublesome event draws attention to it—often negative attention.

Over the past thirty years, ordinary newspaper readers/TV viewers would have been conscious of the Congo crisis beginning in 1960, which led to the creation of an independent Zaïre. They would have read occasionally about the military coups and the general failure of newly independent African states to keep the democratic institutions put into place at the hour of independence. The worse the failure, the more lurid the reporting. In the 1970s, spectacular tyrants like Idi Amin in Uganda or "Emperor" Jean Bedel Bokassa of the Central African Empire got more space and air time than the spectacular but peaceful economic progress and comparative freedom of an Ivory Coast or Cameroon.

Natural as well as human disasters claimed their share of attention. The great sahelian drought of the early 1970s stretched across Africa from Senegal to the Sudan and Ethiopia. In 1973 alone, more than 100,000 people died of starvation and disease brought on by malnutrition. A decade later, drought returned. This time to Ethiopia, the Sudan, and south as far as Zimbabwe and South Africa—with dramatic starvation in Ethiopia. Again, the disaster attracted press and TV coverage. Internationally-famous rock stars attracted still more attention in their efforts to raise money for the victims.

Such spectacular events left the old myths in place. Some of the oldest and most pervasive myths are the simplest. In the popular mind, Africa was associated with lions, and lions with jungles. In fact, only about five per cent of the African landmass can be classified as "jungle"—if jungle means rain forest. And for centuries, Africans have been clearing undergrowth in the rain forest to cultivate crops in the shade of the larger trees. During the past half-century, the forest belts have been among the most rapidly developing regions in Africa, and the destruction of the remaining rain forest is one of the most pressing threats to the environment.

For that matter, lions never did live in the rain forest, but in the open grasslands. They and the other animal life of the open savanna of Kenya and Tanzania have attracted tens of thousands of tourists from overseas. They appeared weekly in the TV nature series, and from time to time in spectacular films like *Out of Africa.* Neither the nature films nor Karen Blixen's picture of settler life in Kenya are inaccurate. They tell what they want to tell very well, but they tell next to nothing about the life of ordinary African people. What they do tell helps to reinforce the old view of Africa as the place on earth that most abounds with wild animals. The North American public now knows a lot about those animals, but none of that knowledge helps to dispel the older and more deeply ingrained myth of Africa as a savage continent. An accurate picture of animal life high on the slopes of Mount Kilimanjaro can easily coexist with the cartoon image of the missionary in the cannibal stew pot—itself part of the myth of savage Africa.

That myth has been around in Western thought since the seventeenth and eighteenth centuries. Even then, it was not created out of European observations in Africa itself, but out of philosophical necessity. If, in the European view, "we," the Europeans, had the one true religion and the one true civilization in the world, then someone else, somewhere must represent the other extreme—the non-civilized. Savagery could be located almost anywhere the European knew little about, but Africa was a favorite place.

The savagery the Europeans imagined at the opposite pole from themselves could be seen as good or as evil. It could represent people with only the most rudimentary technical knowledge—people without fire, virtually without language, who practiced unspeakable cruelties on one another, of which cannibalism was the most excusable because it allowed some, at least, to survive. None of this picture was ever true of Africa. The European encounter with cannibalism came from the Caribbean and the South Pacific, not from Africa. Non-agricultural hunter and gathering societies were very few in Africa before Columbus. They were far more common in the Americas or in Australasia. Africa was far more skilled in metallurgy than either Australia or the Americas. Most African societies were fully within the iron age when Europeans first made contact with them. And they continued to make iron and steel for several centuries after contact, in spite of competition from European imports.

Yet another root of the myth of the savage Africa in Western thought was the existence of a European trade in slaves from Africa. The fact that most of the slaves shipped to European-dominated plantations in the Americas were from Africa was one of the sources of negative racist attitudes. The need to justify the trade as compatible with Christian morality was another source of the savage myth. After all, the myth said, taking people away from such savagery was a step up, even if that step took them into a life of slavery for themselves and for their descendents.

Later on, as the slave trade began to taper off and Christian missionaries appeared in Africa, the missionaries helped to keep the myth of savagery alive. The more "savage" a place, the greater the missionaries' mundane as well as supermundane rewards. Their undeniable fortitude, and the hardships they bore, were translated into the imagery of "savagery" by home congregations and missionary societies. This was so, even when the missionaries did not literally depict a savage Africa—and many were level-headed observers who did not. They knew better, as their papers show: yet the image they cast before them was that of heroes doing battle with cannibalism, lust, and depravity—the forces of "darkness."

The myth of a savage Africa lives on today just as racism in the United States lives on today in spite the Civil Rights revolution of the 1950s and 1960s. Like racism, it tends to take subtle forms. One of these is the use of terms like "tribe" and "tribalism" in the news media. They use the term "tribalism" to analyze African affairs, but not for other parts of the world. In fact, the term became common in European writing about Africa only in the nineteenth century. In the era of the slave trade, Europeans usually talked about different African "nations," but the rise of European racism and cultural arrogance was accompanied by a shift to "tribe."

The image even includes the opposite myth: the "noble savage" also lived on—though with no more basis in empirical reality. Just as the Europeans needed a bad example overseas—however imaginary—as a measure of their own attainments, they also needed a good example to measure their own short-comings. The image of people overseas who, however unenlightened, yet had a natural nobility, served that purpose. It could take several different forms. As the Europeans struggled with the problems of a complex and increasingly technical society, it was useful to imagine other people who were free to practice the simple virtues born of innocence, closer to nature, and somehow free of the incessant struggle for power and domination that marked European class and international relations. For such people, the Christian virtues of faith, hope, and charity were said to come easy.

Various forms of this image turn up in Western literature about Africa and Africans. Perhaps the most famous of all is the contrast between the natural innocence and Christian virtues of the slaves like Eliza and Uncle Tom in *Uncle Tom's Cabin*; in contrast to the moral failings of the drivers and planters who had the benefit of the full Christian message, yet failed to measure up to its demands. And a similar myth is still alive. Only a few years ago, Alex Haley's *Roots* portrayed an eighteenth-century African society on the banks of the Gambia River, apparently innocent of the evils of the slave trade. There, the people went about unarmed, and the European slavers filled their ships by kidnapping. In fact, the Gambians were themselves sellers of slaves, and they were heavily armed. The Gambia River had been an artery of the trade for more than three hundred years. In the eighteenth century, the present-day rural village of Jufure, the home town of Haley's hero, Kunta Kinte, was a thriving center of that trade. The Kinte family have been traders by tradition and were no doubt involved in the slave trade themselves. One can only guess that Haley wanted to show the innocence of the Africans as a literary device to highlight the crimes of the European slavery and planters—much as Harriet Beecher Stowe had done more than a century earlier. But it nevertheless reinforced an ancient myth about "savage" peoples.

Nor are all uses of that myth favorable to the image of Africans. Only a few years after *Roots* appeared as a television spectacular, a similar picture of innocence with more obvious political intent appeared in the South African movie, *The Gods Must be Crazy*. There, the San people of the Kalahari (whom the movie called bushmen, though the word has fallen out of use in academic circles) were shown leading an innocent but good life, in tune with nature, but so far removed from understanding of the modern world that they could not even recognize a coca-cola bottle. The implication was clear: such people are better off under the benevolent guidance of an *apartheid* regime than they would be trying to face the modern world on their own.

Either version of the myth of a savage Africa neglects the fundamental fact that European and African cultures and social organization have a great deal in common, developed over a very long run of history. They have more in common, for example, than either does with the cultures of Eastern Asia or with North American Indians or Australian aborigines. Agricultural techniques and traditions belong to a single cultural sphere. Market organization was also similar. Religions were variations on the same basic themes. Family organization reflects pretty much the same values, even though Africans tended to be polygynous and Europeans claimed to be monogamous. The same kind of similarities are not found among the Chinese or the Aztecs. In much the same way, Europeans and Africans share a common set of diseases and immunities to disease, that others, like the American Indians or the peoples of the Pacific, lacked. As we shall see, this deep similarity was to become one of the fundamental reasons why the Americas came to be occupied today by descendents of Africans and Europeans.

Among the other myths, one of the most generalized and difficult to tear away is the matter of race. This is especially true for Americans, both black and white, since we live in a society that is extremely conscious of race. But Europe too was a racist society from the nineteenth century onward, and is now increasingly troubled by racial conflict, growing out of the great immigration from overseas after the 1950s. There as well, color or physical appearance have far too often carried social implications.

This book is about all of sub-Saharan Africa because the cultures and the histories of sub-Saharan societies have much in common. Many commentators in the past have associated this common experience with a common race. But all sub-Saharan Africans do not belong to a single race, even if comparatively recent arrivals like the European-derived minorities of Zimbabwe and South Africa are left out of account.

We have to go back to the beginning and recognize that no such thing as an unmixed race exists, that no scientifically viable measures exist for defining a similar group of people as a "race," a "sub-race," or any other fixed grouping. For geneticists, the word "race" means an interbreeding population with distinct and heritable characteristics. The trouble comes in trying to define those characteristics. In ordinary usage, the characteristics are simply the visible, physical appearance, but there is no scientific reason for "counting" the shape of a person's nose and not his or her hæmoglobin characteristics or proclivity for heart disease. As an everyday badge of racial identification, North Americans recognize as "black," "Negro," or "Afro-American," anyone with any apparent degree of African descent, measured by skin color, facial configuration, hair texture, and so on. But this is a socially-conditioned definition of race. Geneticists estimate that about 25 percent of the gene pool circulating within the Afro-American community is European, more specifically from the British Isles. This means that more of the ancestors of the "typical" Afro-American come from Britain and Ireland than from any particular region of Africa.

Just as our assessment of race is socially conditioned, so is the Africans'. Westerners in the past tended to believe that cultural characteristics like language were heritable, not learned, and language was sometimes used as a part of racial classifications. When Africans think of social groups or racial groups, they too tend to include a lot of learned characteristics as criteria for membership. Thus, even the most stereotypically African-appearing of Afro-Americans cannot easily "pass" for African in West Africa. Africans will almost universally classify them as "European," from the way they walk, talk, and carry themselves.

Even when they use physical traits as a guide, Africans tend to see one set of traits, while Americans and Europeans see another. They see "racial" differences within Africa that we, as outsiders, are not conscious of. Sometimes this recognition is no more significant than the ability to guess a stranger's nationality in Europe— whether Swede or Italian, Pole or Spanish. At others, recognizable physical appearance marks ancient social divisions between superiors and inferiors. Even though

Rwanda and Burundi in central Africa each has a common, Bantu language and a common culture, the physical difference between the Tutsi, the former masters, and the Hutu, the former subordinates is usually clear even to outsiders. Or, on the Kenya coast, nearly everyone is conscious of the difference between the physical type of the socially dominant Afro-Arabs, of the descendents of former slaves from the region of Malawi, and of the up-country Kikuyu and Luo who now hold many government posts — to say nothing of the Wazungu, or European tourists whose spending helps to support the economy. Similar differences in physical type go along with important social distinctions in Ethiopia.

The point is that the racial myth — the belief that physical type is a guide to inherent ability or cultural characteristics — is completely exploded. What remains, however, is the fact that physical appearance can and does still serve to demarcate certain social groupings, in the same way a learned accent helps to identify the social class of an Englishman to other Englishmen.

In North America, the African cultural heritage and African racial heritage have mixed in a very complex way. We tend to think of the United States as settled mainly by Europeans, which is true; but our common myth fails to distinguish the timing of the European arrival. The median date for the arrival of our African ancestors of Afro-Americans — the date by which half had arrived and half were still to come — is remarkably early, about 1780. The similar median date for the arrival of our European ancestors was remarkably late — about the 1890s. It was not until the 1840s that more Europeans than Africans crossed the Atlantic each year.

This early arrival of our African ancestors has had important consequences. Anthropologists used to write a good deal about the survival of "Africanisms" in Afro-American culture. They were right, but they sometimes failed to point out that these Africanisms were aspects of African culture—not a physical inheritance. They came with the African immigrants through the slave trade; they remained strongest within the Afro-American community, but many also became a part of American culture at large, first in the South and then to the rest of the country. Afro-American cooking, for example, has many traits from Africa; but gumbos with their African-derived okra are now part of a much broader tradition of "southern" cooking, partly traceable to Africa, partly not. African music made an enormous and formative contribution to the creation of jazz and its successors in popular American music, which in turn has done as much as any other tradition to set the tone of popular music throughout the world. Just as Afro-Americans share a racial inheritance from the British Isles with Euro-Americans, all Americans share a cultural inheritance from Africa.

One of the most difficult and persistent sources of myth about Africa comes from a blind-spot in American thinking about the rest of the world. This is caused by the long-term rivalry between the United States and the Soviet Union, which has dominated world international relations since 1945. Far too many American political leaders see Africa only as a group of small countries that can help or hinder the greater rivalry with the Soviets. To see the world as polarized in this way has been a disastrous error of more than one American foreign policy. It stands in the way of any real understanding of how the world came to be as it is, and the ways in which it may well change. It sees African nations either "with us" or "against us." We may see the world that way, and the

Soviets may as well; but Africans do not. Africans are not principally concerned with big-power rivalries. They are not for or against Russia or America, they are *for Africa,* sometimes defined in their own minds as only their own country, or even for their own group within it. If we are "for Africa" defined this way, they are for us, and if we are against Africa, they are against us.

Western courting of African countries to keep them out of the clutches of the "Communists" has risen and fallen with changing administrations in Washington. The Reagan years were peculiarly blind to the fact that regimes labelled "Marxist" were not by that token simply captives of the Soviet Union. Nor were regimes that found it to their interest to support the United States, like Mobutu's Zaire, genuine friends of democracy as we understand it. In the past thirty years many African governments have "changed sides," as Egypt switched from Russia to American support in 1972, Ethiopia changed from American to Soviet support in 1974, or Somalia changed from Soviet to American support in 1975. Several African governments have adopted names like the People's Republic of Benin, or the People's Republic of the Congo, but this does not mean that they have "gone Communist" in the sense of modelling their institutions on those of the Soviet Union, or joining the Warsaw Pact. Nor have others that claim to be friends of the United States "gone Western" in the sense of instituting genuine democracy. African countries are not, cannot be, concerned with the struggles of the titans in world affairs. They have enough trouble trying to assure economic development of their own countries and the welfare of their own people.

One last point must be made clearly—although it is easier to do today than it was a few years ago. The West does not so much have an African problem as Africa has a European problem. The white South Africans talk about a "native problem," but it is they who are the troublesome minority in an African country. Elsewhere the settlers from Europe have tended to make the best of African rule, and few African governments have been more than temporarily anti-European. Yet all African societies live in the shadow of a broader European culture (including in this context both the Americas and the Soviet Union).

Even before the period of colonial conquests, the West in this broader sense began trying to extend its cultural influence into the rest of the world. Christianity was and is an expanding, proselytizing religion. Perhaps more important, nearly simultaneously with its overseas conquests, the West discovered the power of industrial technology, which made it possible for people to produce and consume material goods on a scale completely unprecedented in the world's earlier history.

The rest of the world, including Africa, very much wants to have control of this technology for its own purposes. Once they see how rich others have become, they are no longer content to be poor. They may actually be better off than they were before the colonial era, but the contrast between their relative poverty and the wealth elsewhere automatically makes them deprived. Africans, in their pre-colonial life, were not a deprived people. Lives of tremendous dignity and valued rewards can be lived without the trappings of Western civilization, but once the material possibilities are known, a new day has arrived. And this relative deprivation is not simply in contrast to Europe, North America, and Japan; Africans are also conscious of what has happened in recently industrializing countries like Korea, Taiwan, and

Riverside Bathing, Kisangni, Zaire.

Singapore. They see other people becoming comparatively rich without becoming completely Westernized. And Africans do not want to *become* European in their culture; they want to keep what they value in their old way of life, but the path is beset with difficult choices, with most outcomes too difficult to predict.

We think our task in this book is to present briefly and as accurately as we can the facts about African society past and present. We know that we must, necessarily, be affected by the needs and myths of our own times—but we also hope to be among the first ones to correct whatever distortions appear as time passes, as more research is done, and as we all live longer and learn more.

Chapter Two

THE AFRICAN CONTINENT

AFRICA IS A PART OF THE WORLD ABOUT WHICH AMERicans and Europeans can no longer afford to be ignorant. Realization is fast developing that to understand its present, one must understand something of the ecological environment, the history of the pre-colonial period that is sometimes called "traditional" Africa, the history of colonial Africa, the momentous events of the independence movements, and the quarter-century since most of tropical Africa gained its independence. One must also consider something of the cultural values and outlook with which Africans view the world, and something of African achievements and aspirations.

SIZE, SHAPE, AND GEOLOGICAL COMPOSITION
OF THE AFRICAN CONTINENT

Perhaps the most staggering aspect of Africa is its sheer size, and its cultural and geographical diversity within a greater similarity. It is 5200 miles from Tangiers to Capetown—approximately the same distance as that from Panama City to Anchorage, Alaska. It is 4600 miles from Dakar to Cape Guardafui, the easternmost point of the African horn—only 65 miles less than the airline distance from New York to Moscow. Africa is a big place—over three times the size of the continental United States.

The African continent is a vast plateau: only 10 percent of its land area lies at less than five hundred feet above sea level, compared to 54 percent for Europe and 25 percent for North America. The African continental plateau is a vast shield of ancient hard rock. Except for a few incursions of the sea, it has been a land area since Pre-

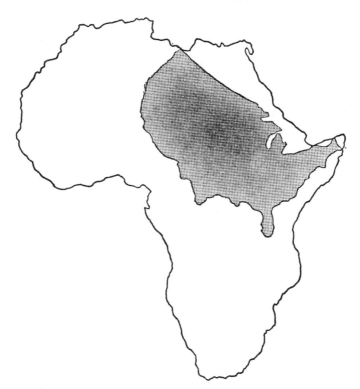

Figure 2. Africa, with the United States superimposed.

Cambrian times—for more than five hundred million years, give or take a few million. The entire continent has been raised and lowered at various times in geological history; but only in the extreme north and south has there been any building up of great folded mountains similar to the Rockies or the Caucasus. Rather, the main form of land movement has been the faulting that produced the Red Sea and the Great Rift Valley that is filled with Africa's Great Lakes.

Geologically, the whole of the Arabian peninsula must be considered as unitary with the African continent. The Rift Valley that cuts through the whole begins in Anatolia, in northern Turkey, stretches through what is now the Jordan Valley and the Dead Sea; it then follows down the length of the Red Sea (which is best thought of as an inland lake with a small opening into the Indian Ocean), and down through Lake Rudolf. At the south of Lake Rudolf, the rift divides and spreads out around Lake Victoria, but joins again at the head of Lake Nyasa, runs down the Shire River and the Zambezi, and finally out to sea, where it continues as a valley in the ocean floor. It extends through more than seventy degrees of latitude—almost one-fifth of the way around the world—and contains some of the deepest lakes on earth.

Because Africa is a great and ancient plateau, it is also a land of swells and basins: the rivers and the basins of Africa are more prominent in African geography—and, indeed, in recent African history—than is the case with any other continent. The vast basins of the Niger, the Nile, the Volta, the Zambezi, and the Congo empty into the sea, but those surrounding Lake Chad and the wastes of the Kalahari have no such outlets. The entire basin-dented plateau falls off, in steep escarpments, to the narrow coastal plain that surrounds the entire continent. The Niger-Benue and Zambezi-Shire, alone among the major rivers of Africa, do not somewhere plunge in falls and rapids over the scarps, making effective navigation from the sea an impossibility.

CLIMATES AND VEGETATION

If we oversimplify, Africa can be divided into five major physical and vegetational zones. At each end of the continent, and occupying only a small portion of its surface, there are equable Mediterranean and Mediterranean-type climates and vegetations. Coming inland, there are vast desiccated deserts and arid plains. Coming still closer to the equator are the wide savanna regions, covered with grass and widely spaced trees. Then along the equator there are humid and forested lands. Finally there are highland areas throughout the continent which respond to natural forces that override the climatic effects of latitude and of rainfall.

The humid forested lands straddle the equator in the Congo Basin and appear again in the coastal areas of western Africa that have the highest rainfall. Many of the most densely wooded areas take the form of gallery forests along streams and, at certain altitudes, surrounding the high hills. The forests vary from one extreme of dark tropical rain forest that might, with some justification, be called jungle; here little undergrowth can survive because the sun never seeps through to give the smaller plants light. At the other extreme, there are wooded areas open enough that they can be distinguished from savanna only by scientific criteria. Between the two extremes are many types of woodland.

North and south of the humid zone lies the savanna. The savanna lands occupy by far the greatest number of square miles of Africa's surface. Their landscape is typically made up of rolling stretches of tall grasses, with intermittent bush and scattered trees. The inland valleys are broad and usually have gentle slopes at their sides, merging over large areas with the plateaus. Only where the streams descend rapidly over the scarps from the highland areas is that pattern broken.

Figure 3. Climatic regions of Africa: (1) tropical rain forest; (2) tropical savanna and summer rain; (3) low-latitude dry climates; (4) undifferentiated highlands; (5) Mediterranean.

Going farther from the equator in both directions, the dry lands of Africa are encountered. In the south is the Kalahari Desert, and in the north, the Sahara and the deserts along the coasts of the Red Sea and Somalia. They

are marked by drought-resistant shrubs and a scant cover
of grass. Some of the semi-arid African regions, where the
desert and the savanna blend into one another, are reminiscent of the American Southwest. The deserts themselves
—the center of the Kalahari and the several vast dry centers of the Sahara—are comparable to conditions found in
Death Valley of North America.

Cities such as Algiers and Cape Town enjoy a climate
much like that of southern France. The crops and cultures,
where they have been subjected to European influence
in these areas, are much the same: based on livestock,
grain, and grapes.

The climatic areas of Africa might be seen as parallel
belts stretching from east to west, a mirror image on either
side of the equator, were it not for the fact that that pattern is seriously upset in the eastern part of the continent
(and a few other small parts) by highland areas in which
altitude overrides latitude. The highland areas of Africa
are divided between steeply mountainous terrain like that
found in Cameroun and the Ruwenzori, and the high,
rolling plateaus such as are found in Ethiopia and Kenya.
Here the climate may be cool and temperate; Mt. Kilimanjaro and Mt. Ruwenzori bear permanent ice fields on
their caps. Vegetation varies from humid forest or savanna
at the foothills to Alpine mountains and tundra, adjoin-
ing barren glaciers.

One of the most distinctive aspects of the African landscape is that—once the scarp is climbed—it contains few
impassable barriers, either for human beings, other animals, or plants. The climate therefore depends primarily
on winds, the position of the sun, and altitude, more or
less modified by the changes wrought by man. Because
the terrain barriers are neither sudden nor insurmount-
able, the weather can "follow the sun." When the sun

comes north in June, July, and August, it brings rain to the
lands that lie between ten degrees and twenty degrees
north of the equator. Similarly, during November, De-
cember, and January, rains come to the areas between ten
degrees and twenty degrees south. Each enjoys a long dry
season during the wet season of the other. In the humid
forested lands, rain is often well distributed throughout
the year, although short dry seasons may occur, depending primarily on the winds. The climates of eastern Africa
are complicated by the monsoon winds coming in from
the Indian Ocean, as well as by the high altitude. There
are also parts of the west coast where the pattern is disturbed by winds created by the currents of the South Atlantic and the drought of the Sahara. As a general rule,
rainfall throughout the continent tends to be heaviest when
the sun is overhead.

Thus, the climate throughout the middle part of Africa
exhibits an alternating wet and dry season, in a band
crossing the continent; there is a stretch along the equator
that has two wet and two dry seasons during the year;
some areas show local variations, making it seem that
there are no wet or dry seasons at all.

The amount of rain is usually far less important in determining the climatological variations within the African
continent than is the number of months during which it
falls. Rainfall maps have a way of hiding almost as much
as they reveal about all of Africa: agriculture is possible
only during the rainy months. It may be noted, nevertheless, that the savanna zones get from twenty-five to thirty-
five inches per year. The high temperature and pronounced dry season lead to rapid evaporation and hence
discourage the growth of forest and limit the types of agricultural activity that can profitably be pursued. The most
typical trees are those that are drought-resistant, such as

the acacia or the locust bean. On the other hand, the areas of heaviest rainfall along the equator have broad-leafed evergreen trees, but as one goes away from the equator in either direction, or as one gains altitude, the trees give way to deciduous varieties. Along the equator, there is little range of variation in temperature from one season to the next, and temperatures drop only a few degrees at night. Rainfall may go to over one hundred inches.

The dry lands may receive less than five inches of rain a year, and sometimes the heart of the desert areas may go for years with no rainfall at all. When rain does fall, it may come in torrents that dump several inches within a few hours, creating floods and erosion that give way again almost immediately to desiccation. This very high variability in annual rainfall causes Africa's periodic droughts. In certain regions, rainfall will vary 20 percent to 40 percent from the mean in any year. These belts of highly variable rainfall cover the Sahara and the belt of savanna country from Senegal on the west through to southern Somalia on the east, including all of Ethiopia. South of the Sahara, the similar region of highly variable rainfall runs along the west coast from the Congo mouth southward, and inland far enough to include most of Angola and Namibia.

SOILS AND AGRICULTURE

Most African soils are typical tropical soils and suffer from the disadvantages that all other tropical soils suffer from in greater or lesser degree: they are devoid of humus. Humus is the vegetable mold in the soil that results from slow decomposition of organic matter. In the so-called temperate zone there are at least some months during the year in which the oxidization of vegetable matter is slowed

to a near standstill—winters enrich the soil not merely by
the aeration that results from alternate freezing and thaw-
ing, but also from the fact that humus can decompose at a
rapid rate only for half the year. The soil thus remains
enriched in the sense that crops and other growing plants
can live off a "current account" rather than off the "storage account" of fertility in the soil. Soils can, with much
greater relative ease, be maintained by suitable farming
practices. In tropical climates, humus oxidization goes on
more or less at full speed the year round. That means that
much of the fertility that might be used by plants is in fact
"wasted" and that there is only a very small "storage
account" in the soil in any case.

There is a further difficulty about tropical soils: they
are easily leached. That is, the nutrients and minerals are
washed out of them and flow away, either into the sub-
soil or into the sea. The lack of humus content and the
ease of leaching interact with one another to ensure that
tropical soils are thin, and that they never achieve the
richness of the soils of the temperate zones. Tropical soils
have a humus content of 1.8 percent of total volume, or
less. The humus content of soils in upper New York State
or in Ohio runs from 10–12 percent, and in the richest
Iowa farmland, as high as 16 percent. African soils are
indeed poor.

Since poor soils are easily exhausted, they can be worked
only for short periods unless expensive and tedious steps
are taken to maintain them. Few tropical peoples have
ever had the technology or the knowledge to take the required steps. Rather, they have "mined" the soil of its nutrients by a method of farming known as "shifting
cultivation."

Shifting cultivation is a method of farming in which
land is cleared, either of the forest or of the grass that

grows on it, and farmed without artificial fertilization.
When the natural fertility of a farm so made has been exhausted, the farmer clears another patch and repeats the
process, while the first patch is allowed to revert to fallow,
and ultimately to regain fertility by natural means. The
entire process may take as few as five or as many as thirty
years, and some authorities (and some African farmers)
claim that never again is the land as good as the first time
it is cleared. This method of dry farming is widespread in
the tropical world: in the Philippines and Southeast Asia,
in much of tribal India, and in tropical America. In Africa,
farmers in some areas utilize the grass or tree limbs that
they remove by burning them, and using the ash as fertilizer. Indeed, in parts of central Africa, notably in Zambia
and the surrounding areas, the process may amount to lop-
ping branches off the large trees, burning them, and planting corn in the ash beds. The few exceptions in Africa are
to be found in the Nile and Zambezi valleys and a few
other areas in which there is a permanent, rich, alluvially
deposited soil, maintained by seasonal flooding, and in
those small areas in which European forms of agriculture
are practiced, primarily in the extreme north and south
and in some highland areas.

Shifting cultivation is, seen from the standpoint of modern technology and the needs of the modern world, a
wasteful method of farming, and the agricultural experts
of the world, including tropical Africa, are working on improvements in the system. But in most areas the method
provides short-term security and, indeed, plenty for the
African societies that practice it. Africans are willing to
make changes, but those changes must be fully tested; the
people must be convinced that the changes are for the
better—that greater plenty and fuller security will result.
Mere introduction of the plow, for example, is not suffi-

cient: deeply plowed land leaches faster than does land which is merely scratched on the surface, and the oxidization of humus is speeded up by aeration. Fertilizer is expensive; green manure crops require as much labor as do crops from which a more immediately apparent return is reaped. Compost requires new and improved means of cartage in a continent accustomed to head-loading. Moreover, the cartage requires more and different animals, differently used, which in turn demands new types of roads and paths. Changing the pattern of African agriculture is a monumental task; many mistakes have been made, and many more will probably be made, before the job can be finished.

There are peoples in Africa who are primarily or even solely dependent on their herds. Such peoples always occupy the savanna areas, and most are nomadic or transhumant. Nomads do not merely wander; they proceed in more or less fixed patterns or routes that may take several years to complete. If the cycle of movement is one required by the seasons and is repeated in an annual cycle, it is called transhumance. There are some places where mixed farming and herding is done by the same peoples, and others where herders and farmers cooperate with one another to the point of mutual dependence. Herding is restricted for the most part to the savannas and some of the highlands. The humid forests present conditions in which only goats can be kept; in a few places, even goats cannot thrive. Goats and donkeys can live in any parts of the desert that will support human populations, although a few of the human populations (particularly the San of the Kalahari Desert) do not keep them. Chickens are ubiquitous among the settled peoples of the continent, many of whom also keep ducks and pigeons.

In the past the major hazard for livestock has been

endemic sleeping sickness. Although the problem has not
been fully solved, there has probably been more research
and effort expended on controlling sleeping sickness than
on any other single health factor—certainly for animals.

In Africa, as everywhere else, resources must be available in two senses: not only must they be physically present, but they must be culturally valued and used. This
cultural availability may change rapidly in some instances
and so make possible rapid changes in a very short time.

In the post-war decades, much of the tropical world
passed through what was called a "green revolution,"
where agricultural production rose rapidly even in the
face of rapidly rising populations. In India and in Latin
America, these gains were made possible by new fertilizers, new varieties of seed, and the spread of new knowledge of tropical agricultural techniques. But the green
revolution by-passed Africa. In all the "developing
world," indeed, sub-Saharan Africa is the only major
region where per-capita income and per-capita food
production declined between about 1960 and the late
1980s.

The food crisis had several causes. The underlying
conditions created one of them! The African environment is not well suited to the new technology of the Asian
green revolution—the new seed varieties were tried, but it
often turned out that the African seeds and techniques
were already the best available for their peculiarly bad
conditions. This may be one reason why many people
who had worked the land before independence, when
they moved into the cities, were so often unemployed or
under-employed. At independence, around 90 percent of
the population was rural; by the mid-1980s, only an estimated 77 percent still lived in rural areas, and only 71
percent was involved in agriculture.

A second important factor was the rapidly rising African population. The current growth rate is estimated at about 3.2 percent per year for sub-Saharan Africa as a whole, and as high as 4 percent in individual countries like Kenya. Though total agricultural production has increased, it has not increased fast enough to keep up with population growth. Many countries also have to depend on agricultural exports like coffee and cocoa, so that food for local use may be even less. It has been estimated that per capita food production in 1982 was 11 percent less than it had been in 1969. After the serious drought of 1983-84, it was down 16 percent.

In spite of the sad record before and into the early 1980s, some improvements began to show a more hopeful future after the drought years. When African countries became alarmed about declining food production, they began to take steps to make sure that the price structure was not rigged against the farmer. Some individual countries, like the Ivory Coast, had never been part of the general failure in any case. The government of Rhodesia under white rule had given favorable treatment to white farmers. After Rhodesia became the independent Zimbabwe under African control in 1980, the government set out to help the black farmers as well. By 1985 they had more than doubled their yield per acre in maize, and produced three times as much maize as they had done in 1978.

MINERALS

Mineral resources other than gold were not much used by African societies before the beginning of the Christian era. Gold from sub-Saharan Africa, however, began to reach the outer world in three separate streams that began about the twelfth century, perhaps even earlier. One stream from West Africa reached across the Sahara by camel caravan, to be minted in Morocco into coins that circulated throughout the Muslim world and even in Europe. A second stream moved overland from Ethiopian highlands to Egypt. The third came from the placer gold diggings in Zimbabwe, being exported overland to the east coast and then north by sea in the hands of Muslim shippers mainly from Arabia. They sold most of the gold to India, though some reached the Muslim world as well. It is not possible to be precise about the size of these streams, but the Zimbabwe and Ethiopian sources exported on the order of 500 kilograms each in a good year. The West African supply was somewhat larger, perhaps 1500 kgs. a year. The total may have been as high as 2.5 metric tons in a good year, though probably close to 1 to 1.5 metric tons as an annual average. For the time, that was an enormous quantity, with a really significant influence on the monetary systems from India to Gibraltar.

Then in the 1880s, Europeans discovered the gold of the Witwatersrand in South Africa. It lay in comparatively small, vertical deposits of low-quality ore, but in enormous quantities. If it had been discovered earlier, neither Africans nor Europeans had the industrial technology to work such deposits; but the machinery was available in the 1890s, and South Africa rapidly became the most important source of gold anywhere. In the mid-1980s, South Africa alone produced more than 70 percent of the world's gold, and additional supplies came from Zimbabwe, Zaire, and Ghana, among others.

Other metals had an early importance in long-distance trade. Copper mining began in Central Africa in the second or third century of our era. By the time Vasco da

Gama visited the East African coast in 1498, copper
objects from either Zaire or Zambia were available for
sale there. In West Africa, the copper trade was even
more important, since West Africa lacked its own
supplies. The trans-Saharan trade before 1500 A.D.
included very large copper shipments, mostly from North
African or Saharan mines, but some from as far away as
central Europe. The famous bronze statues of life in
Nigeria were produced at this time out of copper from the
Sahara or from Europe combined with tin from northern
Nigeria.

As with gold,the quantities of copper mined increased
enormously with the coming of the European and their
machines for digging deep mines and working the ore. By
the mid-1980s, Zambia, Zaire, and South Africa together
supplied about 17 percent of the world's copper production.

Africa is almost a solid chunk of iron ore—most of it
low-grade, though in some areas of Liberia and Guinea-
Conakry, the content runs as high as 84 percent. The
early mining technique in the Nimba Mountains on the
Guinea-Liberian border was merely to cut off the trees,
let the thin topsoil wash away, and use surface mining
methods on the naked, rusting hills. In the mid-1980s,
however, Africa accounted for only about 9 percent of
world iron-ore production, mostly from South Africa,
followed by Liberia and Mauritania.

Iron was made in many parts of pre-colonial Africa.
The southern fringes of the Sahara are littered with the
remains of earthen furnaces which could turn out either
wrought-iron or steel. In a few places in West Africa,
smiths still make their own iron using the old methods,
though today they are likely to recycle truck springs to
make tools in the traditional shapes. Most iron used

today, however, is a product of Africa's new iron
industry or else is imported from Korea or Japan.

Diamonds are one of the continent's most important
assets. In the mid-1980s, Africa accounted for more than
80 percent of world diamond production, both industrial
and gem stones.

All of these minerals—the gold, diamonds, iron, and
copper—were explored and set into production before
the colonial period ended. Oil, however, was new in the
post-war era. Especially during the period of very high oil
prices, lasting from 1974 to the early 1980s, oil had an
enormous influence on African development. Those
countries that had large supplies readily available, like
Nigeria, passed through an economic boom followed by a
bust. Those that had none, found their economic
development sharply curtailed by the rising cost of energy
that was essential for transportation, industry, and
modern agriculture. The extent of Africa's potential
wealth in oil is still uncertain, but, by the mid-1980s,
Africa already produced about 4 percent of world crude
oil, much of it off-shore on the continental shelf of the
Gulf of Guinea in southern Nigeria, Gabon, and Angola.

Since the Second World War, many minor minerals
from Africa have also increased in importance. These
include mica, quartz, tungsten, bauxite, uranium,
chrome, tantalite, columbite, cobalt, zinc, and mangan-
ese.

Africa's main economic claim to world attention has
been minerals, and it will probably continue to be
minerals for some time to come.

DISEASES

Africa was long called "the white man's grave," and
with reason. Strangers arriving on the tropical coasts

once died at rátes as high as 50 percent in the first year of
residence—not because they were white, but because they
lacked immunities appropriate to the African disease
environment. Black people born in and raised in North
America or the West Indies also died at very high rates if
they came to Africa as adults.

But the fact remains that lowland, tropical Africa may
well have the most intractable disease environment in the
world. Over the past century or so, the struggle of
modern medicine to deal with that environment shows
some victories and some defeats. The most notable
victory was a victory for all people everywhere. In 1980,
the World health Organization announced that it had
succeeded in eradicating smallpox, the last cases being in
eastern Africa.

Another notable victory came in the early 1980s, when
teams from the World Health Organization and
cooperating African governments managed greatly to
reduce the incidence of onchocerciasis or "river blind-
ness." This disease exists in many parts of the tropical
world, where it is carried by a fly with the descriptive
name of *simulium damnosum*. In Burkina Faso and parts
of northern Ghana, it used to be so serious along certain
rivers that as many as 50 percent of middle-aged people
would be blinded for life. Many other fertile valleys were
simply left unoccupied because of the disease. The international campaign against its carriers and intermediate
hosts, however, seems to have reduced it to minor
proportions in West Africa.

The most striking defeat has been the failure to deal
with a new arrival, the acquired immune deficiency
syndrome, usually known by its initials, AIDS. Some
authorities believe that AIDS may have originated in
Africa, but that was not certain at the time of writing. It

did, however, spread more rapidly in Africa than on other continents. Two-thirds of the cases reported so far have occurred in the United States, but authorities think there are even more unreported cases in Africa. In the United States, the principal, but not the only means of spreading the virus, is unprotected homosexual sex relations. In Africa, the main route of transmission is heterosexual relations. One possible explanation for the more rapid spread in Africa is the fact that certain combinations of a gene called "Gc" have greater resistence to the virus than others do. The dangerous combination occurs more frequently among people of African descent, and the least dangerous occurs most frequently among people of European descent. Asians come somewhere between.

Some diseases are easier to control than others. Yaws has been stamped out in wide regions of the continent. The curative drugs are cheap and can be distributed on a mass basis wherever health services reach all those who are infected.

Schistosomiasis is quite different. It is said to be the most widespread of all human diseases, and that 150,-000,000 people suffer from it chronically. It is caused by parasites of the genus *Schistosoma* that live in fresh water. They enter the human body through the skin and lay eggs which pass back into the water through human waste. After a complex cycle in the water, with snails as an intermediate host, the parasites are again ready to infect anyone who goes wading to fetch water, to wash clothes, or merely to cross a stream. Clean, piped water and efficient sanitation can end the disease but these simple controls are far too expensive for most African countries. In the past, most of the drugs available against schistosomiasis had serious side effects or were very expensive. In the late 1970s, however, a number of new drugs appeared, which were both cheap and harmless to most patients.

For Africa as a whole, about half the population suffer from schistosomiasis; in some rural areas everyone over the age of two is infested. The disease is rarely fatal or even incapacitating, so it escaped notice until recent decades; but doctors now realize that progressive damage to the intestinal tract, lungs, and liver are a serious drag on the victim's vitality and contribute to early death. The new drugs show some possibilities of control, but general eradication is still years away.

Tropical Africa's bad reputation for health comes mainly from such insect-borne diseases as malaria and yellow fever. Yellow fever (which probably originated in Africa) is carried by *Aedes aegypti,* a mosquito that is fairly easy to control. A simple inoculation can protect the individual. Yellow fever is unlikely to be a serious threat in the future, but it played an important role in African history. Infection in childhood is seldom fatal and produces a lifelong immunity. Only strangers who came to Africa as adults died at the first infection.

Malaria was equally dangerous in the past and continues to be a serious problem, harder to control than yellow fever, yaws, or schistosomiasis. It has been wiped out by effective mosquito control on some of the African islands like Mauritius and in North Africa. In tropical Africa, however, intensive mosquito control was tried for fifty years and failed. For a time people hoped for success with DDT, but resistant strains of mosquitos appeared. After the war, treatment with chloriquine looked promising, but this time the parasite itself evolved new resistant strains. By the early 1980s, an anti-malarial vaccine appeared to be theoretically possible, but it is not yet tried in practice.

The principal carriers in tropical Africa are the mosquitoes *Anopheles funestus* and *A. gambiae*. Together they help to guarantee that most of tropical Africa is a hyperendemic area, where virtually everyone is assured of receiving an infective bite. In addition, Africa is one home of falciparum malaria, the type that is most often fatal. Every child therefore fights a life-and-death struggle with the malarial parasite during the first years of his life. As many as half may die before reaching the age of five. The survivors are infected during the remainder of their lives, but rarely suffer from clinical symptoms. They acquire an apparent immunity that hides the progressive damage to the liver and other organs. Before the development of tropical medicine, strangers paid a price in adult mortality similar to that paid by Africans in infancy. With modern drugs, Africa may no longer be the "white man's grave," but it continues to be the "black child's grave" to a degree far beyond the range of recent Western experience.

Sleeping sickness, or trypanosomiasis, is also an insect-borne disease. The vector is the tsetse fly—actually several different flies of the genus *Glossina* carry several different parasites of the genus *Trypanosoma*. Both the disease and the flies arc peculiar to Africa; even there they are confined to restricted regions in the humid tropics. Some are found in the forest, while others thrive in wooded or brush-covered savanna. These flies cannot survive, however, in open grassland, so that clearing the brush is one means of control. Like other forms of disease control, this one requires expensive and continuous effort.

Unlike malaria or schistosomiasis, trypanosomiasis is not, in most areas, a direct problem for the human population. Although most types are fatal to people, people are not infected as often as domestic animals or wild game. In the past, epidemics have carried away as much as two thirds of the human population of some small regions, but such occurrences are rare. The continuing and serious problem is with animals, because without cattle a diet containing enough protein is difficult to acquire. One result is the prevalence of kwashiorkor, a form of malnutrition caused by the lack of milk and meat that domestic animals could provide. Kwashiorkor in infancy can be permanently damaging.

These diseases are an obvious hindrance to African development today, and they have played an incalculable role in the African past. Three quarters of all the world's cases of schistosomiasis are in Africa, and Africa appears to have far more than its share of hyperendemic falciparum malaria. Yellow fever originated in Africa, and trypanosomiasis is still confined to that continent. Tropical Africa also had—and has—the full range of diseases common in Europe.

In addition to the impact of disease on Africans themselves, disease contributed to Africa's isolation by keeping visitors away. Traders who crossed the Sahara from North Africa found that residence in the sudan brought disease and death. When they therefore stopped at the desert's edge, tropical Africa lost an opportunity to keep in close contact with the world north of the Sahara. After the fifteenth century, when European traders began to arrive by sea along the African coast, they made the same discovery—that their death rates were astronomical. A few—but only a few—found it worthwhile to take the risk in order to buy gold and slaves. Africa thus remained largely isolated from the great civilizations that stretched from Spain and Morocco to China.

Internal transportation was made difficult across wide belts where domestic animals could not go because of trypanosomiasis. In these regions all goods had to be carried by human porters. Enforced dependence on human power alone was a serious constraint. Without animal power, the wheel is of little use. On the west coast, even the early European colonial officials were forced to abandon wheeled transport and to have themselves carried in hammocks slung from a pole, or paddled in canoes along the coasts or up the rivers. Westerners are now so used to non-human sources of power that it is hard to conceive of societies in which animal power was missing, and all work had to be organized within the limits of what man himself can do.

Chapter Three

THE PEOPLES OF AFRICA

IN TODAY'S WORLD, ANY WESTERN DISCUSSION OF THE peoples of Africa must revolve about the question "What is race?" The differences between races cannot be specifically defined physiologically, but rather depend on cultural points. The continuity of physical types in modern man has no "natural" breaking points—there are only stereotypes from which all persons are removed in at least some degree. Only by fiat can the distinctions be made.

RACE

The trouble with "race," as a concept, is that it is two concepts. The two are hopelessly intertwined by our emotional and cultural notions into false unity on the basis of a mere word. "Race" has become the idiom in which the twentieth century has cast some of its practices of and ideas about persecution. It has, moreover, been utilized as a technical term by the biological sciences, and particularly by genetics. Then, it has been blandly—or, sometimes, aggressively—assumed by the Western world that the popular idiom and the scientific concept have some sort of bearing on one another.

"Race" as a social problem is what might be called a "cultural displacement." That is to say, just as some neurotics displace their difficulties into an idiom which

41

ensures that they need do nothing to correct them, and which has little if anything to do with the "cause" of the neurosis, so the whole "race" question is created by something that is of quite a different order from the biologist's and geneticist's problems in which the term has scientific meaning and validity.

The task to be performed in this chapter, then, is twofold. It is important to understand the biological definition of race and review the European attitudes toward Africans that have culminated in the "race" concept as it is generally understood in the Western world, and as it affects Africa.

A race is, in biological science, a group of organisms, the members of which share a statistically significant proportion of their genes. The point at which "statistical significance" is reached is a matter for special determination in the specific problem before the scientist. In some situations, and for the purposes of some problems, the proportion can be rather small; in others, it must be defined as being much larger. In the latter case, the members of the "race" are fewer and are more nearly homogeneous than in the former. There is no point in nature, however, at which one race becomes another race—"race" is part of the analytical equipment of science, *not* part of the data.

Races are interbreeding populations, and because the members of interbreeding populations are material and take up space, and further since they must meet in order to breed, every "race" has a geographical dimension: an area in which it is represented. Changes in the geographical dimension (which is the same thing as mobility of individuals) usually result in changes in the available genes, and hence ultimately in change of the "race."

To repeat, a race is (to a biologist) a group of plants or

Young girl in Kano, Nigeria.

animals that share some of their genes, the proportions
being dependent on definition.

It is wrong, however, to think of races as immutable or
even as very old. The length of time that it takes to create
a "race" depends (in addition to the definition, either
social or scientific, of what characteristics make the difference) on how large, how homogeneous, and how
isolated the group of interbreeding animals may be. All
of the characteristics which mark the socially recognized,
"phenotypical" races of today are (with the exception of
the color of skin, hair, and eyes, which are linked) determined by different and independent gene combinations.
There is no genetic correlation between jaw shape and
hair texture, between musculature and bone formation in
the wrist and the presence or absence of epicanthic fold
on the eye, all of which are among the criteria for determining the racial types with which we in the modern
world are familiar. As the interbreeding of present-day
"races" occurs with the breaking down of geographical
and social barriers, the known "races" are changing. If, at
a later date, new geographical isolation or new social
barriers again create fairly small interbreeding populations, a new set of races may result.

In short, race is a scientific concept for classifying con-
geners. The class so set apart is also temporary, when
seen in the sweep of geological and cultural time.

But race also means something else in the modern
world, as a glance into any dictionary—or, indeed, into
the newspaper—will show. The word is derived from the
Latin term for "root," and it has been used in English,
even within the last few decades, to refer to sex (the female race), to all of humanity (the human race), to
members of a profession (writers are a peculiar race), to
nationalities (the French race), to language groups (the

Semitic race), and to religions (the Jewish race).

Moreover, in the Europe of the eighteenth and nineteenth centuries, "race" was the idiom in which democratic revolutions were organized, propagandized, carried out, and fought. In the Europe of the twentieth century, race has been one of the idioms in which the totalitarian revolution has been waged. And in the United States of the late twentieth century, "race" is the revolutionary cry with which new standards of equality and justice are being demanded.

The first book on race with scientific pretensions is generally considered to have been that of a German named Blumenbach in 1806. To read it today is almost impossible—in fact, it leads to little except greater regard for the magnificent achievement of the Darwinian revolution of the 1850s and 1860s. Blumenbach still subscribed to the "degeneration" theory of race, based on the myth that man was created perfect but had everywhere degenerated to greater or lesser extent.

Documents from the eighteenth century did, of course, recognize the physical differences that we today associate with race. But they did not consider them of telling significance.

Modern notions of racism developed out of the social revolutions of the late eighteenth and the nineteenth centuries. In France, the change from the feudal system to a modern industrial system was explained in terms of race—and Europe to this day means something quite different by "race" than does America. In the United States, the monumental social changes that followed the Civil War (which occurred within a few years of the Darwinian revolution, though the results collided only decades later) gave rise to many of the present-day beliefs about "race" in the United States. On both continents, a type

of nobility and feudal or demi-feudal system was giving
way to a new type of society, based on contract and the
market. In Europe, the nobility under the tutelage of men
like the Comte de Boulainvilliers and Gobineau began
to think of themselves as "Teutonics" in contrast to the
revolutionaries—their former serfs and yeomen—whom
they called "Alpines" and "Mediterraneans." During the
reign of National Socialism in Germany, "race" was again
the idiom for social revolution, when "racial purity" was
correlated with stamping out the people and institutions
of one of the most progressive and powerful of Europe's
minority groups. It was, in America, not until the social
revolution created by the Civil War and Reconstruction
had crippled old institutions that "race" was primarily a
weapon to be used against Negroes; the "yellow peril"
seemed of far greater moment even at the turn of the
century, and may in fact again seem so before the turn
of the next.

The facts of the matter are, of course, that heritable
differences among human beings exist and can be seen
with the naked eye; that scientific definitions of geneti-
cally interrelated groups of plants and animals exist and
are pinned to words in the common language; that social
problems exist that have, for almost two centuries now,
been expressed in an idiom of "race." No one has as yet
"proved" any verifiable association among the three mean-
ings. Yet because words mean precisely what one intends
them to mean, the racial attitudes of the modern Western
world are adamant. Western scholars do not ask what
peoples with other cultural traditions and histories think
about the physical differences that are visible to all.
Rather, they assume these differences to be explained by
their own concept of "race," and when they investigate
race they do not question the concept. The number of

studies that contain any information at all about what other people make of these physical differences is minuscule.

Race is, like "gravity," a concept, not a thing. But while gravity explains a great many empirically verifiable facts, nobody has ever shown scientifically that "race" explains anything—its unscientific use to "prove" points has never been more than special pleading. In short, it would seem that social scientists have hold of a wrong concept. Biologists can use the notion; social scientists cannot— except insofar as populations believe certain things and hence bring them about by cultural means. We are dealing here with the problem of metaphor: when is a word or an image to be understood clearly and unequivocally and when is it metaphorical and equivocal?

RACES IN AFRICA

It always pays to be suspicious of any list of races, for all the reasons just outlined. It is convenient, however unscientific, to mention seven principal physical types in present-day sub-Saharan Africa. In approximate order of their numerical importance they are: 1) Negroes, 2) Ethiopian/Somali (formerly called "Hamite," sometimes Erythriote), 3) Caucasians, 4) Indians, 5) Khoisan, 6) Orientals, 7) Pygmies.

Let us say again that no race is pure. Some physical anthropologists have abandoned the concept of race altogether. They may still want to identify physical differences between people, but they do this by looking at a bundle of twenty or more different characteristics. These characteristics do not all vary together. Blood type and skin color are inherited separately by different genes.

Even characteristics that seem to go together do so more
by chance than by any scientific law. In America, we
know that "sickle cell trait" is found among blacks but
not among whites. But in Africa some whites have it as
well, and it is very rare among blacks in certain places.
We also know why. This trait gives some protection in
childhood against falciparum malaria, even though it
may lead to an early death from anæmia. In regions of
endemic falciparum, like West Africa, it tends to breed
in; in non-malarial areas like the United States, it tends to
breed out. In earlier times, when the deep forest still
existed in West Africa, it was a virtually malaria-free
area, because the mosquitoes that carry the disease there
like to live in the open. Africans from those recently
deep-forest areas, therefore tend to not have sickle-cell
trait; though the cutting of the forest may, over time,
cause it to increase.

The physical types on our list are those visible to the
superficial observer—sometimes in stereotypically classic
forms, sometimes in various mixtures. Negroes and
Caucasian types are familiar enough. Negro-appearing
people are the dominant population in sub-Saharan
Africa. People of the other types are either scattered or
dominant in a comparatively small region.

The Ethiopian/Somali type is dominant in those two
countries and in Djibuti—broadly the eastern peninsula
called "the Horn of Africa." They are probably a
stabilized mixture between people from Arabia and
Africa, but they are recognizable as a different physical
type from either. Past authorities had them classified as a
separate "Hamitic" race, sometimes called a sub-class of
Caucasian—because Amharic, one of their main
languages is similar to Arabic and Hebrew. But that myth
had to be abandoned after it was found that languages

are learned, not inherited.

The Khoisan people are another distinct physical type of purely African origin, fairly short, with wiry hair and a yellowish skin, and found mainly in the southwest—in parts of Botswana, Namibia, and the Republic of South Africa. The name "Khoisan" is a made-up word derived from San (the hunting and gathering peoples formerly called Bushmen) and the Khoikhoi (the cattle-keeping people who once occupied the hinterland of the Cape of Good Hope). Most authorities think that they and the pygmies of the forest belt further north may well represent the remains of a broadly scattered but sparse population that occupied the whole of central and southern Africa before the Bantu-speaking Negroes moved in from the north during the past three thousand years. Pygmies live mainly in the tropical forest, where they continue to specialize in hunting, though they have mixed physically and culturally with their Bantu-speaking neighbors. Pgymies and Khoisan may have descended from common ancestors, but they look different today.

The groups we have called Caucasians, orientals, and Indians are all recent immigrants from elsewhere. The main Caucasian group is the settler minority in South Africa and Zimbabwe. Other Caucasians include some North Africans who live south of the Sahara, as in Mauritania. In the Nilotic Sudan and scattered down the East African coast, the immigrants came from Arabia, but they have mixed with their Negroid neighbors for several centuries. In the cities everywhere, scattered Caucasian communities from Europe and North America are far more numerous than they were during the colonial periods. They tend to live concentrated near buildings labelled "Hilton."

Some of the orientals came far earlier. Their largest

and oldest settlement was on the large island that is now
the Malagasy Republic. They came by canoe from
Indonesia and settled on the then-uninhabited island.
Negroid peoples from the African mainland came later,
so that most Malagasy today are mixed, though their
Southeast Asian origins are visible. Other orientals are
the Chinese communities of South Africa and the
Mascarene Islands—Réunion and Mauritius—and in
smaller numbers in most African cities.

The Indians are also mostly urban people, except in
South Africa, Réunion, and Mauritius, where they
represent the descendants of migrant sugar workers.
Substantial Indian communities, mostly engaged in
commerce, are found up and down the East Africa coast
and its hinterland. They are very important economically
there, and Kenyans of Indian descent are about 3 percent
of the population. Other, smaller and more scattered
Indian communities are found in West Africa as well.

Some authorities would like to sub-divide the Indians
into several different physical types, just as others in the
past have tried to distinguish "true Negroes," "Bantu,"
or "Nilotes" among the Negroid-looking Africans. The
effort has some merit for trying to trace pre-historic
migrations across Africa or India, but such distinctions
have little value for understanding recent African history.
Race is, after all, in the eye of the beholder.

CHANGING EUROPEAN VIEWS OF AFRICANS

Dogmas concerning the visible differences between
Africans and Europeans have undergone many changes in
Europe and America, and we know a great deal about
these shifts in racial attitude—both among ordinary people
and among scholars and scientists. At the same time, we

have almost no information on ways in which African peoples react to "racial" differences. But we do know that their own reactions are sometimes quite different from the patterns found in our own culture. Black Americans in modern Africa, for example, sometimes find that African villagers consider them to be "Europeans" (that is, people of Western culture), who merely incidentally happen to be black.

Great difficulty inheres in any attempt to explain to laymen that science can say nothing about the attitudes, endowments, capabilities, and inherent tendencies of different groups of human beings as they are determined by the stereotypes of race. The difficulty arises because in the early days of scientific discussion it was assumed, even by scientists, that such differences did exist. Race, indeed, appeared at one stage to be the major determinant of the course of human history. Twentieth-century science has recognized that its predecessors were mistaken. The twentieth-century populace has not quite caught up.

Racial doctrines of the eighteenth and nineteenth centuries came in part from popular views, formed by several centuries of association between Africans and Europeans.

Up to the 1840s, the Americas as a whole received more Africans by way of the slave trade than its total number of immigrants from Europe. Especially in Brazil, the Caribbean, and the southern American colonies, Africans were known only as slaves. In these societies, and ultimately in Europe as well, Negro skin color, hair texture, and facial features were associated with the status of slavery. Prejudice based on culture and that based on social rank were blended together and expressed as a "racial" prejudice.

The problem of defining the nature of people whose

culture and appearance was different was not new to Europe. The Spanish had faced the problem in their American empire shortly after the discovery of America; it was not until 1537 that a papal bull stated unequivocally that non-Westerners, specifically American Indians, were officially human beings. They were, by papal fiat, declared to have full spiritual equality with Christians. This position, be it noted, was very like the Muslim one as late as 1850. But Protestant countries of northern Europe postponed the question; they had at that time no large overseas empires, though the English had had a "native problem" in Ireland since the Middle Ages, and some of their attitudes toward the Irish were very like those they adopted in regard to Africans.

By the eighteenth century, north Europeans began to have large "sugar colonies" in the Caribbean as well as economically important plantations in southern North America. Then, and especially in the last quarter of the century, Europeans began seriously to consider the Africans' "place in nature." The prejudices of the older planters was joined by new attitudes, one of which was an increase in the cultural arrogance of Europe. As the Industrial Revolution progressed into the nineteenth century, Europeans found their technological superiority increasing rapidly. Where, only a few centuries earlier, they had had no measurable superiority over the technology of China or the Islamic civilization, Europeans were now creating the first industrialized society the world had known. Few people are capable of viewing the world over the long perspective of time, and it was easy to equate technological expertise with a general superiority of Europeans over all other peoples.

As Europeans sought to explain their increasing dominance in the world, it was only "natural," in the culture they were creating, to turn to the scientists. As it happened, some of the most spectacular scientific advances of the eighteenth and early nineteenth centuries were in biology. Scientists like Linnaeus, Buffon, and Couvier were at work classifying all of the animal kingdom, laying the basis for the classification by genus and species that is still used.

The work of the biologists must, however, be considered in terms of the cosmographical background of the times: a central concept known as "the great chain of being." According to this dogma, all living beings could be fitted into a hierarchy, with apparent but very small differences between each. In this pre-Linnaean mode of classification, man took his place "naturally" at the highest point on the scale, while the smallest organisms were considered to be at the bottom—and therefore inferior.

Before the major revolutionary aspects of Linnaeus' work came to be understood—indeed, it would seem that he himself never grasped the point that his classifications would destroy the concept of the chain of being—his simple classification of the human races on the basis of skin color came to be adopted. Indeed, the classification of human beings by skin color goes back to the Egyptian papyri, though the concept of "race" almost surely does not.

In any case, Linnaeus named the four races to be the white, yellow, red, and black races. Narcissism, if nothing else, assured that Europeans would be at the top of the scale, for no two differentiated types in the great chain of being could be precisely equal. The hierarchy demanded ranking; ranking was carried out, in an idiom of "race," on the basis of subjective evaluations of the cultures that travel writers had associated with the various races. Vol-

taire, Rousseau, Hume—and most of their contemporaries
—made the basic mistake of equating culture with race
and ranking races on the basis of their own attitudes toward various cultures. This error was perpetuated into the
early twentieth century.

Linnaeus, still under the influence of the concept of
the "great chain of being," changed his classification in
1758 so that the genus *homo* included the orangutan and
several fabulous beasts of the "abominable snowman"
variety. The philosophical concept—the great chain of being—was preserved, but the reputation of Africans in Europe was sacrificed to it.

Both the new cultural arrogance and the "varieties of
mankind" became embroiled in political issues. Colonial
policy-makers took up positions; pressure groups such as
the anti-slavery leagues took up theirs. Data, however,
came from the same sources—the xenophobia of the travelers and planters, and the racial rankings of the biologists.

Throughout the debates about the abolition of the slave
trade, the similarities between Caucasians and Negroes
were minimized to the most basic in order to attract as
many followers as possible to the cause—Christians
claimed that Africans were "fellow creatures." Few would
care to deny so minimal a claim. The initial issue of the
slavery abolition movement had little to do with race, but
it was very soon dragged into the matter, and in many
cases argument proceeded on whether or not the "sav-
ages" were in fact "naturally" inferior. The equation of
slavery with race was thereby more or less taken for
granted; at least the question was begged by an assumption for the most philanthropic of purposes. The stereotypes of "the Negro" began to appear, and qualities assigned to it that often could not be observed in individuals.
Even Wilberforce argued that Africans, being men, were

nevertheless "fallen men." They were degraded by their savagery. Throughout, there were some voices raised that "the Negro" was not a valid abstraction because of the very diversity within all African populations. Except for the philosophical background, which was changed radically in the nineteenth century, most of the argument remains with us today.

The xenophobia of the written accounts, the position of the Negro in the "great chain of being" (echoes of which were still heard in the early twentieth century when the "missing link" was still being sought by some), the minimization of the similarities among all men in order to achieve philanthropic purposes—all these things came to influence the stereotype of the African that was being built up. The eighteenth-century position can be summed up as a change from the intellectual habit of looking for similarities in all men to the habit of looking for the differences among men in order to achieve scientific classification, to maintain self-images, and indeed to achieve moral distinction. It also ultimately led, in later days, to the simplistic and specious doctrine of the physiological determinism of character.

The early decades of the nineteenth century were marked by two important advances: the idea of the "great chain of being" was giving way to the ideas that were ultimately to be organized by Darwin into evolutionary theory, and ideas of anatomy were becoming more and more precise with the development of scientific clinical medicine. In both spheres, questions began to emerge to challenge the stereotypes that had developed. Men such as Winterbottom, a doctor who worked for years in Sierra Leone, began to question the old stereotypical myths: that African women could give birth without pain; that Negroes had better eyesight, but that in other matters they had less sensitive nervous systems than Europeans; that Negro brains and Negro bones were of a different color. Scientists such as James Pritchard even made claims that the usual classifications into races were conventional and arbitrary. Pritchard frankly admitted that he disliked African culture, but also claimed that there was no physical limitation to the potential achievement of African peoples—or any other. Another of Pritchard's achievements—but few noted it—was to notice that physical characteristics that had been used as classifiers: skin color, hair form and color, skull shape, facial features, all varied independently of one another.

Pritchard made, however, a mistake of exactly the same order as his predecessors. Instead of defining race by a general cultural criterion, he merely picked a precise one: language. In his effort, which we indeed know was right, to give up the determination of a "natural" division among the races, in which physiological differences "cause" other differences—he has the dubious honor of being the first anthropologist writing in English to fall into the opposite trap and make a total overt confusion of race, language, and culture.

The pseudo-science of phrenology was also instrumental in spreading the idea of linking physical traits with mental ability. Phrenology held the stage for some decades, only to be proved wrong on every point. Unfortunately it too left a residue of prejudice from which anthropology was long in freeing itself: the idea that head shape was meaningful did not disappear until well into the twentieth century.

There are many early-nineteenth-century theories of racial origins that depend on natural selection, but the mechanisms by which they worked were not known until the *Origin of Species*. The main point is that it was during the decades from 1820 to 1860 that the change in philosophical background was made, and a vast array of knowledge added. The interesting thing, however, is that in this whole period there was no change in the cultural prejudices exhibited by Europeans. They merely began to justify them in terms of different theories. It was even held by one author that African physical features would change as they became more civilized. With the new ideas of the survival of the fittest, and stepping up of the anti-slavery activities, and the further development of British humanitarianism, it became stylish to press the claims of the Africans *because* "they were inferior." Here we have some of the earliest suggestions of what was ultimately to become "the white man's burden."

Travel literature grew. Culture shock experienced by missionaries and other travelers was almost invariably reported in terms of the inferior qualities of the people who were being visited. Even the stanchest supporters of individual Africans said no more than that because some had become "civilized," all could become so. What we now know to have been the achievements of African culture were not recognized until well into this century.

During the early part of the nineteenth century, the most important single problem for British social theorists was human progress—by which they meant European progress. The forerunners of theories of cultural evolution kept pace with the forerunners of theories of physical evolution. The two constantly interaffected one another, and given the cultural chauvinism of the time, the African people came out with a very low ranking in the eyes of European moral historians. Historians of this period were also busy working out the comparative histories which were to culminate in the works of Spengler and Toynbee.

The claim was made by most that the "human race" developed in Mesopotamia and stayed there until after the flood, after which it moved out. Civilization went northwest. The Africans, such historians either said or implied, obviously had taken another direction.

At the same time, humanitarians began to lose what belief they had that the major cause of African "barbarism" was to be found in the chaos resulting from the slave trade. Against the commanding presence of the idea of the survival of the fittest, such a view seemed difficult to maintain. By the time Mungo Park and other travelers actually penetrated the interior of Africa it became necessary—if the stereotype was to be maintained—to deny that African Negroes could possibly have created any of the civilizations that were found. George Combe, a prominent phrenologist of the 1840s, went so far as to claim that the people of the western sudan, though resembling Negroes in other respects, could not possibly be real Negroes because of their achievements in civilization. The stereotype was now working overtime and being manipulated to cover up new facts.

In science, the Darwinian revolution corrected most of the errors of early nineteenth-century biology, but it allowed the racist error to stand. Indeed, it underwrote it without providing any confirmation of it. It made it possible to claim, with a new scientific "surety," that superior races were marked by their superiority—and to people interested in "progress," that meant technological proficiency.

As early as 1841, the old idea of the moving focus of history (one version of which was "westward the course of empire") was taken up by Thomas Arnold in his inaugural lecture as Regius Professor of History at Oxford.

He set the old idea in terms of race. According to him, the force of world history came from a series of creative races; the Greeks, the Romans, the Germans, the English. Gustav Klemm, in 1843, distinguished between active and passive races; progress was seen as the result of the contributions of a monolithic succession of great races. Perhaps the first influential proponent was Dr. Robert Knox, the Edinburgh doctor who was supplied with corpses by Burke and Hare. Although he was not personally implicated in the murders that these two performed, his reputation was nonetheless ruined. He wrote a book called *The Races of Man* and turned to lecturing about race, which he called "transcendental anatomy." His racism was nothing if not thorough. As he put it: "Race is everything; literature, science, art—in a word, civilization depends on it."

In Knox's view, the dark-skinned peoples of the world were first to evolve, but reached the maximum achievement possible to them and became stagnant. The light-skinned peoples evolved later and had to wage war to the death against the stagnant earlier "races," who would eventually become extinct because they were "incapable" of civilization. Knox, like so many of his contemporaries, included among the dark races the southern Europeans or Mediterraneans. By the light races he meant the Saxons —the people that latter-day dictators have called Aryans. Soon the theory of racial determination of history became all but general—only The Ethnological Society and a few individuals held out against it.

As historians began to use racial explanation, other commentators introduced the factor of race into almost every other aspect of contemporary affairs. Every failure of European work in Africa became a further sign of the basic inferiority of Africans.

Thus, just as the eighteenth century had reduced the common elements of the races to a minimum, the middle of the nineteenth was able to destroy the intellectual foundation of racial egalitarianism.

It is hard today for us to understand that in the middle of the nineteenth century the study of language and the study of race were considered to be approximately the same thing. Gobineau claimed, and most of the authorities of the age agreed with him, that the hierarchy of languages was precisely the same as the hierarchy of races and that some languages were superior to others in a hierarchal arrangement more or less reminiscent of the "great chain of being." Languages evolved very much as races had evolved. In an opposite view (but proving the same point) it could be said that God had given language to man in the Garden of Eden, and that all known languages were greater or lesser degenerations following Babel. Tonal languages, being harder for Europeans to learn, were placed lowest on the scale. Latin was "obviously" highest. Linguistic studies also went into African oral literature and smashed once and for all the theory that Africans had no myth and no tradition of the past. History began to be reconstructed from linguistic similarities.

The climatic theory was still very commonly subscribed to, however, and was reinforced by the high mortality rate of Europeans in West Africa. Diet, ecology, and sexuality all came in for examination as being effective differentia among races and among the levels of civilization achieved. Missionaries also began to enter the field in force at this point, and it was they who pointed out that African religion was not merely the absence of religious truth but was "a positive evil." These men in their writings very often equated their own "worst passions" with the deified forms in African religions.

It was not until late in the nineteenth century that historical and ethnographic data in any quantity began to be collected in Africa and brought to bear on the problems at hand. It was not, in fact, until the 1920s that any large amount of ethnographic data became available, and it was only after World War II that African history emerged as not merely a recognized branch of the subject, but indeed one that might ultimately change the nature of historiography. Indeed, it was not until the revolutions of independence in 1960 that it became possible for Europe, for the first time in centuries, to examine Africa with uncommitted eyes. The stereotypes are still in the way, but it is beginning to be possible to see beyond some of them.

MODERN POPULATION PROBLEMS

Africa is, except for Australia (and Antarctica, which hardly counts), the least peopled of the world's continents, and in population per square mile it also ranks next lowest to Australia. Even if the population density is measured in people per square mile of arable land, Africa is far below the world average. Yet many parts of Africa are already meeting problems of population pressure, and present tendencies suggest that these problems will become more severe in the decades and years ahead.

In the distribution of its people, as in other matters, Africa is a land of contrasts. In scattered regions here and there, people are so few in relation to usable land that land is available to anyone who will put it under cultivation. Elsewhere, population problems were present at the beginning of the colonial period; a few areas had already reached densities comparable to those of the best farming areas in Europe—and the population continued to grow. Uneven population distribution is especially marked in East Africa. In mainland Tanzania, an estimated two thirds of the present population lives on 10 percent of the land, while one third of the country is uninhabitable. In nearby Kenya, more than one third of the people live on less than 2 percent of the land. But over most of the continent, tropical soils and rainfall conditions cannot, given present technology, support dense populations. It is only there that tillable land is sometimes free, because the quality of the soil is too poor to justify the labor required to farm it.

Until recently, little attention was paid to the problem of overpopulation in Africa. One reason for this neglect was the fact that obvious overpopulation was limited to a very few areas of high density, like eastern Nigeria, Rwanda, or Burundi. But arid and semi-arid lands can also be overpopulated in relation to their productivity. Large parts of the Sahara, the arid horn of Africa in Somalia and northern Kenya, and Botswana are now experiencing population pressures, though the population is actually very sparse indeed. Population pressures made their appearance rather late in Africa, compared to other continents. In East and Central Africa, indeed, the impact of migration, colonization, and European diseases was so serious that the population probably dropped slightly between about 1880 and 1920. In some places, it dropped heavily, but in the middle colonial period it began to recover. For Sub-Saharan Africa as a whole, estimates suggest a population growth rate of about 0.6 percent from 1900 to 1930, then 1.3 percent between 1930 and 1940, 2.4 percent in the 1960s, and 3.2

percent today, with no sign of decrease for several decades to come. Keep in mind that an increase of 1.7 percent annually was enough to qualify as a "population explosion" in the history of nineteenth-century Europe. The present growth rate in Africa is the highest of any major region anywhere in the world, and it goes on in the face of death rates that are high compared to those of other continents. The outcome is not predictable, but the price being paid in retarded development is already becoming clear in some of the fastest growing countries, like Kenya.

Chapter Four

MAPPING AFRICAN LANGUAGE
AND SUBSISTENCE AREAS

COLONIAL ADMINISTRATORS IN AFRICA WERE UNDER
the illusion that African societies tended to be mutually
exclusive, when in fact many of them ran together and
intermixed. The early scholars and travellers made a
similar assumption that everyone in Africa belonged to
some "tribe" or other. Then came the anthropologists
who wanted Africans straightened out and classified for
their own reasons. For better or for worse, they carried
their concern a step farther than it should have gone.
They also wanted to get back to a picture of Africa as it
must have been before contact with the outside world
disturbed what they conceived of as a long period of
relative stability.

This imaginary world is sometimes called the
"ethnographic present," because anthropologists wrote
about it in the present tense. They left out the colonial
administrations, recent changes in custom, and the men
who had to migrate to the mines to support their families.
They also left out the "minority" who happened to be
present in the place they wanted to describe as having a
"whole culture." But these "minority" communities had
often been there for centuries—foreign fishing villages
set down in the midst of farming communities, nomads
who crossed and recrossed the territory of settled people,
traders belonging to trade diasporas that could stretch for

hundreds of miles. When these others had been excluded, the subject group could be studied and placed on a map. The map-maker's problem was to get everybody located in about the right place—either to govern or to study him.

For a time in the 1940s into the early 1960s, some anthropologists went a step farther. They began trying to generalize about the individual ethnic groups—the former "tribes." They tried to make maps that would identify similar ethnic groups, so as to place together in "Cultural provinces" or "culture regions." It might have been possible, following this approach, to create a map of Africa, divided into "culture regions" equivalent to states on a map of the United States, "ethnic groups" equivalent to counties, and sometimes "sub-groups" equivalent to townships. It was a useful exercise, but it is not done much any more.

Reality was simply too complex. Each distinct culture trait had its own distribution, for intricate reasons connected with the history and the environment. To create an accurate map of cultural types, it would be necessary to have a large base outline map, and then a series of transparent overlays. Each could show the distribution of some feature of culture—a house type for one, a particular group of myths for another, language for a third, art styles, and so on. To be accurate would require an enormous number of such overlays, each showing a different distribution. Some mythical themes or folklore motifs are worldwide. Kinship systems may also spread over great distances, but undergo dramatic changes in new settings.

Perhaps the sharpest breaks in such a map would lie along lines of environmental cleavage—like the desert fringe between the Sahara and the savanna. Certain things people can do in a region of rainfall agriculture cannot be done in the desert, and the reverse. The farmers want to buy meat and milk, which the nomads have to sell, and the pastoral people need to buy grain. These lines marking off environmental zones and ecological possibilities are therefore places where trade has been most intense over a very long run of history. Where trade is intense, people exchange more than mere goods, so that aspects of savanna culture will stretch out into the desert and aspects of desert culture reach far south into the savanna country.

The question, then, is what can be mapped? Culture areas are certainly still useful for classifying museum collections, but not for understanding the compexities of the African reality. In this chapter, we present two maps, one for language and one for ecological adjustment. Both will be explained in some detail, but with the advance warning that they represent a kind of "ethnographic present," a photo taken at the moment of colonial conquest in the late nineteenth century. Many changes, which cannot easily be mapped, have taken place as a result of enormously important movements of people over the past hundred years.

THE LANGUAGES OF AFRICA

African languages have sometimes, in the past, been said to be so simple that they contain vocabularies of only a few hundred words or so difficult as to be unlearnable by ordinary Europeans or Americans. Obviously, both statements are absurd. African languages are highly developed and fine instruments; they are as expressive and as expandable as their speakers care to make them. It is true that some African languages contain consonantal sounds not elsewhere found: the four clicks of the San languages, which have been taken over by some of the surrounding Bantu-speakers, are probably the most famous. The double consonants of the west coast languages—*gb,* pronounced by releasing *g* and *b* at the same time, is a case in point—are also to be noted. African vowel systems tend to be simple like Spanish or Japanese rather than complex as in such languages as French and English.

Many African languages are tonal—a fact that scares off many potential speakers who are preconvinced that tone is difficult and who hence refuse to sing. Such people may be assured that they can, if they lose their *amourpropre* and try, learn to speak African languages. Speakers of Indo-European languages can learn most African languages with somewhat greater ease than they can learn a language like Arabic or Chinese, or even one like Hungarian. On the other hand, they should not confuse a smattering of kitchen Swahili or trader Hausa with knowing an African language.

There are many languages in Africa; 800 is the traditional number. Joseph Greenberg, in the latest edition of his classic monograph *Languages of Africa,* found adequate records to consider and classify 730, but says the number may be well above the traditional 800. The problem should be familiar to us: in the same way that we had problems in differentiating men from pre-men, and the races of men from one another, so it is difficult to distinguish one language from another. The divisions in nature are not always precise—a man-made criterion must be added to make sensible classifications. Although there is still dispute in many cases about whether different languages are only different dialects, linguists are now carrying out studies of interintelligibility of languages. We shall soon have a good and full record of the languages spoken by Africans.

The vicissitudes of classifying African languages can be traced back to 1810. Every few years a basic change has had to be made in the classification, following upon better information. Greenberg in America, A. N. Tucker in Britain, as well as French, German, and Soviet scholars found it constantly necessary to revise their classifications as more and more information became available. However, this branch of African linguistics is entering into a new era of certainty, so that Greenberg could begin his 1966 report with the statement that it "contains a complete genetic classification of the languages of Africa." Certainly he (or anybody else) had never made that claim earlier.

The Greenberg classification contains five major language groups, shown in the accompanying map. Far and away the largest of the language groups, covering the largest geographical area of the continent, is the group that Greenberg calls the Niger-Kordofanian group of families. Its most important member is the Benue-Congo family of languages, which subdivides into six subfamilies. One of these subfamilies contains the well-known "Bantu languages" which cover most of central and southern Africa—but all are closely related to one another, reflecting the fact that it has been only in recent centuries that the Bantu peoples have spread into the forest regions and down the eastern and southern highlands.

The second large group of languages is called the Nilo-Saharan. It includes the languages spoken by the Nilotes, as well as many spoken in the western sudan and the area of the middle Niger River.

The Afroasiatic group of languages contains Semitic languages that are spoken in Southwest Asia as well as in North Africa; it also contains Egyptian, Berber, and

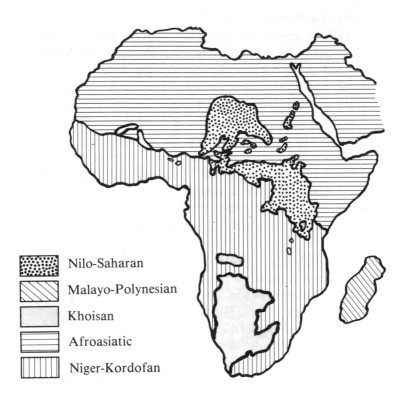

Nilo-Saharan

Malayo-Polynesian

Khoisan

Afroasiatic

Niger-Kordofan

Figure 4. Language areas of Africa (after J. H. Greenberg).

Cushitic languages, as well as various languages spoken today around Lake Chad, of which the most significant is Hausa.

Linguists used to assume that these languages must have entered Africa with immigrants from Asia. With some, like the Arabic spoken in Algeria and Morocco and the western Sahara, this is certainly true. It only happened in the eleventh century A.D. and later. Most authorities now believe, however, that the original home of this language family was probably somewhere around the Ethiopian-Sudan border in eastern Africa. Of the four major branches of this language, only the Semitic branch extends into Asia at all. The others, with their many individual languages are all spoken in Africa. This does not mean, however, that the ancestors of the people who speak Hebrew or Arabic ever came from Africa. Languages can be learned. Thus, the black Hausa-speakers of northern Nigeria speak an Afro-Asiatic language, which used to be thought of as a "white" language. The only language group that even vaguely corresponds to physical appearance is the Khoisan, but even here the distinctive clicks have worked their way into the languages of indubitably Negroid people like the Zulu.

The final language group spoken in or off the shore of Africa is Malagasy, spoken all over the island of Madagascar by people whose ancestors came from Africa, as well as by those of Malayo-Polynesian descent. Malagasy has a further distinction being one of the first languages of Africa to be written down. As long ago as the 1820s, missionaries helped develop a system of writing Malagasy with Western characters. As a result the Malagasy national archives today contain government documents in their own language going back a full 60 years before the French conquest of 1895.

Even beyond our language-map of Africa in the ethnographic present, the colonial languages have been around for a century or more. In most of Africa, they are the official languages of law, politics, journalism, and education. Africans educated in Europe began using them well before the colonial period had even begun. Africans have published books in European languages since the eighteenth century, several dozen of them before the colonial period. They still do. English and French have become the ordinary vehicle for African authors who want to reach a wide audience, and the names of Chinua Achebe, Amos Tutuola, and Ousemane Sembène have become internationally known. Only recently, the first Nobel Prize in literature to be awarded to an African went to Wole Soyinka for works written in English.

The presence of English, French, and Portuguese traders on the coast—in some numbers since the seventeenth century—made for the creation of new, mixed languages. These are usually called "pidgins," so long as they were no one's home language (from the pidgin-Chinese word for business); but in time they came to be established as the first language for many speakers. At this stage they are called "creoles," after the similarly mixed Afro-European languages of the Americas.

In the Cape Verde islands and in Guinea-Bissau, Portuguese-African creoles have existed for centuries. They are formal languages with their own grammars and dictionaries. In the Indian Ocean islands of Réunion and Mauritius, the normal language is an Afro-French creole, though the official languages are French and English respectively, and the majority of the population is descended from immigrants from India. In Sierra Leone, a similar creole, called Krio, is the normal language of discourse in the Freetown area, and it serves as the language of trade in the interior markets. In this case, it is not only a creole, but a *lingua franca.*

The original lingua franca was the variant of Italian that served as the language of commerce in the Medieval Mediterranean. But today the term, lingua franca, means a language used for communication by people for whom it is not the home language. In East Africa, for example, Swahili is Bantu language with many Arabic and English loan-words. It means it is the language of the coast, and is the home language of no more than perhaps 50,000 people. But it serves as the second language for many millions. It is the official language of Kenya and Tanzania. In Tanzania all children must be educated in Swahili through primary school, so that everyone will soon speak it, and it continues as the principal lingua franca far into eastern and central Zaire. It is too early to say whether or not it will become the home language of most Tanzanians, but that seems to be the intent. Other linguae francae are spoken elsewhere, such as the Lingala of the lower Congo basin, but not quite so widely as Swahili, mainly because the official European languages take over the role.

Language is an important policy issue all over Africa. African governments and intellectuals know that they need access to one of the world languages, preferably English. At the same time, they want to preserve their African heritage, hence Tanzania's decision for Swahili education. But young Tanzanians must pay the price of having to learn a second new language, English, at the secondary and university level.

Other countries began with English, or even switched to English. Ethiopia has Amharic as an ancient written language, but it adopted English-language education after the Second World War—when it was already an independent country, not a British colony—partly because Amharic was not popular with the non-Amharic-speaking majority, partly because English provided an easier and quicker access to the broader world, and since few technical works had been translated into Amharic.

MIGRATIONS

In mapping African languages, we placed them where they were about the beginning of the colonial period. But languages move when people move, and the actual languages spoken in Africa have already begun to shift with the massive movements of people in the twentieth century. Most Africans already spoke two or more languages with varying degrees of competence. As they move, they learn to speak more of them, and with years of residence in a foreign place to speak them better. This is one reason why the use of European languages and other linguae francae has become so important in this century.

African migrations have taken two different forms, temporary and permanent. In the colonial period, mines, plantations and European-controlled farms needed labor, but they preferred to hire workers for as long as they needed them and no more. This led to a widespread practice of labor migration. The employers rarely paid enough for a man to move his whole family and set up a new residence, so workers moved for shorter periods, leaving the family at home. Sometimes the labor period was one or two years, as in the southern and central African mines. Sometimes it was seasonal. Where the rain, and hence the farming season, was limited to three or four months in a year, farmers were under-employed. They could go off to another place looking for work. This kind of migration was most common in West Africa, where savanna conditions made for seasonal underemployment, but work could be found in the forest belt in mines or new cash crop farming of coffee, cocoa, or cola nuts.

After the Second World War, the enormous growth of

cities added another magnet drawing immigrants in hopes of finding a job. Often, the hope never became a reality. In recent years, the urban work force in many cities is more than 50 percent unemployed; but work, if it could be found, was preferable to the depressed conditions of rural agriculture. This movement was based partly on the "push" of rural poverty combined with the "pull" of the "bright lights" of the cities. Even though the pull was an unreal expectation, many people, especially young men, would take the risk on what is sometimes called the "Vegas principle"—even though they knew that the chance of success was small, they would make the gamble; because success in finding a job would leave them much better off.

Over the decades, these tropical African migration patterns often turned into permanent residence. A man in Burkina Faso might go south to the Ivory Coast to work two or three dry-seasons in a row. Finally, he might be able to move his family as well. People often kept in touch with the home village, but only for visits. In the process, the migrants and their families became bilingual. Over the longer run, it became customary for them to use the new local language, even at home. Sometimes French or English could become the new home language.

As temporary labor migrations turned into permanent shifts in the population, a whole new distribution of people and a new mixture of languages came into existence. In the 1920s, for all of West Africa to the west of Nigeria, the population of the forest belt made up about one-third of the regional total. By 1985, it was more than half. This meant that more than a quarter of the now-permanent population of the forest belt had come from the savanna. In especially prosperous countries like the Ivory Coast it was more than half. This part of West Africa had no well-developed African lingua franca to serve the place of Swahili, which means that many of these people will have switched to French as their home language before the end of the century.

The second area of mappable culture comes from the fact that Africa can be divided into a number of over-lapping zones or belts, where the traditional subsistence tended to particular patterns. Needless to say, we are concerned here with those belts as they were near the beginning of the colonial period. We cannot easily take account of a country like Nigeria, which today exports oil and imports much of its food from overseas. We can, however, show a point of departure from which African agriculture moved.

The subsistence areas are also important for other aspects of culture. The crops people grew, whether they herded or farmed, even the kind of animal they herded correlates widely with other aspects of their way of life. Subsistence activity shows a close correspondence with the working habits of both sexes; with the size and com-position of work groups; with trade; with diet patterns; indeed, even with musculature. It is also true that subsis-tence patterns are those least changed by the colonial experience.

The staple products, and therefore diets, of Africa can be classified meaningfully by the source of food. There are a few remnant groups who still subsist on a foraging economy: the Pgymies are primarily hunters and gather-ers (although trade with neighbors brings them vegetable food); so are the San. The most important group of

Pepper seller in the market, Ibadan, Nigeria.

foragers are the fishermen on the coasts and rivers. Fishermen are among the few Africans who do not show some dietary deficiencies; they usually trade a part of their catch for one of the' starchy staples, or else the women of the group grow some grain or tubers.

African herders are primarily cattle herders, although the Sahara shelters a few peoples who keep camels, and the Serengeti plain and other areas in East Africa are the home of peoples who keep large flocks of goats (that animal being all but ubiquitous on the continent, however). Herdsmen's diets are either a milk staple or (in a few parts of East Africa) a diet in which a source of protein is a mixture of blood and sour milk. Almost all herding peoples add starchy staples to their diets, either by harvesting their own cash crops or, more commonly, through well-integrated methods of trade with settled agricultural peoples.

By far the greatest number of Africans are farmers. They can be sensibly divided into three groups: those among whom grain crops are the major staple, those who grow root crops, and those who grow tree crops. Bananas are the basis of the diet in a belt stretching westward from the vicinity of Lake Victoria to the Atlantic. The grain changes from one area to another of the "grain belt" and there is a variety of root crops, but these distinctions are of somewhat minor importance when it is realized that Liberian rice farmers and Rhodesian maize farmers use very similar methods of cultivation, and the yam cultivators of Nigeria and the manioc farmers of Congo would quickly be at home in one another's work habits even though cultivating manioc takes much less work.

Camel herders are found throughout the inhabited Sahara and on the Saharan fringe, both north and south, as well as in the eastern Horn. The "cattle belt" of Africa runs from the Atlantic in Senegal, along the corridor between the forests and the desert with only a few breaks; it turns south along the Nile and from Lake Victoria proceeds both eastward and southward, and eventually swings back to the Atlantic in Angola, between the forests of the Congo and the Kalahari Desert. In much of the area of East and South Africa where cattle are the greatest concern, cattle nevertheless do not actually form the subsistence base, or provide the staple part of the diet, and these areas must be included in the "grain belt," the staple being maize or sorghum. Cattle do, however, form the basis of the morality and prestige activities of the men of the tribes of that area, and many pastoralists get grain in exchange for dairy products.

A great deal has been written about the East African herding peoples who tap blood from the neck veins of their cattle, mix it with sour milk, and eat the mixture. Actual studies by food economists, dieticians, and geographers, however, have recently indicated that blood accounts for at most a few hundreds of calories a week. Milk and butter are much more important, but some starchy staple enters the diet of almost all African herdsmen. They seldom kill animals for meat, but do of course eat those they sacrifice.

The grain belt of Africa forms a crescent, inside of and overlapping with the herding crescent. There is another, smaller grain belt along the Mediterranean coast, in which the staple grains are barley and wheat grains from Southwest Asia via Europe. South of the Sahara, however, the grains are of a different sort. Farmers from Senegal south through Liberia and into the Ivory Coast grow an indigenous African variety of rice as their staple food. They grow it either as upland rice or sow it into patches

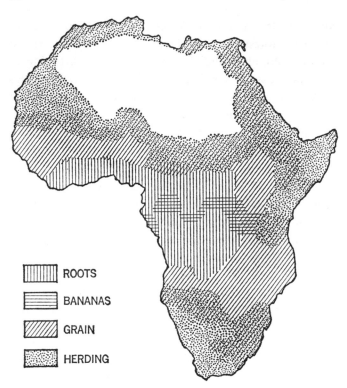

Figure 5. Subsistence areas of Africa.

which they have cleared out of the forest. Although rice
has remained a staple in this area, much of the acreage
has been put into Asian rice, which is considered even by
Africans themselves to be superior.

As one proceeds westward from Senegal, the grain
changes to sorghum and millet. Still further east, in the
southern sudan and Ethiopia, the primary grains are eleusine, teff, and fonio. As one turns south, east of Lake
Victoria, maize and sorghum are the staples; there is some
pearl millet in the southern Congo area and in a few
others, but aside from that, maize and sorghum form the

staples all the way to the southern end of the continent.

Throughout the grain-producing areas of Africa, the mode of agriculture and the nature of the diet are similar. The chief agricultural implements are the hoe—short-handled in most places but long-handled in parts of Rhodesia, Zambia, and Zaire—and the long knife called a matchet in western Africa and a *panga* in Swahili-speaking areas. In some places the digging stick, with or without a metal tip, is still to be found. The plow, pulled by oxen, is found today in parts of eastern and southern Africa. In most places—but there are, as usual, exceptions —the heavy work of clearing the land is done by men, who also prepare the fields for planting and may even do the planting. The women then take over—if they have not indeed been doing the work already—and take care of weeding and harvesting. It is also the women who carry the grain back to the homestead or to the drying platforms. It is stored in granaries which are made, in most areas, something like the houses but smaller and usually set up off the ground to give some protection from termites, rats, and other pests. These granaries—and the food in them—are often the property of the household head, but the food is just as often considered the property of the woman, who is obliged to feed her children from it as well as her husband who provided her with land and cleared it for her.

Except for rice, which is cooked whole, grain in Africa is ground—traditionally by hand, on stone, today often by hand-operated mills or power mills at the village or town center—and cooked into porridge. A thick, malleable porridge is Africa's bread. It provides most of the calories of most African diets. It is eaten dipped into a sauce prepared of meat or vegetables or both. Oils and fats are plentiful—the particular one varies with the part of the country from shea butter to palm oil to peanut oil to sesame oil and many others. They are part of the sauce, not of the porridge.

A woman's day is taken up with farming, grinding the meal, cooking the porridge and the sauce. Yet most African women find time to attend markets, visit relatives, and even sometimes to rest.

Men's work is more strenuous, more varied, and—like farmers' work everywhere—seasonal. During the time of clearing land, African grain farmers may put out almost unbelievable amounts of work in a day. They have, moreover, to carry out the political and judicial affairs of the country, which in most African societies takes a lot of time on the part of many of the men.

The subsistence area based on root crops forms a core in the Congo basin, with a long strip along the Guinea coast. Crops are yams, manioc, taro, sweet potatoes, and a few other minor root crops. None of these roots, it would appear, is indigenous to Africa. The yam is Malaysian, and manioc is South American. Root crops, as food, are generally considered by Western dieticians to be inferior to grains, because they are short of some of the essential vitamins and minerals. Their culture puts a little more work on the men of the community, who must, in this shallow soil, make two-foot mounds in which to grow yams, or smaller ones in which to grow manioc or sweet potatoes.

Roots are either cooked green or else dried and made into a flour, then mashed or stewed into porridge and eaten with sauces.

Dates form a staple in a relatively large area of the Sahara, and, in a large stretch across equatorial Africa and a few spots on the west coast, bananas are the principal food crop. These bananas are not the sweet bananas that Americans and Europeans eat for breakfast or dessert, but are plantains — scarcely sweet, much starchier, and of a less oily consistency. Plantains are cooked and, like the grain and the roots, made into porridge.

It is important to note that not only food, but drink, follows these general areas. Again to oversimplify, herders drink honey beer—except those who are Muslims. Some make beer from traded grain. In the grain belt, arguments rage about the virtues and faults of beer made with maize, sorghum, and millet. In the banana country, bananas are mashed and made into beer. The root crop country is approximately the same as the oil palm country, where the staple beverage is palm wine.

Westerners who are thoroughly familiar with the market economy and with the particular tensions and insecurities it brings would do well to remember that subsistence economy also brings its own tensions: one is totally dependent for one's food during the next year on one's own labors, and on the fruits of one's fields, more or less ameliorated by dependence on kinsmen. Droughts and floods, locusts and birds are personal enemies. Religious myth and ritual, like insecurity, center around food production. Many Africans are, today, entering market economy and adjusting to new types of insecurities. But with most, even now, subsistence is a major psychic as well as practical problem, and in creating it one must work and must cooperate with kinsmen and with the forces of the gods.

Part Two

AFRICAN INSTITUTIONS

Chapter Five

AFRICAN ARTS

ALL ART CAN BE SAID TO HAVE TWO SWEEPING CHARAC-
teristics: it embodies a message within an idiom of communication, and it arouses a sense of mystery—a feeling
that it is more than it appears to the intellect to be.
"Good" art is that which, no matter what its cultural origins or uses, can arouse this sense of mystery in many
persons, from many cultures (although all of us are probably blind to the arts of some cultures and some ages).

In that sense, Africa has an extensive "good" art. Its
ineffable quality can be widely perceived, and it has taken
its place in museums and in the collections of many art
lovers.

Yet art also bears a "message" from artist to viewer.
The message must be carried out within an idiom that,
like language, can be broken down into a sort of gram-
mar—the parts of sculpture or the parts of music, analo-
gous to (but probably more complex than) the parts of
speech. In fact, it is impossible for an artist *not* to convey
a message, whether his metier be measured realism and
calls up the calm of a forest twilight or it be abstract,
which is to say that it is art about art itself.

Art then may be valued either as a message-bearing
comment or as mystery. It may in fact be valued for both
of these things at once. Usually, however, it is not. Too
often art appreciators—those who prize the mystery for

itself—object to the people who intellectualize and put
into words the messages that are conveyed. On the other
hand, anthropologists and others who use art to get at
the temper of a culture (much as critics use it to get at
the temper of an age or of a creative mind) usually deni-
grate the mere appreciator. Fullest comprehension implies
both.

The mystery of good art comes across cultural barriers.
The message probably does not. In order to appreciate
the art fully, something of the cultural background must
be known to make the message clear.

ARTISTIC COMMENT

Art is of the essence in analyzing culture because it
supplies the media in which some of the most perceptive
and original thinkers in any society communicate their
experience. Therefore it is to the arts (as well as to the
sciences) that we must first turn to know what the people
of another culture—indeed, of our own culture—may be
thinking. It is, ultimately, not art that holds the mirror up
to nature—it is social and natural science. In art, everything is simplified, stripped to its essentials; the mirror of
art is a burning glass.

Art then includes communication, comment, and criticism. The message may be trite or propagandistic. The
message may be extremely distasteful; it may also be obscure. Yet artists are thinking people—which does not
mean that they are intellectualizing people. So are
consumers and critics of art. They are the people on
the receiving end of communication. The critics translate
for us, who may have less perceptive vision, what it is that
the artist is saying—the postulates that lie behind his mes-

sage. Artists may hate critics. If they do, it may be because the critic was obtuse, but it may be because the critic was extraordinarily perceptive and the artist is unable to bear the bold statement of his message in an idiom and in a symbolism different from that which he himself gave it.

African art can be understood on three levels. It can be studied as form and technique. In the second place, the purpose and the meaning—the aesthetics, indeed—of the art must be garnered not merely from the artists but from the critics in the society. Finally, African art can be evaluated for its impact on Western (or some other) art—an impact that was, earliest and strongest, that of the mystery rather than that of the message.

THE FORMS AND TECHNIQUES OF AFRICAN ART

The forms of African art that have become widely known outside of Africa are limited to sculpture and music. African music is coming into its own as one of the world's great musics that has several specific contributions to make. Undoubtedly the most dramatic of the special attributes is its polyrhythmic structure. Polyrhythms are complex combinations of fairly simple but different rhythms, all played concurrently. Western music has the "classic" situation of "two against three"—the triplet played against two "full-value" notes during the same time span. Rarely, in Western music, a third rhythm may be added. In African music, on the other hand, five such rhythms are common, and as many as a dozen at a time have been recorded.

Although African dancing has been for a long time one of the two favorite sights of tourists in Africa (the other is watching big game), few outsiders have been able to realize its full quality and artistic achievement. The point of African dancing in many parts of the continent, at least, is for various parts of the body each to accompany one of the rhythms in the orchestra so that the poly-rhythms in the orchestra are reproduced by the dancer's body. The head moves in one rhythm, the shoulders in another; the arms in still a third, the trunk in another, and the feet in still another. Once the viewer has learned to see and feel the polyrhythms in the dance as it reflects the music, he can appreciate that African dancing both demands great precision and allows great freedom of ex-pression to the dancers. African dancing is still a folk art; there have been a few attempts to produce it for the stage—notably the African ballet companies sponsored by several African countries—but too often the European and American audiences have not been sufficiently sophisticated and the individual dances have been cut too short to give the dancers sufficient play for their imagination and the variations that each dance requires if the rhythms are to be fully explored.

In African literature the great form is the dramatic tale. African tales have affected the literatures of many lands, particularly of the southern United States and the Carib-bean area, where the so-called Brer Rabbit stories have become standard. Collections of African folk tales are also quite common, even though they are usually studied only by specialists. In all of these manifestations, however, the true quality of the original has been left behind in Africa. The mere tale on a page will produce little more than would the retelling of the plot of *As You Like It* in two paragraphs, with a moral tacked on at the end, fable-fashion. These dramatic tales in Africa have a theatrical quality. They are told and acted out before audiences who participate in musical choruses and in spoken responses. The individual taletellers may be assisted by a dozen or more people who are costumed and "cast" as in any other theater art. The taleteller also makes up songs, centering around the situation of the tale; he teaches the choruses of the songs to the audience and assures himself audience response whenever he needs it. The stories of the tales are well known. The achievement of the individual artist is to be found in the music and in the version of the tale and the way he manipulates the dramatic elements in it to enlarge or point his moral. The result is living theater. It cannot be overemphasized that African folk tales, written on half a sheet of paper in a Western language, lose all but the so-called "plot" of the original. The art is gone. Again, it should be noted that the dramatic tale demands of its performers compliance with a certain set of activities, and then encourages individualization and free expression.

Africa has produced novelists like Chinua Achebe, who are known world-wide. Playwright and poet Wole Soyinka has been produced in Africa and Europe and North America — and won the Nobel Prize for Literature. A host of young writers in English and French — and a few in African languages — are garnering fine reputations today. Several American and European universities added courses in African literature in recent decades, and in the last twenty years, African universities have also added them.

African painting has a long history, but is comparatively unknown in the West. The earliest cave paintings go back several thousand years, but as yet have not been dated with any great precision. Experts do, however, know the marks of various periods of such paintings —some of the earliest are huge representations of human

A traditional Senufo artist, working to the tune of a Western radio (Ivory Coast).

beings eleven feet high and animals as much as twenty-six feet long. Rock painting in the Sahara is still being done today, but the figures are miniatures rather than the gigantic murals. Rock paintings have been found and studied in most parts of the continent—the picture is becoming clearer, but expert opinion says that it will be some decades before a real "history" of African painting can be written. Since the middle of the twentieth century, African painters have appeared in great number, and some, such as Selby Mvusi, have acquired international reputations.

Nevertheless, the best known of African arts, outside of Africa at least, is sculpture. Most African sculpture, except that done in terra cotta, is produced by a subtractive process—material taken away from a core instead of added to a core. Soapstone carvings are to be found in areas of Sierra Leone, and iron sculpture in several isolated places in Africa. Ivory was a favorite medium in the Kingdom of Benin and in Zaire, and ivory sculpture is carried on in many areas today. However, the major media for African sculpture are wood and various alloys of copper, tin, and zinc that hover around bronze and brass.

African carvers work almost exclusively in green wood. The carver must know a great deal about the qualities of different woods, so that they will not crack too much when dry, although cracks appear in most pieces of African art —even in Africa, let alone when they are subjected to the high and dry temperatures of American and European homes and museums.

Woodworking is done with an adze and is finished with a knife. In some parts of the continent, some sculptors use rough leaves as sandpaper—or, today, sandpaper. The carvings may be painted with all sorts of mineral and vegetable colors (and today with imported paints), the most common being lampblack set by the sap of any of several trees.

Indigenous African sculpture falls into three main sorts: one is the figurine, which may vary from small and simple figures only a few inches high to elaborate carved house posts, stools, or other functional forms. The figurines are fundamentally adaptations from the tree trunk, with the heaviest weight at the bottom, proceeding in columnar form. The next form is the mask. African masks are among the best known in the world and artistically are among the most satisfying. They come in three main shapes: those that are worn over the face, those worn on top of the head, and the "helmet"-type masks which fit down over the head. The third form is decoration of various useful objects, ranging from doors to spoons to bobbins.

African bronzes are all cast by the lost-wax method. Each piece is therefore unique. In this method, the technique is fundamentally additive, rather than subtractive as it is in carving. Over a core of some sort—usually dried mud in the traditional forms—the sculptor models in wax whatever he wants to reproduce in metal. To this he adds, also in wax, several long, tentacle-like appendages. When the core is thoroughly dry and the waxen model completely set, it is covered by several coats of the finest pottery slip clay available. The whole is then covered with coarser pottery clay. The mold is then heated and the wax runs out along the passageways that result from the melting of the tentacles. The molten metal is poured into the hot mold—a skilled task if one is to avoid air bubbles —and exactly fills the space left when the wax melted, and reproduces the original image.

THE HISTORY OF AFRICAN ART

Except for Egypt the earliest sculpture that we know to be unequivocally African comes from the Nok culture, from about 600 B.C. to A.D. 200 in the sub-Saharan sudan area. The distribution of Nok culture is a fairly narrow area between Katsina and Katsina Ala in northern Nigeria. It was discovered in the course of tin-mining operations.

Nok art, as we know it, is almost entirely a pottery or terra-cotta art. Most terra cotta, even in Africa, is done by an additive technique in which the sculptor starts with a core and adds more clay as the sculpture progresses. However, Bernard Fagg found some examples of Nok terra cotta that showed forms which would be more suitable to a subtractive technique, like carving, and was able to infer that carving in wood (necessarily lost to time and the elements) was also present. Nok art which has been preserved is done in fine pottery, excellently fired: hollow figures, three-quarter life size, in some cases. Such an art is technically very demanding. Nok culture is now represented by several score of examples — heads, limbs, and some furniture.

The earliest bronze sculpture so far found in Africa is from Eastern Nigeria, and is known as the Igbo Ukwu style. It has been dated to the tenth century A.D. Discovered, excavated, and thoroughly documented by Thurston Shaw, these sculptures are in a style that both is unprecedented and, as far as we now know, had no followers.

Among the finest pieces of measuredly naturalistic sculpture ever produced are the bronze heads of Ife in Nigeria, which date from about the twelfth century A.D. Because they are in a measured and classical naturalistic style, it was assumed when they were found, in the early twentieth century by Frobenius, the German ethnologist, folklorist, and adventurer, that Africans could not have made them. Therefore, "obviously" it was the Portuguese who did them. The fact that there was no technique of this sort known to the Portuguese at this time was not allowed to intrude against the stereotype. Once carbon-14 dates· made the age fairly precise, it became necessary to admit that they could *only* have been done by Africans.

Frobenius turned up a good many of these Ife heads in terra cotta and one in brass. The brass piece that he discovered he "bought" (in a manner of speaking) from the family in charge of the Olokun Grove. The British administrative officers on the spot refused him permission to export it. After considerable contretemps, Frobenius returned the bronze, and some of the terra cotta. In the 1940s, however, Leon Underwood, a well-known British sculptor, discovered that the head Frobenius had originally discovered was a sand casting, whereas all the other Ife heads were lost-wax castings. No African artists had ever done sand casting. The assumption is unavoidable either that Frobenius had not returned the original or else that he was not the true discoverer, and discovered only the copy. Except for that original piece and one other, which is in the British Museum, the complete set of brass heads (but not of terra-cotta heads) is now in the possession of the Oni of Ife and housed in his small but magnificent museum.

Another ancient art that deserves attention is that of the Kingdom of Benin, some 110 miles southeast of Ife. Benin art flooded Great Britain, and indeed the Western European museums, at the very end of the nineteenth century. At that time, 1897, the consolidation of European power in Africa was being carried on most furiously, with the colonial powers, in accordance with

Brass Worker, Bida, Nigeria.

the Berlin Conference, busily occupying the territories they had claimed. The Ashanti in the Gold Coast fought and held out for some years. The people of the Kingdom of Benin (not to be confused with the present-day Republic of Benin west of Nigeria)—who call themselves Bini—also fought. The Bini had a form of religion in which a royally sponsored art, made by highly organized craft guilds, was a major component. The content of the religion embraced safety, salvation, fertility or increase; sacrifice at altars played a major part. The art was based on altarpiece heads of cast bronze, each of which supported, on its top, a carved elephant tusk. The tusk swept back and up from the head. An altar might have more than a dozen such pieces, magnificently wrought and carefully preserved. Most of these pieces are, today, still in the British Museum, although a small number of them were returned to Nigeria, where they are to be found in the Benin branch of the Nigerian Museum, as well as in several of the other Nigerian Museums.

The other major component of Benin art was the bronze plaques which were set into mud walls and pillars of the house. There are a large number of such plaques known. Some are of historical importance: since they show Portuguese in medieval European armor with arquebuses and crossbows that we know from other sources, we can reasonably assume that they show as accurately those aspects of African culture to which we have no other direct contemporary evidence.

Benin is well known for the fact that during its last years human sacrifices were performed in the most gross exaggerations. There were sacrifices made just before the capture of the city by the British—almost frenetically performed sacrifices aimed at staving off the encroaching enemy—an orgy of human sacrifice that seems to have been

far worse than any which preceded it. The first major
work on the area, R. H. Bacon's work of 1897, is called
Benin, City of Blood. Only in later years was the precise symbolism of these sacrifices determined; the word
"Benin" was, in parts of Europe, synonymous with depravity at the turn of the century. Today, when these
matters have been forgotten, there is a new, derivative,
but hopeful art being made in Benin. The organization
of guilds is still more or less intact, and it would seem
that royal or governmental patronage may lead to an ef-
florescence of art, in a new set of styles containing some
traditional elements.

The African art that is best known in the West and
best represented in African museums stems from the late
nineteenth and early twentieth centuries — from the era
just before the culture and ethnogeography of Africa
were frozen in place by the colonial era.

Although scholarship today has created many refined
classifications of African art, such classifications, like
race, are most easily left as three major stereotypes. In
this way, we can avoid the many contradictions of
experts. The major classification is the one created by
William Fagg of the British Museum in the early 1950s,
which is still the most generally useful. He divided
African art into three major "culture areas": the Sudan,
the Guinea Coast, and the Congo Basin. Trying to put
the elements of style from the three areas into words inevitably erects a screen between the viewer and the artist.
Thus, the student of African art, or any other, must learn
at the same time that he makes the classifications for
scholarly purposes to supersede them for purposes of
direct communication. Because it is more abstract than
other African art, the art of the sudan has a quality of
quietness and inwardness and intensity. The Congo Basin

provides a more flamboyant, decorated, exaggerated, extroverted (it has been called) kind of art. The Guinea coast lies stylistically as well as geographically between them.

Westerners have often, in the past, confused the examination of the place of art in society with the historical development of art. They have been wont to seek for the "origins" of art rather than to perceive its uses. Origins and histories of individual art styles and forms can, of course, be usefully made; but "the origin of art" is too amorphous a question. Sometimes religion is the assigned "cause," sometimes something else. Art can no more have a cause or a single origin than can language. Just as apes did not suddenly one morning awake to find themselves human, so art did not, one day, suddenly spring into being from the fertile mind of some prehistoric genius. Art is a form of communication, and therefore it grows with culture and develops with the beast—and it has always been so.

Although decorative and other secular art is to be found in most parts of Africa, many forms in African art are indeed associated with religion. So is much of Western art and every other art. This fact has led some art critics and some anthropologists to exaggerate the claims of religion for art. It is quite true that many pieces of art have religious associations. Of course African art has a religious connotation—but the very same claim can be made for its having a political connotation or an economic one or a domestic one.

African masks are one of the most common art forms and are worn as part of a costume. In the court or the ritual, the symbolized forces of politics and religion can be made carnate, so that the drama of justice or of myth can be reenacted. The myth is not assumed in most societies, as it is in our own, to be pseudo-historical and about the past. The myth is rather used to explain—indeed, to communicate—the here and now. Much African masked drama is a reincarnation of the basic myths of creation, the power structure of the society, the myths of history and religion, and even the myths of settlement patterns. One of the best ways to assure the efficacy of the myth is to sanctify the objects which Westerners call art. Then it is possible for the priests, or the kings, or simply the public to loan their human vitality to the mythical principles that are symbolized.

Figurines are not "worshiped." They may be used as symbols of forces, ideas, historical events, myths, which are very real in society and held sacred. That is a grave difference. The "heathen" do not "bow down to wood and stone." Neither are saints' symbols in our own society worshiped. Rather they stand for something important and holy. Figurines can be consecrated in that same sense, and for the same purpose.

Giving living reality to the myth through drama and art is the most vivid way of making people recognize their dependence upon the myth and upon the society whose members live more or less by it.

Sometimes, too, African art is for fun. We would even say that some "art" may be no more than playful decoration added to the basic ideas for producing something that is "needed." Art supplies a "need" that is felt or expressed. It is art, in one sense, if it is decorated and goes beyond the mere need. Omitting taste (criticism within a culture cannot omit taste but comprehension across cul-

tures probably must), art is decorated, needed objects.
The communication in it is greater if it is great art; so is
the mystery. But art for fun both supplies needs and is
decorated. As with the Jefferson Memorial, the image
draws attention to the principle.

Art permeates African culture, which in turn permeates
African art. Art is not set aside from "real life" — it cannot
be among a people who do not traditionally make such
distinctions.

THE AESTHETICS OF AFRICAN ART

It is critics and scholars rather than artists who create
aesthetics. Only in a hopelessly intellectualizing culture
such as that of the modern West does the artist have to
become his own aesthetician. Therefore, for social
sciences it is from the critics that the greatest knowledge
is to be gained. It is the critics and the consumers of art
who relate art to the rest of culture and therefore create
data for social scientists.

The screen that comes between the viewer and the artist is the thing that has been intellectualized and nurtured
among Westerners. We should be made aware of it.
The screen becomes readily apparent if one compares a
"primitive" with a "modern" piece. The earliest piece in
an exhibition of Portuguese art in London some years
ago was a fourteenth-century crucifix about eighteen feet
high, done in wood, magnificently displayed so that as
one came in the door he was hit by it. It was immediately evident that the sculptor had had absolutely no set
of principles between him and the wood. There it was—
indeed, there he was, immersed in the idea. The communication was immediate.

Around the corner in Cavendish Square, Epstein's madonna is perched high on a convent wall. The Epstein intensity is of a completely different nature from the intensity achieved by the unknown Portuguese artist of the fourteenth century. Sir Jacob Epstein had to settle down and create an intellectual aesthetic. In our era, it is necessary for at least some people to intellectualize the aesthetic: to verbalize all communications first, even when the ultimate medium is not verbal. For the Portuguese artist, such intellectualization or verbalization was not necessary. What he was saying about his belief and his convictions and his vision was a direct representation—almost a union between him and the wood. Epstein may have achieved something greater, but he has not achieved that union. Their achievements may, indeed, be all but incomparable, joined only by the word "art."

It is such direct union that can be discerned, felt, in the greatest pieces of African art: there is no intellectualized aesthetic or verbalized purpose between artist and art.

There *is*, however, a screen of "aesthetic" between a piece of art and the viewer, probably in all situations. There is certainly such a "screen" between African art and the European—indeed, for most modern African—viewers. Whatever disadvantage may be felt here can be turned to advantage if one completes the process—creates a full intellectualization so that the screen is known and hence can be systematically disregarded. Directness—or a reasonable substitute—can thus be achieved by the viewer as well as by the artist.

Until very recent years, the aesthetics behind African art were seldom verbalized. The study of African aesthetics done by most European and American scholars warped the subject to one degree or another—a translation difficulty from which there is no escape. Today several universities in Africa have introduced courses in African art, and the process of verbalizing the aesthetics is under way. However, it is generally agreed that the best places to study African art are still the U.S. and France.

There is, for example, a great deal of discussion among students of African art about whether African sculpture is "portraiture," but only comparatively little sensible discussion of what defines "portraiture." It is a phony question. The use of small figurines in the Ivory Coast, for example, is as a place or site into which the spirits of departed ancestors can settle. In Western portraiture the point is to capture the personality—we are told by our severest critics that we overvalue the cult of the personality. Likeness, even the caricature of individuality, is prized. If you doubt that caricature is prized in twentieth-century Western art, examine Graham Sutherland's painting of Maugham or Epstein's bust of the ninth duke of Marlborough, or almost any of the Sargent portraits. It is the very individuality that our religion, our culture—and, of course, our art—make us seek to recapture. The Ivory Coasters are seeking something quite different when they make the figurines for shrines to contain the spirits of ancestors. They are after a principle that lies behind both the religion and the kinship system. Strip the personality—and the principles of humanity, of ancestorhood, remain. With us, it is the personality that must be kept, not the principle or the relationship.

Getting at these ideas is difficult precisely because, among other reasons, the people we study do not look at such problems intellectually. We must find out what we require of art before it is possible to discover what somebody else requires of it. A background in traditional aesthetics doesn't help much in that process.

One reason that some educated Africans do not like African art is not merely that it is associated with "backwardness" and therefore injurious to their *amour propre;* rather it is that they have actually lost the culture which allows them to see immediately the relevance of much of this art, to respond to it, at the same time that, for whatever reasons, they have not been interested in "appreciating" it through intellectualization. They have the same problems the Europeans have in looking at it. Yet, to appreciate African art fully, there is no better experience than to attend one of the fine African museums and note the reactions of the Africans— some of them directly from the farthest villages— and their rapt attention.

There have been very few systematic attempts to get at the aesthetics of African art. The most notable one is documented in a slim volume by Hans Himmelheber called *Negerkünstler,* about the Atutu peoples of the Ivory Coast. Himmelheber went into the area armed with first-rate interpreters, and with questionnaires. He found nineteen artists with whom he spent several months. He watched them work and he filled in his questionnaires. In the book, written in German, one of the questions he reports that he asked was "when you are working, *fühlen Sie noch Schöpfungsfreude?"* ("do you feel any joy in creation?"). The question was asked in French, interpreted into and answered in Atutu, recorded again in French, and reported in German—yet Himmelheber is aware of the difficulty and says specifically that he thinks that his interpretations came through the buzz of language pretty well. The reaction he got was: "Good heavens, no—not that!" Artistic joy is something that all Atutu denied.

Himmelheber could not help being put off when Atutu

artists claimed that they worked mainly for money. Himmelheber was a little sentimental here: artists in our society do not expect to make a lot of money (neither do the Atutu), but they like to make a living at their art. They *all* do it for money, in one sense: yet we have a sneaking suspicion — left over from the nineteenth century — that doing something for money is a sign of the prostitution of talent.

African taste in art, like taste in art everywhere else, is created ultimately by the consumers. The second most important function in any art tradition is that of the critic. We in America have assumed that only the people who create have a God-given right to criticize. Americans dislike the notion of criticism—criticism is tantamount to carping. We have a special term, "constructive criticism," under which we are allowed minimal expression of our critical capacities.

Everywhere there is an exchange of views between the artist and the critic-consumer. Realization of this point makes us see that most of the comment about "preserving" African art is the grossest sentimentality. Unless the art conforms to the cultural patterns and values—the views of the society and the ideas behind the expressed views—it is meaningless. Thus, art is "cheapened" by African workmen for Europeans. The reason is simple: the only "feedback" is that of the market place. There is a widespread and mistaken belief that only the bad taste of Europeans has "spoiled" African art: that African art has gone to pot *because* of the European curio trade, etc. The real reason it has "gone to pot" is that the demands of the consumers have changed. African art, obviously then, has no glorious future—if that future is measured solely by the nineteenth-century tradition. But then neither do

copies of the French impressionists. A tremendous body
of modern African art is being produced. Much of it is
plastic art, as the tradition of great African art would lead
us to predict.

Today African artists want to be recognized as artists,
not just African artists. Their subject matter is drawn
from the world in which they live—which is the present-
day world, not nineteenth century Africa. They do not
sculpt like traditional Africans any more than Pollack
painted like Whistler—and for the same reasons. Like
other Africans of talent, no matter what their field, these
artists are pushed all out of proportion by demands made
by both Africans and Europeans—indeed, by two
streams of evaluation and criticism.

For African artists to do "authentic" African art would
be equivalent to the most distressingly precious folkloring.
Folk song in our own society can be made viable only
when it is modified and recast into the late twentieth-
century idiom of performance. The same is true of
today's African art.

If there were no African artists we might decry the
"death of African art." But the continent is full of them,
as it is of writers and musicians. As everywhere else, artists in Africa are "oddballs." Everywhere they are specialists, given a different set of moral demands by the public.
Artists are special people—that is as true in Africa as in
Paris or London. African artists are trained today, and
they always have been. The training may be formal as it
is among the Ivory Coast people in which an apprentice-
ship may last up to five years; during that time the ap-
prentice is made to copy the master's work and live in
the master's household. In such a way, style is handed
on: yet individual styles are immediately distinguishable
to the aware eye. Today artists are trained in universities

and art schools as well as by traditional means. So are artists everywhere.

Frank Willett, who is both an art historian and an anthropologist, claims that the first piece of carving made by African hands to reach modern Europe arrived in 1504 on a Portuguese trading ship. African workmanship in leather and probably in gold had been known for centuries before that.

However, African art burst upon the awareness of the Western world only at the turn of the nineteenth to the twentieth century. Army men like Pitt-Rivers and Torday brought back large collections of art along with good ethnographic description—in fact, Pitt-Rivers built two fine museums (one in Oxford and the other on his estate in Dorset) to house his collections. The Musée de l'Homme in Paris and the Royal Belgian Museum at Tervueren also acquired large collections.

Several painters and sculptors working in Paris in 1904 and 1905 began to notice African sculptures brought back from the colonies: Maurice de Vlaminck, Derain, Picasso, Matisse, Vollard, and Maillol were only some of the artists who were greatly affected by African art in the early twentieth century.

No one should jump to the idea that Picasso's women who look two ways at once, or anything else about his work, is a copy of something he discovered in African art. There was little direct, stylistic influence, although some can be discovered by latter-day critics. Rather, what happened was that with the discovery of African and other exotic art, the way was discovered for breaking out of the confines that had been imposed on European art by tradition—perspective, measured naturalism, and anti-intellectual sentimentality. African figurines could give the "modern" artist courage to foreshorten, to emphasize by changes of scale, to adjust scale to message. Looking at African art made such artists know what some of the earlier great painters had already known—El Greco stretches his human figures—that one sees passionately quite differently from the way one sees mensuristically. To get inside the vision, it was necessary to get outside the inherited canons of art. And African art was one of the means of getting out.

Yet, African art had been present in Europe for many years. It had never really been looked at by artists before the late nineteenth and early twentieth centuries. Some of the best collections in Europe are to be found in Germany, in Switzerland (especially Geneva and Lugano), in Belgium and in France.

Americans coming now to the study of African art should know that an interesting process has been occurring during the last twenty years. When the first edition of this book was published, in 1963, the finest collections, almost without exception, were in anthropological museums. During the last twenty years, art museums have begun to collect and display African pieces. The Chicago Art Institute and the Museum of Primitive Art in New York are examples. And in September, 1987, the new National Museum of African Art was opened in Washington, D.C., as a permanent part of the Smithsonian Institution.

Looking at plastic art, however, is no substitute for handling it—and unfortunately, museums cannot allow their specimens to be handled. Tactile sensations are as important in learning about African sculptures as are visual sensations. It is easiest to learn if one can get it into his hands. The memory of it, like the sensation of it, comes through the muscles and the sense of touch as well as through the eyes. Dahomean brass sculpture (from the present-day Republic of Benin) is tactilely sinewy and tough and not at all delicate as it appears to the visual sense: actually, of course, the combination tells one a great deal about Dahomean culture. Some African wood carving is in heavy, earthbound wood; other is in wood so porous and so light as to seem almost spiritual. To make such remarks is *not* so much to interpret African art (which they do not) as to prepare one for the fact that there is more in it than the artists put there and that the something more is derivative of the cultural image of the human condition. The more we know of the human condition, and the specific picture of it which lies undelineated behind the pieces in question, the more the art can be made to mean.

African art, like any other, must mean something to the artist and something else to the viewer or the critic. The anthropologist tries his best to make the African artist's view as palpable as possible to the European viewer, and such is a worthy intention. He is not, however, within his province if he claims that any other interpretation of it is wrong. Art is embodied vision. African art speaks both for the culture and for itself. Like all art, speaking for one human culture allows it, in some degree, to speak for all.

Chapter Six

AFRICAN FAMILIES

THE FAMILY ARISES FROM THE MAMMALIAN HERITAGE of the human being. Family life is a universal—it is to human beings what the herd is to cattle or deer, the school to fish, or the flock to ducks and geese.

A great deal of effort, energy, attention, imagery and imagination must go into the perpetuation of the species, the control of sexuality in order to avoid social chaos, and bringing up children to be "human," however that may be culturally defined.

The family is the most economic way of controlling and satisfying fundamental needs of the human animal: the need for secure and predictable companionship, for food, for sexual expression and regulation, for reproduction, for teaching and training the young.

Family life is a universal. It has often and correctly been said that the family image is at the foundation of the images of all social relationships. Whether we make the statements from a psychic or a social, a historical or an evolutionary point of view, it is incontrovertible.

Kinship is, actually, a simple business. It springs out of the fact that a man marries a woman and they beget and bear children. These are "the facts of life." On such facts, several changes can be rung; and only a few of the possible changes are not found institutionalized and valued somewhere. Therefore, it behooves us to look at African

111

kinship practices in order to understand Africa and better understand ourselves.

There are two kinds of kinship. One is a relationship of descent; the other is a relationship of sexuality. Each may occur in two modes: the direct mode and the shared mode.

"Male" assumes the existence of female. "Child" assumes the existence of parent. Such are the direct mode relationships. But co-wives assume a common and shared husband, with no direct "organic" relationship. Just so, siblings assume a common shared parent (perhaps more than one), with no direct "organic" relationship no matter how many genes they may have in common. These are indirect modes of kinship.

Out of these differences, and the relationships which exhibit them, all kinship groups have to be built. The only building blocks are those of sexuality and descent, which English-speaking Westerners see as the relationships of husband-wife, mother-son, mother-daughter, father-son, father-daughter, brother-brother, sister-sister, brother-sister, and co-spouse relationships. The blocks can be compounded into great edifices; nevertheless, the blocks themselves are of a very precise nature and number.

American families contain all the relationships except those of shared sexuality. African families, being polygynous, contain all the relationships familiar to Americans, plus that of co-wife to co-wife, and the ramified relationships of half-siblings and of "father's wife-husband's child."

In all cultures, such kinship relationships must be given a more or less restricted content. It is necessary to know what husbands are supposed to do, as husbands; and what wives are supposed to do, as wives; what fathers are supposed to do, and what daughters are supposed to do.

Then, on the basis of these understandings, human beings can act more or less comfortably as they make their compromises between reality and the ideal.

The content of the mother-child relationship shows greater similarity from one society to the next than does the father-child relationship. The brother-brother relationship can go all the way from the minimal content which Americans give it today to the maximal content that some African patrilineal societies give it, where it is fundamental. The husband-wife relationship, and the kind of content that it involves, can vary just as widely: from the maximal content that Americans give it to the minimal content that some African societies give to it.

What, then, is polygyny? A married man marries a second or third woman, and they produce children. The content of each husband-wife relationship will be altered; the relationships of the co-wives and half-siblings have been added. The difference between monogamy and polygyny is contained in this: it is possible, even if it is not usual, to create a deeply intense relationship between husband and wife that probably most men cannot enter into with two women at once. If the intense and unique quality in that relationship is what is most highly valued, then polygyny must be opposed. But if something else—say security of position and many children—is most highly valued, polygyny is not a contradiction. Indeed, the added relationship among co-wives may provide some of the very cultural content and psychic satisfaction among adults which modern Americans try to cram solely into the husband-wife relationship. And it is no more fair to say that a rewarding husband-wife relationship cannot develop in polygyny than it would be to say that intense community of interest among women cannot develop alongside monogamy.

The birth rate in a polygynous situation is never higher than the birth rate in a monogamous situation. It is usually lower. A man may beget many more children in polygyny than in monogamy. A woman does not bear any more. We can cease to worry about the birth rate in polygyny, because the moment that enforced monogamy comes into the African situation, the birth rate always soars (although monogamy is not the only factor—enforced monogamy is always accompanied by many other factors which change the way people live). African women do not, in their indigenous cultures, bear more than one child every two and a half or three years. They achieve this spacing by the only sure means—continence during the time they are nursing a child. When the situation changes so as to favor monogamy, their inclination and opportunity to shun their husbands for such a long period of time are usually reduced. In the indigenous culture, polygyny gives security to both husbands and wives during the time when a mother withdraws from cohabitation with her husband during a nursing period. The number of men in any society who can undergo such a long period of celibacy is small. If you are a wife in a polygynous society, would you rather have your husband at home with your co-wife or galavanting around the countryside?

Americans think that the impossible thing to share is the husband. If American women would really look into their souls, they know that it is really the kitchen that they would refuse to share. And the wives of African polygynists do not try. There are separate houses for each wife or for each group of wives; there is also usually a separate sphere for the husband.

Obviously, to make polygyny work it is necessary constantly to re-create a situation in which the rewards and

obligations among co-wives are as neatly and precisely
stated as are the obligations and rules among parents and
children, husbands and wives. There are some things that
a co-wife must do to be a good co-wife. There are others
that she must *not* do if she is to be a good co-wife. If she
does the one cheerfully and well and refrains from the
other, she is by definition a good co-wife, whatever her
husband's other wives may do.

Examining divorces in Africa shows that some women
leave their husbands not because they do not like their
husbands but because they do not like their co-wives.
Living in an impossible situation, whether that
impossibility is created by husband or co-wife, leads in
some societies and under some conditions to divorce.
There are African women who divorce their husbands because they can't stand their co-wives; there are others who
stay with impossible husbands because the co-wives are
congenial. A good senior wife or mother-in-law may be as
important in providing security, pleasant surroundings,
and a rewarding place for a woman to bring up her children as is her husband.

If they have separate quarters and an established code
of behavior known to everybody, it is possible for co-wives
not only to live next door, but to share their husband
and even to become quite fond of one another. They
have a great deal in common. The ideals of polygyny always are such that harmony among co-wives is possible.
At the same time, in many African languages, the word
for co-wife springs from the same root as the word for
jealousy. The situation is fraught with difficulty—but are
not all family relationships fraught with difficulty: the
husband-wife relationship in monogamy? The parent-child
relationship everywhere? The polygynous family is more

complex than the monogamous family, and there are certain difficulties built into it. But the rewards involved may be great: it is possible, in a polygynous family, to spread your regard, your love, and your dependence over a wider range of people. You don't put all your emotional eggs in one basket. For this reason alone it can be seen to have great rewards. A large group of people has the welfare of each member at heart. And in the worst of all possible situations, the very number may dilute the hate pointed at each one.

Women in polygyny have grave trouble only when the interests of their children are involved and when real or supposed slights from the father toward one set of children or the other affect the smooth running of the whole. A woman, as a co-wife, can learn to accept all sorts of real or fancied slights. The same woman, as a mother, will have difficulty in accepting either real or fancied slights to her children. Here is the source of the difficulty: tension between my mother and the mothers of my half-siblings.

Polygyny has nothing to do with the position of women in society. African women, by and large, have a high social position: legal rights, religious and political responsibility, economic independence. Where there are kings in sub-Saharan Africa, there are queen-mothers. At the basis of every secret cult of men, there are women: the innermost secret of every religious club barred to women is the male's ultimate dependence on women. Women are often excluded from rituals, but there are two things that initiation into religion and society involve: initiation into society is a ritualized teaching to the novitiates that they embody, in themselves personally and in their relationships collectively, the moral force of society—they are themselves the gods (not God) and the sanctions. Initiation is also a ritualized teaching to the initiates that women must stand behind and support men. In the Ivory Coast, for example, initiation has two denouements: one when the masked dancers who have represented the gods and the social forces suddenly take the masks off and put them on the boys themselves; the other when the innermost hidden secret of the men's religious societies is exposed to them—and turns out to be a woman.

Women in Africa are not, in short, a deprived group as they were in the nineteenth-century Western world. African men ritualize rather than deny their basic dependence on women.

The next myth that must be banished is that polygyny has anything to do with the concupiscence of the male. Polygyny is a state into which most African men enter with a certain trepidation. If you think that one wife can henpeck a husband, you should see what three in league can do. If co-wives live up to the ideals of the roles, even just barely, no man exists but is under greater strain and control than he would be if there were only one woman involved. The man who has a strong senior wife is a fortunate individual, because she will run the household and will straighten out the fusses among the co-wives. He will not have to bother. If he does not have such a wife, two thirds of his energy goes into administration.

Men must treat their wives in accordance with the station of the wives—not necessarily with absolute equality, unless the society dictates that their stations are those of absolute equals. The greater number of societies lay down quite precise obligations on the part of the husband, but others insist that the obligation is to make the personal adjustments necessary to keep all the parties contented.

It is all but inevitable, in all probability, that polygynists have favorite wives. It should never, however, show
up in the way the husband carries out his obligations:
clothing them, feeding them, giving them children. Occasionally romantic love enters into this situation. There
was an old Tiv chief with seventeen wives who loved
them all, but loved one of them in the sense given that
term by the troubadours and adapted by latter-day American marriage counselors. The senior ones had given him
families and had comforted his years. But unfortunately
—and even he considered it unfortunate—he "fell in love"
with one of the younger ones. It kept him from being a
good family man; it kept him from being a good chief.
Romantic love occurs in an African familial situation
about as commonly as it does in a European or American
one. The difference is that Westerners have a series of
myths which make them simulate romantic love to see
them over the time between initial attraction and the regard that sensitive and sensible living together, breeding,
and growing together can foster. The myth makes it possible for Westerners to select their spouses on something
besides random choice—indeed, under it they can arrange
their own marriages.

Old-fashioned Africans select their spouses by "giving
in to their parents' wishes." But in most cases in which
the parents' wishes do not correspond with their own,
they elope. Seldom do Africans make their children marry
someone they do not like, although they sometimes (by
refusing to refund bridewealth) make their daughters stay
with husbands they no longer like.

The other aspect of African family life that is most
likely to be misunderstood is the institution of bridewealth. Initially, the European observers who went to

Africa said that Africans bought their wives. In a sense, that is true. It is *not* true that wives enter the market place or that they are commercialized or anything of the sort. It is easiest to explain by noting that part of the marriage contract in any society is that the wife gets certain rights in the husband and he gets certain rights in her. The rights of each are the obligations of the other.

Initially the husband has to make a bridewealth payment that is tantamount to posting a bond that he will carry out his obligations, thus guarding his new wife's rights. The analogy can be carried too far, because the nature of the bond and the purpose of the bridewealth changes, and ultimately its nature is in the sphere of legitimizing the children. But, in return for his "bond" and his obligations, the husband gets certain rights.

To sum them up quickly, a man may get in his wife domestic rights—the right to establish a domestic unit with her and to her domestic work and time and care. He may get rights to her extradomestic economic substance or labor; such was the case in the late nineteenth-century West, but is seldom so in Africa. He gets sexual rights in her and obligations toward her. Finally, he may or may not get the right to filiate that woman's children to his kinship group. In most African societies, traditionally, a man acquired such rights in exchange for cattle or ceremonial currency such as spears or pieces of iron, or else for service of the sort Jacob performed for his two wives in the Book of Genesis. The difference between matriliny and patriliny can be summed up by determining whether it is common to transfer the rights to filiate the children.

It is these rights that the bridewealth purchases, these obligations that it symbolizes. If a woman "has cows on her back," as the East African idiom has it, then her children belong to the man and the social group that paid the cows. This is a matter of legitimization. It is, indeed, a symbol of legitimization.

If the marriage breaks up, the bridewealth must be returned, totally or in part.

Polygyny does not necessarily mean that some men do not have wives, but only that men marry later than women (although it is also true that women beyond the age of menopause seldom remarry, whereas men never grow out of the marriageable population). Polygyny must also be distinguished from concubinage. Concubines are not wives, for all that in some places they have legal rights. In many societies there are, besides concubinage, several "degrees" of marriage, and in some there is allowable sexual and other relationships which may not be granted the status of full marriage. Indeed, in the Roman Republic there were two forms of marriage—heiresses would not marry by the ritual that gave their husbands control of their property, but rather formed a recognized, common-law union in which this economic right was not transferred. There were, thus, two "types" of "marriage": one involved the acquisition by the husband of all the rights; the other of only part of them. Many—probably most—African societies exhibit just such variation in the possible marriage arrangements.

Rights in women are considered, in most African societies, to be heritable. If my father or my older brother dies, leaving a couple of wives, I may inherit his rights in those not my mother. Since all rights involve obligations, it would be more accurate to say that I inherit my father's obligations to his wives. If the widow has several children and her children are members of her late husband's kinship group, she has an important position within that kinship group, even though she is not a member of it. Her

position in life, indeed, may depend upon her children
—thus underscoring the hard fate of a barren woman. Her
natal group has little obligation to her after her initial
marriage—ultimately none. As some Africans put it, "your
wife of long-standing becomes your sister." A woman's
status derives from her being a mother of lineage members. Therefore, it is only sensible for her to remarry into
that group. And most widows are women of maturity
(which may, of course, begin before twenty); they do not
expect from a second marriage what they expect from a
first—sometimes the second may be happier for that
reason.

The result is the institution of inheritance of rights in
widows. In one situation the widow is inherited as a wife;
there is another, quite different, situation in which (to
use the Old Testament term) the brother of the dead husband raises up seed, which is to say that the widow moves
in as his "wife," but that the dead husband remains the
legal father of any children that she bears. Such an arrangement is called the true levirate. The new husband
acquires domestic and sexual rights in the widow; he does
not acquire rights to filiate her children, which are thought
to be part of the "spiritual property" of the dead husband.

It is possible, in most African societies, for a widow to
decide not to remain with her deceased husband's people.
She therefore probably marries someone else and the
bridewealth is adjusted.

American and Western European society does not
cope very well with widows. They are an anomaly. They
occupy an insecure position, are to be pitied, particularly
if they have young children; they are not quite to be
trusted, although the divorcee has in the twentieth century taken over the role assigned to the widow in the

nineteenth. African societies cope well with both divorcees and widows—getting them back into families quickly and simply. Loneliness is not an indigenous African problem.

In addition to families, there are other sorts of kinship groups in Africa based on a more limited range of relationships than are families. Extended families can attain only a certain size—after that, the members cannot know all their kinsmen, or respond equally to them all. Since the functions of the family are usually associated largely with households, the household limit—certainly the neighborhood limit—is, in most cases, the effective limit of the family. But certain types of limiting kinship groups can gear their purposes to other ends and still use kinship amity as the sanction for carrying out the cooperation of the group and the achievement of its ends. The descent groups contain fewer relationships, but can control much larger numbers of people.

There are two sorts of descent groups: patrilineal descent groups, which include the father-son and father-daughter relationships and the three sibling relationships. The matrilineal descent group includes the mother-son and mother-daughter and the three sibling relationships. All of these, being limited in the way that they are and specifically not being able to take care of the basic functions of bearing and rearing children, can be brilliantly adapted to political and economic ends.

Descent groups may contain several million people and use the sanction of kinship obligations—"blood is thicker than water"—to reward their members and bind them to "right" courses of action. These groups can be called lineages; some types are called "clans." The word "clan" in the anthropological literature is used broadly—it may cover any kinship group that is not a family, and even some extended families (the Chinese *tsu*, usually called a "clan" in English, is in fact a type of extended family).

Unilineal descent groups are very widespread in Africa and were—indeed, still are—the basis for most of the extrafamilial social organization. They form political groups, religious congregations, and even production and land-owning units. They are still strong. They are strong among the educated as well as among the "bush" people.

The strength of unilineal descent groups will wane only when the tasks they perform can be done by some other means with less emotional and social outlay of energy. Unless they are given other tasks, they will probably become less influential before the effective police systems, contract law, and large-scale political institutions that are now becoming commonplace in Africa. The unilineal descent group can do all these political and economic jobs, with the sanctions founded on specialized kinship obligations. However, in the present day, the size of the operation makes it more efficiently done by state and contractual methods.

There are some societies in Africa in which unilineal descent groups are not found, but such groups are overwhelmingly present in many more. It is loyalty to the descent group, as well as to the family, that is under discussion when Africans talk about their obligations to "their" people.

In addition to the economic and political purposes that such groups can be made to serve, they are often central to religious ritual and belief. They are, moreover, often associated with the history and the view of the cosmography. They are, in short, one way in which the small world

of the family can be tied to the greater world and ultimately to the supernatural.

African children grow up in an intense situation of kinship, family, and lineage. They continue throughout their
lives to learn and to be bound by their family obligations
and family histories. Perhaps even more importantly, they
learn from a very early age to spread their love and regard, their rewards and their worry and concern, over
larger groups of people.

Among the Tiv of eastern central Nigeria, for example,
a child when he is about six months old is assigned to an
older sister or brother, preferably the same sex as the
child; the older becomes the nurse of the younger. For the
next three or four years—almost until the younger child
is ready to become a nurse, they accompany their nurses
everywhere. When they cry, the nurses take them to their
mothers. When the nurses go out to play, the babies go
with them. The bond between a child and his nurse becomes an enduring bond. Old men often introduce men
just older than themselves who had been their nurses.
Children learn a great deal about the culture from one
another and especially from their nurses. In our society,
children more and more learn from adults.

Tiv children, as an example, are allowed to go any
place, so long as they keep quiet. They can go into the
most solemn court proceedings and sit down and listen.
The moment one of them makes a noise, out they all go.
Older children of eight or nine often get interested in court
cases or political meetings. When their younger charges
will not behave, they have to go away; therefore they become very adept in silencing the babies. There is nothing
from which children are excluded, unless they misbehave
and intrude. As a result, they tend to be well-behaved
children, aware from an early age of what goes on in adult

culture. The abrupt break such as Westerners know, between children's culture and adult culture, is not to be
found.

African children get into their cultures early, and there
are no abrupt shifts. After they are twelve or thirteen,
and sometimes earlier, boys form groups that range the
countryside, hunt, and (where there are cattle and goats)
tend the herds. Girls by this time are more closely kept at
home and are on the brink of marriage.

At marriage, the vast majority of girls shift homesteads.
They leave the households in which they are daughters
and join those in which they are wives and in which they
will become mothers. Men do not undergo this kind of
change, but continue to live imbedded in a group of their
own kinsmen.

It is probably impossible for anyone who has never lived
in a kinship-dominated society to realize the combination
of security and bondedness that it implies. In discussion,
Africans always emphasize the positive factors: a group
of their own, on which they can depend totally and to
which they owe allegiance, a group which transcends them
and gives them position in society and in history—importance and status as well as physical necessities or even
wealth. Nevertheless, they do, to some extent, chafe under
the demands of their kinsmen. Until the present century,
there was no "way out" of the kinship situation. There
was no place to go if one were exiled. The kinship sanction
was sufficient to control all of one's behavior. Modern
Westerners would see such a fate in terms of the lack of
individuality and freedom. Africans do not. Although today many of them do leave when faced with choices in
which they consider that they must give more than they
get, few intend to stay away for good.

Africans who felt it necessary to maintain their relationships within their kinship groups have discovered ways and means that have made them all but geniuses in personal relationships—at least it is so at a kinship level. The story is told of a South African chief whose murder was attempted by his brother. The brother got out of prison several years later. The chief met him and welcomed him back to the fold of the kinship group. The balance between individuality and security is solved quite differently in a kinship-dominated society from the way it is solved in a contract-dominated society.

Parenthood is important everywhere. It is trebly so in a society in which rights to the most important parts of all aspects of life are dependent upon kinship, and when most of one's status derives from kinship factors. Only on the birth of a child does a woman become truly a kinsman in her husband's group. Only on the birth of a child is a man assured of the "immortality" of a position in the genealogy of his lineage, or even of security of esteem among the important people of his community. Only on the birth of a grandchild is a man in a position to be truly sure that his name and spirit will live in the history and genealogy of his people. This factor, combined with that other factor that is so true everywhere—that grandparenthood allows a perfect and rewarding position for summing up the meaning of the life cycle—makes grandparenthood enviable, and elderhood the finest estate.

Many Africans express concern lest the kinship groups to which they are bound will wither and perish in the course of industrialization and mechanization of the new Africa. They are determined that, if possible, no such fate will befall them. It will be an interesting experiment. From it we may learn whether or not it is truly modern technology and the development of contract which destroys the ramified kinship system, or whether Western reasons for abandoning it were quite different from those they themselves use to explain their distrust of all kinship groups save the nuclear family.

Traditional house design in Kano, Nigeria.

Chapter Seven

LAND AND LABOR

POLITY AND ECONOMY ARE OF A PIECE. WE ARE USED to separating them for analysis, as political science and economics, or political and economic anthropology, but we also blame our political leaders for recession and credit them for prosperity. In fact, it is unfair to praise or to place blame for conditions beyond a leader's control, but no American political program or platform is without a large economic component. The term political economy is coming back into fashion, involving law and international relations as well as production, distribution, and consumption.

SPACE AND TERRITORIALITY

On the broadest scale, human beings are animals; they therefore take up territory. They must exploit their territory for their nutritional needs, and the way they will do so is at least minimally predictable. It also calls for some kind of systematic relationships with others of their species, aside from their immediate kin. It implies, in short, some minimal "political" order.

The African view of space tends (with few exceptions) to be based on social relationships. The Western view of space, on the other hand, is based more often on exploitation. In order to understand the African idea, it is important to underline the dominant outlines of the Western concept — one we scarcely know we hold.

Terrestrial space is a "thing" modern Westerners cut into pieces they call parcels, which they can buy and sell on the market. This is rare in other societies (and it used to be rare in our own). Our neighborhoods are nevertheless the result of buying and selling, renting and leasing homesites. Our local communities are the long-term result of mixed motives, choices, and decisions that had, at some time, to be expressed through market purchase or lease.

Such was never the case in traditional Africa, and it is rare even today outside the cities. In the older Africa, a community was built fundamentally on relationships within social groups based on some principle other than purchase or lease. That community as laid out on the ground, given territorial meaning by the social relationships among its members, and these relationships, not "ownership," established a person's right to make use of a particular plot of ground.

Think about the map of the world that Westerners are taught. Maps are records of astrally determined points and lines on the surface of the earth. These records are made by representing the grid which we imagine to cover the earth, according to a known scale, on a flat surface. We discovered that if a surveyor takes a sextant and "shoots the stars," that place can be relocated on the map. We are the only people in the world who use seafaring instruments to determine our position on the ground.

After the position on the earth is astrally determined, measurements are made of the plot by other surveyors' instruments such as transits and plane tables. These measurements are also translated to the paper. And it is whatever corresponds to the representation on the paper that you "own." In this system, a piece of property is determined by its position in relation to the stars, not its location between North Salt Creek and Squaw Butte or its position between the Joneses and the Smiths.

The Western map is, as a matter of fact, a strange kind of map. All the peoples of the world have maps of one sort or another—usually they are not written, but the raw material is there for a "map." A view or image of the terrestrial world. None save modern technical civilization have maps in which precision is so essential. There are a few peoples who divide up the world by natural boundaries such as rivers and hills. Most, however, see it in terms of social relations and the juxtaposition of social groups.

In order to understand the way such peoples are associated with the land and with one another in terms of land, and hence the way the political power system and the economic system of exploitation work, it is first necessary to understand the way they see themselves in relation to the earth.

African societies did not split land up into pieces at all. Here we shall mention two methods by which an area can be made into a socially recognizable "map." One of these is by a series of specific terrestrial points which are given particular recognition and either economic or ritual meaning by the people concerned. The Plateau Tonga of Zambia traditionally hooked their social organization to the earth not by means of anything we would ourselves consider land tenure, but by means of a set of rain shrines, each of which is associated with surrounding villages, and each of which is specifically placed on the earth—possibly but rarely subject to move on ritual authority. Opportunity for individuals to move from one village to another is great, and one's acceptance as a resident in a village automatically carries with it not only fealty to the shrine but a right to make a farm nearby on any land not farmed at the moment nor claimed as fallow by another resident. Tonga farms can be cultivated for five or six years before the soil is exhausted. Tonga can be seen to have short-term "farm tenure," as it were, in the village area near the shrine.

The bedouin Arabs of Cyrenaica are another well-documented example in which community lands were attached to points—in this case to saints' graves and wells. Or so it was before their grazing lands turned into oil leases and they themselves sought employment in the Libyan oil industry. Many remaining pastoral societies, and most of those that practice shifting cultivation nevertheless see the land in this sort of association with society. The pastoral Fulani, with their long, sweeping cycles of movement, and the slash-and-burn peoples of the Congo forests, with their relatively short moves, can all be included in this classification.

In the other mode of connecting society to space, the social organization is conceived in terms of pure space, and is only incidentally linked with the physical environment by vicissitudes of farming or other land uses for very short periods of time. The Tiv of central Nigeria are an example of a farming people who are characteristic of this type. They see geography in the same image as they see social organization. The idiom of descent and genealogy provides not only the basis for lineage grouping, but also of territorial grouping. Every "minimal lineage" is associated with a territory. This minimal lineage (two or three hundred males derived from a single ancestor, whose wives and daughters live with them) is located spatially beside another lineage of precisely the same sort—that is, from the brother of the ancestor of the first group. In reference to the father of the two apical ancestors of the two minimal lineages, they form an inclusive lineage, and their territories form a single spatial unit. This process continues backward genealogically for several generations, until all Tiv are included; it continues spatially until the entirety of Tivland—some two hundred miles in diameter—is seen as a lineage area, segmenting into increasingly smaller lineage areas.

This "genealogical map" of Tivland moves about the surface of the earth in sensitive response to the demands of individual farmers as those demands change from year to year. The "map" in terms of which Tiv see their land is a genealogical map, and its association with specific pieces of ground is of only very brief duration—a man or woman has precise rights to a farm during the time it is in cultivation, but once the farm returns to fallow, the rights lapse. However, a man always has rights in the "genealogical map" of his agnatic lineage, wherever that lineage may happen to be in space. These rights, which are part of his birthright, can never lapse. A mathematician friend has suggested to me that whereas the Western map, based on surveys, resembles geometry, the Tiv notions resemble topology, which has been described as "geometry on a rubber sheet." The Western map is necessarily rigid and precise if the principle of contract is to work; the Tiv map is constantly changing both in reference to itself and in its correlation with the earth, thus allowing the principle of kinship grouping to work. For the Tiv, the position of a man's farm varies from one crop rotation to the next, but neither his juxtaposition with his agnatic kinsmen nor his rights change in the least. Tiv, like Tonga, might be said to have "farm tenure" but they do not have "land tenure."

Thus, instead of seeing their maps primarily in terms of "property," Africans see something like a map in terms of social relationships in space. They emphasize the spatial aspect of their social groups and provide themselves with a social map, so that they are left free to question the ways in which they attach either social groups or individuals to exploitational rights in the earth. In the past they were usually imprecise, because group membership was the valued quality. Westerners, on the other hand, think about their map in terms of property and values, and see the social system which results as fundamentally a series of contracts and hence open to question. As a result, in any situation of change, Westerners question the social system that lies behind land usage, while Africans question the property ideas associated with the systems of land usage.

This relative inability on the part of Westerners to question whether or not a land system is in fact a property system—that is, the assumption that it always is, even if land does not enter the market—or is what they have come to call by that astonishing term, "a free good," has led to the continued life of a silly concept called "communal ownership." Now, in a technologically developed, contractually oriented society like Europe and America, communal ownership can and does exist. That is to say, the commune, whatever its nature, can be viewed as a jural person. As a "corporation aggregate," it is capable of owning property under the law. The difficulty arises because this fiction has so often been used by Westerners to make sense out of African land systems, where it not only explains nothing, but makes understanding the system on the ground more difficult.

Sir Henry Maine pointed out long ago that in a community based on kinship, the land is an aspect of the group, but not the basis of grouping. Notions of "communal ownership," manipulated by people who assume property and market as the basis of society, have made the land the basis of grouping in a system in which spatial extension and concomitant rights to exploit the environment are mere aspects of the social group. The indigenous basis of grouping is kinship in some parts of Africa, while in others it is a village community similar to those Maine studied in India and Europe. In no place in Africa did the basis of grouping depend indigenously on contract.

Property, in the Western sense, and its resultant contractual relationships, are the fundamental basis of grouping in the Western type of national state. In a developed market economy, a land market emerges—with whatever agony to the people who must see it to fruition. Therefore, as African societies become Western-type national states, as they come to have more fully evolved market economies, the problem before them is how to preserve certain of their valued kinship groups. One answer is similar to one found by some of the more prosperous of American Indian tribes such as the Osage. They are turning their kinship groups into corporations aggregate before the law. This means that they can maintain at least some of the valued qualities of the kinship group at the same time that they are making themselves into corporations—sole or aggregate—which are the units of "modern societies," based on contract and on the market.

The Osage, when they struck oil, turned their tribe into a limited corporation under the laws of the state of Oklahoma. The Yoruba people in the western region of Nigeria turned their extended-family compounds into landholding units before the law, under the "Communal Land Rights (Vesting in Trustees) Law" of 1958.

This law, in brief, makes a matter of legal record the change in the nature of the Yoruba lineage group called the *ebi,* though it does so in legal language which eschews mention of the *ebi.* The *ebi* in traditional terms was an agnatic descent group which shared a common residence. Every quarter of every Yoruba town had several *ebi,* and on some occasions an *ebi* could split into two or more *ebi.* This body of agnatic kinsmen, with their wives, also had an estate—a more or less precisely determinable area within which they traditionally farmed, and which they protected from encroachment by others. Within the *ebi,* the members farmed not in specific places which they considered their own, but the group moved its farms about within the area so that they could remain as a unit to take advantage of the best soils and to control the system of fallowing. Nobody "owned" anything, but every member had a right to a farm sufficient to support his immediate dependents. These rights to a farm were inalienable. The *ebi* had a head and a council which ran the agricultural affairs of the *ebi* in a kind of committee.

This mode of spatial distribution and concomitant exploitation of the environment left several things to be desired in the new society which has developed under colonialism. In the first place, it granted a man land rights *only* insofar as he was a part of a lineage. The moment he ceased to be an effective member of his lineage, his land rights were forgone until he again became an effective member. Under modern conditions, Yoruba often want to remain members of their lineages, but also want to have land rights of a different sort. Sale of land was impossible in the old system because land was the spatial dimension of the *ebi* rather than a commodity which could be considered "property" and sold in the market, but sale of land became desirable when the economic system changed in

such a way as to make such sales feasible. Immediately, a
sort of pull or pressure was set up between the *ebi* land
unit and the individual. Either a man had to cease being
an individual in the new system, or the *ebi* land unit, as
an institution, had to go.

"The Communal Land Rights (Vesting in Trustees)
Law" is, then, a legal mechanism by means of which this
particular difficulty has been solved. European analysis of
Yoruba land tenure has, from the beginning, classed the
ebi's spatial dimension as "land owned in communal tenure." The *ebi* is certainly a community of sorts, and since
it was associated with land, the European notion of "tenure" was automatically applied without question as to
whether it fit or not. Such an assumption had the result
of turning the *ebi,* in European eyes, into a corporation
aggregate before the law. With this European analysis in
terms of legal corporations, a subtle change was introduced. The Europeans, in the legal system they fostered,
gave the *ebi* a legal reality which it formerly had not possessed. From being only a social group, it now became a
legal entity. Yoruba were late in recognizing what had
happened. But having recognized it, they and their legis-
lators have seen in it a means of preserving the *ebi* as a
social group fulfilling some of the basic needs of what we
would call social insurance and community center at the
same time that they have strengthened the institution of
private property.

Thus, in the indigenous system, the *ebi* did not "own"
land communally or any other way. In the modern system,
the *ebi* of the Yoruba has been turned into a legal entity,
before the laws of Nigeria, and can therefore "own" land.
"Communal land ownership" assumes that the commune
is, before the law, the same sort of unit as the individual.
That idea has penetrated Yoruba cultural values and, in-

deed, communal land ownership under the law is actually taking place.

With changes in the economic use of land—that is, with "economic development"—the dimensions of society are necessarily affected. Land as a factor of production assumes a greater role than it formerly had, compared with land as the dimension of society.

LABOR

If land provides the fundamental dimensions of society, work provides its gyroscope. If one's work is changed, the balance of one's life is changed in the process.

Economists have always viewed labor as one of the "factors of production" along with land and capital, but labor is more than that, if only because it is done by human beings who are part of a society. People at work create not merely products; they also create a web of social relationships. They fraternize with one another in terms of quite specific sets of rules; each takes home to his family at least some residue of these relationships with his pay envelope. Indeed, all of life is involved with one's work habits. In addition to some of the most dominating of one's social relationships, even such fundamental aspects of life as how and when one sleeps, and what and when one eats are influenced by one's work. The concept of the "labor supply" is only one way of looking at the social structure—a way limited by and to certain economic and political problems.

During the Industrial Revolution in Europe and America, work with all its social ramifications underwent a profound change—it entered the market place. The dictum "He who does not work does not eat" became "He who does not sell his labor or his brains on the market does not acquire the means to buy the wherewithal to support himself and his family."

Like the Europeans before the eighteenth century, Africans before the early twentieth century did their work in groups, and by arrangements that were not fundamentally geared to the market. Traditional forms of labor in Africa took place within the sphere of the family, the local government, the age-set, and other such organizations. They specifically did not take place in the form of any organization set up to buy labor and the other factors of production on the market, in order to turn out goods to be sold on the same market in which the labor was hired and the other factors acquired.

Before the colonial revolution, most work done in Africa was done in carrying out obligations within family and kinship groups. The domestic economy was not severed from "the economy" as in our society. People helped one another for an approximate return in kind. The men of a local community, however defined, got together for community work such as road and path construction and bridge building, clearing the market place, or putting up a new shrine. The economy was no more differentiated from the local government than it was differentiated from the family. Part of one's duties as a citizen, to put it into modern terms, was to carry out part of the work of the community. One favorite way of getting sizable working groups together—and some jobs require sizable working groups—was for members of an age-set to work together. The community age-set in most African societies could furnish from twenty to one hundred men. The organization within the set was already established so that few or no new lines of authority based primarily on the job at hand and the purpose in mind had to be established.

It is customary—and correct—to think that the African "production unit" is the family or kinship group. It is necessary, however, to recognize the more basic situation: that kinship groups are less specialized in traditional Africa than are kinship groups in modern America. Production was and is done in family groups because subsistence production does not require any others.

There have been, from so-called time immemorial, a few people in Africa who sold their labor on the market. To overlook this point would be to report falsely and—more serious—to deprive one's self of the most sensible explanation of why the Africans took to market labor with such alacrity when the opportunity came for them to do so. Traders have existed for centuries. Although they often depended on slave labor, more often they were able to hire labor. If they depended on sharing with their kinsmen rather than hiring strangers, their reasoning can be seen because there were no courts to adjudicate their rights.

Thus, most Africans "always" knew that it was possible to hire themselves out and to sell their labor at a going market rate; but only an infinitesimal proportion ever did so. By and large, their work, like their land and like the other factors of production, and indeed like the mode of distribution, was organized along non-market principles and not for purposes of increasing production or creating "economic growth."

In the West, and in the technologically advanced parts of modern Africa, one still works for the sake of one's family, for the sake of one's citizenship, as well as for the sake of one's sanity. But in the West, and in the new Africa, one works in a different social context: that of the "firm." The firm is a type of social organization put together on the basis of the principle of contract—a principle that was very little developed in most parts of Africa, even by the colonial governments who imposed it on their African colonies.

It has often been said, correctly enough, that Africa, for all the fact that she was the home of great legal systems, never developed a reliable system of contract law. The reason is that she never needed it. Law always follows social development, and contract-oriented forms and rights and obligations had not yet taken a dominant enough place in society to make the law follow in spite of itself. In a firm, those aspects of a contractual relationship which lawyers call the "consideration" are of the essence. In short, through firms, people sell their labor. With the establishment of this new type of organization, new types of obligations and rights came into being in African society much as they had come into being in European societies several centuries earlier. Obviously, they are not as painful to African society as they were to European society during the Industrial Revolution because there is a model to go on—it would be a sad comment on us all if some lesson had not been learned from the European experience.

Perhaps the most important point of this discussion is that Africans have always worked—like all other people—but in this century the spread of market forces has changed them into "labor." Labor in this sense not only means work, it also becomes the collective term for that sector of the population that sells its work. As some Africans became labor in this new sense, they took on new identities and obligations. Sometimes these obligations included movement to find a job, or, as in West Africa, it might include movement completely away from the village social setting into a new and rapidly evolving urban culture.

Europeans who came to Africa to establish mines or plantations regarded Africans as labor—a commodity to be purchased when wanted and then returned to the shelf. They also reckoned that African labor was cheap labor, and they wanted to keep it that as long as they could. One rationalization for paying low wages was the argument that Africans were not willing or able to work steadily. The African (it was always in singular) was a "target worker," who would come to work only until he had enough money to buy a bicycle (it was always a bicycle). Then he went home until he needed something else. If this was the motive for employment, then raising wages would only make it easier to attain the target sum, thus reducing labor supply. What the employers failed to realize was that unskilled workers, temporarily away from home, might earn low wages yet still be expensive "labor"—measured by the work done for a given sum of pay.

In the early 1920s, however, some of the mining firms in the southern Belgian Congo (now Zaire), decided to experiment with what they called "stabilized labor." Instead of trying to lure men in for brief periods, they began encouraging them to stay as a permanent work force, bringing their wives with them. Sometimes they even offered to pay the bridewealth for a worker who would agree to become a permanent employee. By such devices the Union Minière du Haut Katanga, the largest Belgian mining company, reduced its labor turnover from an annual 96 percent in the early 1920s to 7 percent in the early 1930s. By the 1930s, the mining companies of the Zambian copper belt also began the change-over to stabilized labor.

In southern Africa, however, the South African and Rhodesian governments (before Rhodesia became the independent Zimbabwe in 1980) discouraged people settling down in the economically developed parts of the country. Whites took the skilled jobs, reserved for them by law. After a time, they discovered their interest in preventing Africans from acquiring those skills. Forcing Africans into a pattern of migratory labor was one way to accomplish this. As far back as 1912, the South African government passed a Lands Act, that laid out a small part of the country as "reserves" for Africans. On the surface, this looked like the American policy of Indian reservations, but Native Americans have a right to buy land off the reservations if they can afford to do so. The corollary of the reserves policy in South Africa was that all the rest of the country—the vast majority and all the most valuable parts—was reserved for the white minority.

After the 1950s, the theory was extended, so that people of African descent had no right even to become a permanent resident of the developed parts of the country, now declared to be "white" areas. They were not "white" because they were mainly occupied by whites, since black people there did most of the physical labor on a migratory basis. They were declared to be "white" because government wanted economic benefits reserved for whites.

The labor pattern that emerged has been called oscillating labor. Workers would leave the "Native Reserves," where they were forced to live, to work for a time in the cities or at the mines. Once there, they were supposed to be short-term residents only and were confined to separate "locations" or urban ghettoes, while their "real" homes were officially in one of the Native Reserves. After a year or two of absence, they could make enough to go home again, only to be forced out by economic necessity after two, three, or five years.

These policies made it possible to keep African incomes at about one-tenth the incomes of white workers. Preserving aspects of the old culture in the reserve, though under frightful pressure, gave most African males a consciousness of the greater world beyond the "Native Reserve" and of their own relative deprivations.

The size of these population movements was very large indeed, in line with the massive population movements elsewhere in the world in this century. The oscillating pattern was very large even by mid-century. In 1951, a South African government commission estimated that at any moment, 40 percent of all males between ages 15 and 65 would be absent from the "Reserves" on labor contracts. By 1960, for the whole of sub-Saharan Africa, it is estimated that a quarter of the wage-labor force were migrants from beyond the national or colonial frontiers. This did not mean a quarter of all workers, since most labor was still set in the community, not for wages, but it was nevertheless a major change.

The absence of so many men on a temporary basis brought enormous changes to southern African society. It imposed an element of social disorder on the all-male societies of the mining camps. It imposed new burdens on the heavily-female society left behind in the "Reserves" in South Africa or in the villages of Mozambique. In effect, the system of oscillating labor forced the women in the reserves to provide much of the family's support, thus subsidizing the low wages paid at the mines.

After the Second World War, even the mining companies came to realize that low-wage labor was not necessarily cheap labor, but the South African government was unwilling to give up the fiction that a "white" South Africa could be kept a racial monopoly area with black labor present only as a temporary expedient. After 1975, the pressure against the whole of the *apartheid* system began to rise, and oscillating labor became one of the key points to attack, and for the white minority to defend.

Chapter Eight

AFRICAN POLITICS AND COURTS

AFRICAN POLITICAL LIFE RUNS AT SEVERAL DIFFERENT levels. At the top, Africans operate within the institutional framework of the colonial state, now become an independent state and member of the United Nations. At this level, African states came to independence with institutions modelled on those of the colonial powers, with occasional borrowing from the federal constitutions of the United States, Canada, or Australia. For the formerly-British colonies, the political model was the "Westminster model," so called after the home city of the British Parliament. The chief executive, usually a Prime Minister, is responsible to the majority of the elected parliament. In the formerly-French states, the model was usually that of the French republic, with an elected President, but also with a Prime Minister, responsible to the majority in the national assembly.

In Africa, these institutions stayed in place only a short time. Two common alternatives emerged. One was an out-and-out military dictatorship, with no pretence at Parliamentary institutions of any kind. The second was the one-party state, in which the party that brought the country to independence became the one official party. One-party states are under the executive control of a strong President who was also head of the party.

147

Elections may be held, but they are more or less openly controlled, and contesting candidates are all members of the same party. Real outsiders cannot run at all, but the one-party electoral system does provide the voters with some small element of choice.

It would be fascinating to trace the movement of African politics at the national level since independence, but that is not part of our objective in this book. We are concerned with the underlying traditions of African political life—those that were there when the colonial period began and that represent the still-living traditions from which African institutions politically develop. Over the past thirty years, these traditions have sometimes seemed less important than the Western overlay of constitutional models and precedents, but they remain the indigenous African way of conducting political affairs, and they have tended to reemerge in various forms in the recent decades of independence.

African politics, like any other, must deal with problems of internal welfare and international relations in terms of geographical space, however that may be conceived. First, how did Africans maintain law and welfare among their peoples? Then, how did they maintain cultural integrity and keep other societies and peoples from overrunning them? Again, in order to discover traditional African answers to these problems, we must at the same time expose our own traditional ideas so that we can recognize those answers when we find them.

There were two basic types of indigenous political systems in Africa, with some intermediary types and a few small societies that fall outside the classification. One of the basic types is familiar to Europeans and Americans because they too now utilize it and have done so for long enough that many of them seem to believe that it is synonymous with order and civilization. That is the political form called the "state." A state is a bureaucracy organized specifically to carry out political activities. The bureaucracy may or may not be based on some other kind of social group such as the family—that is to say, the criteria for achieving entrance into the bureaucracy may be almost any that a society chooses. In a state there is an interlocked system of offices or positions that must be filled by officials. Authority is then made inherent in these interlocking positions, which both reinforce and act as a check on one another. In a successful state, the centralized bureaucracy has not just the authority but the power to carry out public policy within a given area.

States are, with only an occasional exception, multi-ethnic groups which, to be successful, must have a concept of citizenship—that is, a means by which a person can belong to or identify with the state organization. Such an idea of citizenship must go along with, but not ultimately come into too great conflict with, membership in families, local groups, and other social entities.

The central bureaucracy called the state, with its accompanying concepts of citizenship, is a political form that was broadly spread throughout Africa. Such states were found at the edge of the Sahara, and at the southern edge of the forests and in the eastern highlands of the continent —the maps accompanying Part III of this book show the locations of some of the most important of them.

The state, however, is not the only kind of organism capable of carrying out the political requirements of society. A second type of political organization in traditional Africa is called a "stateless society," which may sound to an outsider like a contradiction in terms. Some authorities, thus, prefer the term "non-centralized society." Both have the disadvantage that they are residual categories—but because of the variety within that category, characterizing them by a specific characteristic is very difficult.

Many kinds of non-centralized societies are possible. A feudal kingdom of Medieval Europe was non-centralized to a degree—political power of the kind we associate with a state had become the private property of feudal lords, towns, and even segments of the Church such as abbeys or bishoprics. The stateless societies in Africa were very different from this, being based on ideas of kinship and its functions. They remain hard for Westerners to understand. Colonial officials had a particularly difficult time molding them to Western norms so that they could serve as a part of the colonial structure of authority.

On the other hand, the state form fitted in with political structures the colonial administrations found comparatively easy to understand. They had kings and presidents back home, and they understood the principles of delegating authority from a central point. This is one reason why the British in particular praised the advantages of Indirect Rule—rule through the existing African authorities—rather than pushing indigenous leaders aside in favor of a purely European bureaucracy. Whether they praised the idea or not, other colonial administrations had to rule through existing African authorities. The Europeans were too few on the ground to do otherwise.

STATES

When we encounter a word like "State," we tend to imagine what we already know—an organization with a monopoly on the use of force, along with a bureaucratic organization capable of giving orders and seeing that they are carried out everywhere within certain territorial limits. This is a fair enough description of European states in the nineteenth century and later. Even in Europe, earlier kingship was strictly limited—that is, the state organization was flawed. Royal orders could be carried out as far as the frontiers only when the subordinate individuals and groups with sufficient power were willing to see that it was done.

The same was true in Africa, where kingdoms were also the rule, but the nature of kingship was somewhat different and the building blocks of government authority were different. Most African states were superimposed on older and more intimate forms of social organization. The lineage, or the group descended from a common ancestor through either the male or female line, was one of these infra-state groups. The local village as a geographical unit of residence was another, and the subunits within the village were often the local members of a particular lineage. Lineages, however, usually spread beyond the village, so that the recognition of kin in other villages provided a wider unit of membership.

At the top of the structure, the king often held office because he was a member of a particular royal lineage. And many subordinate officers, such as provincial governors, also held their right to office by virtue of lineage membership. In some West African kingdoms, the kingship rotated through a number of different royal lineages, each taking its turn in furnishing the king.

The powers of the king were considerable, but rival lineages usually found ways to limit them in their own interests. Kings usually had to consult some kind of council, or a group of councils, each with its own sphere of jurisdiction. Other building blocks of political authority cut across the lines of lineage membership. In many African societies, men and women separately belonged to age-grades, or groups born at approximately the same time. Such age-groups held specific duties within the village, and within the state, such as military service. As they became older, they gained the authority of age and their representatives sometimes had to be consulted before an important decision could be taken.

Another such cross-cutting organization was the secret society, common but by no means universal in West Africa. Its importance seems to coincide with situations where certain lineages became especially powerful. The secret society as a grouping could protect the rights of weaker lineages, joined together across lineage lines. Typically, a secret society would be open to all—either men or women but in separate societies—but initiation involved ritual and learning the lore of the society, and it often included ceremonies that specifically cut the new member off from his old lineage connections and united him with others of the society and its guardian spirits. Men's societies in particular had important judicial functions, helping to settle disputes between lineages, sometimes ordering punishments and seeing them carried out by its junior members wearing masks to conceal their identity—and to emphasize the spiritual basis of their authority.

Kingdoms in Africa came in many different sizes. Sometimes they covered immense areas, often ruling through smaller kingdoms that had formerly been independent. These "empires" figure largely in African history, especially in the savanna country both north and south of the forest belt. Other kingdoms were really micro-states, with authority stretching only over a few dozen villages. In West Africa in particular, where micro-states were common, the secret societies had a larger role to play as arbiters of what was, in effect, international relations.

Just as the secret societies held their authority by virtue of spiritual sanctions, so the kingship itself was often held to be a sacred office. The sacredness resided with the royal insignia or even in the body of the king himself. The king might be the physical symbol of the kingdom, so that his person was surrounded by an important set of taboos and restrictions. A king who became old or sick was in some places put to death and replaced by a younger, healthier man who was a more fitting symbol of the kingdom's health and well-being.

One now-discarded hypothesis about African society and history was a belief that this kind of kingship belonged to a larger category called "Divine Kingship" that originated in Egypt and the Middle East and was imposed on sub-Saharan Africa by conquest. Many aspects of West African kingship suggest Egyptian models, but the similarities are far too loose to prove that the model was transmitted from one to the other — or, if transmitted, whether it moved from sub-Saharan Africa to the Middle East or in the other direction. Most kings at most times have tried to claim some kind of religious sanction, from ruling by divine right up to and including the claim to *be* gods, as certain Roman emperors did. There is no adequate evidence that African Kingdoms were created by conquest from across the desert.

The web of government below the level of the king himself could pass through as many as five different levels of delegated authority. At every level, the chief was the delegate of the king to the people, and representative of the people to the king — typically the chief must be acceptable to both. In the central and southern Bantu

kingdoms, people could move about from one chief-
ship to another almost at will, and the chiefs and headmen
were in considerable competition for subjects. Movement,
while not impossible, was much more restricted in the
kingdoms of the Guinea coast, mainly because local communities were organized on a more consistent kinship
principle.

Tribute passed from the lower office to the higher office
in this ladder of delegation, and in fact its presentation
and acceptance symbolized the delegation. A king would
not accept tribute from a man who was not, in his view, a
legitimate chief. A chief would not give it to one who was
not a recognized king. Tribute was generally of small economic value, and sometimes was purely symbolic in that
it had no economic value whatever.

All African kingdoms used some form of "taxation"
in the form of tribute, labor, and calls upon the subjects
for sacrifices, feasts, or celebrations within the kingdom.
Tribute collected at one level of the system of authority
was handed up, in part, to the next higher level so that
ultimately a part of it from everywhere reached the top.

The hierarchy of delegation also acted as a hierarchy of
appeal courts. In some cases, the chiefs and kings had
oracles as well as courts, and a hierarchy of oracles was
established for settling those disputes that could not be
settled through human judicial activity.

The state was one of the most notable features of preconquest Africa. But scattered among the states and
within the states were other, stateless societies, which also
have added much to the political character of the
continent.

STATELESS SOCIETIES

Whereas most members of stateless societies can understand the notion of the state—indeed, their attitude may be that they understand it only too well—most members of states (even African states) confuse stateless societies with chaos. And even those who understand the non-state forms of political organization are aware that without the idea of citizenship that attaches people to a state, modernization is infinitely more difficult, and probably impossible.

"State" is, to repeat, a very simple idea, even though its manifestations may be terribly complex. As with most simplifying ideas, it allows (but obviously does not require) suspension of more complex alternatives. Modern Westerners use the institution of the state to avoid tyranny (the while knowing from experience that a bad state may impose tyranny).

Africans who live in stateless societies tend to see the state as unavoidable tyranny; they seek and find order in other institutions.

There are several organizations that African societies have used as alternatives to state political organizations. A few Africans—less than half of one percent—still live in small hunting and gathering bands. The San and Pgymies are the best known of these people. Another political form is the maintenance of justice and of cultural and territorial integrity through the extended family organizations and the invocation of kinship behavior not only in domestic but in wider spheres.

The classic form of the stateless society—although recent research and analysis indicate that it may be rare in its pure classic form—is a system of checks and balances based on a lineage system. In such a system, there is no single center of power or authority—in fact, there is no authority system at all, and the power of the situation is always based on two centers in opposition or cooperation rather than on a single center with authority. Since there are two centers of power, no single bureaucracy of the sort that characterizes the state can arise.

The band, the extended family, and the lineage forms of stateless organization all use kinship as the idiom of stating their required behavior and for their system of sanctions. They must not, on that account, be confused with one another. The band solution is perhaps more a solution to economic problems than to political ones, and it disappears when the economy is no longer primarily based on subsistence hunting and gathering. The familial solution works with larger, but still strictly limited, sizes of group and has never worked well when the society is faced with more efficient modes of production or with larger groups of technologically more advanced peoples. The lineage solution works better because it can accommodate several million people and can frustrate—indeed, baffle—technologically advanced groups. The family solution is easy for foreigners to understand, and easy for them to demolish. The lineage system is neither.

The lineage system as a solution to political problems at the local level depends on an arrangement of power reminiscent of what used to be called the "balance" of power. It is most often (but certainly by no means necessarily) expressed in terms of kinship with brothers and their groups of descendants balanced against one another —and, at a more distant ancestral remove, large groups of descendants of brothers or other "equivalent" ancestors balanced against one another.

It is a postulate of most of the societies of the world that brothers fight with one another, but that when some-

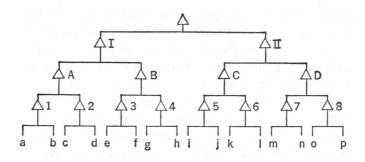

body steps in to stop their fighting, they are likely to join together to turn upon him. Furthermore, though brothers may fight, they must because of their very brotherhood ultimately reach a *modus vivendi*. If we examine the diagram, it becomes quite obvious that if Brother *h* fights with Brother *g*, then anybody who steps in will be regarded as an interloper. If, on the other hand, *h* fights with *f*, *g* will come to the aid of *h*, and *e* will come to the aid of *f*. If the dispute lies between *h* and *d*, then everybody who is a descendant of *B* will come to the aid of *h*, and everybody who is a descendant of *A* will come to the assistance of *d*. In the same way, I and II are equivalent segments in such a dyadic unit.

When we discover that each of the units may contain several hundred men with their wives and children—all the sons and the unmarried daughters—it becomes obvious that a certain narrow band of kinship norms can be used to control warfare and to carry out the legal proceedings. Warfare is in fact stopped automatically by the nature of the system—at the very least it is contained. Outsiders, instead of joining in, are usually peacemakers, because they are kinsmen to both warring parties.

Laws are maintained in this situation not through a system of chiefs, but through opposed sets or councils of elders. If there is a dispute between the members of Lineage 3 and those of Lineage 4, the elders of each group will meet, often on the borderland, often in neutral territory, and they will hammer out a solution to the problem because, after all, they are "brothers."

This kind of system has no bureaucracy which is vested with authority. Rather, all disputes, all solutions, all agreements are hammered out between segments whose power is "equivalent" and who are balanced against one another, with the rest of the outside world having no basis for taking sides one way or the other. In one sense, every court case, every legal dispute which is decided amounts to a treaty rather than to a court decision.

Formerly, the Tiv of central Nigeria organized almost a million people with this system. The Nuer of the southern Sudan organized well over a quarter of a million. The Bedouin Arabs throughout North Africa and over into the Arabian Peninsula were all organized in this way—indeed, there are remnants of such a system in the royal houses of the various Arab states. In such systems there are no officeholders, there are only representatives of groups. The moment that the representatives of Group A finish dealing with Group B, and turn back into their own organization, they are members either of Group 1 or Group 2, and therefore their "authority" is automatically limited. In the same way, within Group 2, they must belong either to *c* or *d*. In just such a way, authority within groups is checked at the same time that power in intergroup relations is given full force.

Early political officials from European countries sought responsible officeholders in such societies. Obviously, they did not find them. But they did of course find leaders, and when these leaders did not turn out to be "responsible" authorities, the government officials tended to

The Chief Alkali of Kano, a Judge in Muslim Law Holding Court in Colonial Nigeria.

underestimate both their intelligence and their actual power. Throughout the colonial period, the inclination on the part of colonial governments was to give such leaders authority—to force it on them. Wittingly or not, colonial officers tried to create some sort of a state organization and bureaucracy. Almost without exception, their attempts were baffled. Even when such peoples clamored for chiefs—and sometimes they did—these chiefs were treated as the external representatives par excellence of the group, or segment of it. Within the group they had little authority and what little they had was considered tyrannous by the people under them.

Stateless societies can be seen to be bicentric organizations—or rather organizations in which two equivalent centers are activated at any particular time. They reach compromises rather than make decisions. Judgments must be concurred in by both sides—there are no sanctions from a higher authority. A state is one type of unicentric organization, and because of its single center—no matter how pluralistic that center may appear—its organs may make decisions, their laws can be stated, judgments made, and sanctions brought to bear. The differences between the two ways of seeing "law and order" are so immense that it is sometimes difficult to see that the "other" system does in fact provide them.

LAW IN AFRICAN SOCIETIES

Although many references to warfare among African societies are found in travel books, in historical source materials, and even in ethnographic accounts, there is still no study of warfare in Africa that pretends to tie that information together. With law, that other primary political function, the situation is far different. The written material on African law is extensive; although much of it written by Europeans is uncomprehending restatement of substantive norms as legal rules—the pigeonholes of common law filled with exotic fauna—there is nevertheless a substantial body of knowledge about African law.

Indeed, Africa is one of the homes of advanced legal institutions. Perhaps the most famous of these institutions are the courts still found among the Bantu states of the southern third of the continent. At least until the end of the colonial period and probably still, the local or provincial chief was one of a number of judges on a large and inclusive bench. The bench included representatives of all the important social groups of the community, whether in any particular case they were seen as territorial segments and communities, as kinship units such as clans, or even as age-sets. The judges formed a regular and pronounced hierarchy, and were seated in a row or an arc. The provincial chief sat in the middle; at his immediate right was the second most senior person (however seniority might be computed locally) and at his left the third most senior. To his right, but farther removed, the fourth most senior, and so on, right and left, until the whole court was deployed more or less in a row.

There were, then, certain areas in which the litigants were to stand or, more often, sit on the ground. There were assigned places for witnesses, for the nobility, for the followers and backers of the litigants, and for the community as an audience. These court sessions were often held out of doors, but there might be a building for them—colonial governments preferred them inside so that regular schedules, based on clock and calendar time, could be maintained even in the face of hostile weather.

There was, in all cases, also a known, and demanded, decorum and order of proceedings. The plaintiff (to use an English term with only a 90 percent fit) made his plea—usually without counsel—and was usually allowed to finish his whole complaint, so long as he spoke well and to the point. The defendant (another translation that does not fit precisely) then made a reply and told his version of the story. Witnesses were called—including what we would call expert witnesses and character witnesses. Then, after the principals had each told his side of the dispute, and after witnesses had been heard, the most junior member of the bench, down at the far end, gave his opinion. His statements probably included moral lectures and statements of the proper kind of behavior that should have been carried out in the situation. His judgment would be followed by that of the man at the other end of the line, his immediate senior, who might disagree, and who added new views and new opinions. The third most junior man followed, and so on until they arrived at the middle where the head chief pronounced the final sentence. He had heard everything that the representatives of the community had to say. He had a chance to weigh the evidence, the judgments, and the opinions of his junior judges. His word on the decision became final.

In the southern Bantu states, there were also well-known and highly effective means for carrying out the decisions of the court. The community, having been represented in the audience as well as on the bench, brought both sacred and mundane sanctions to bear. The decisions of such courts were obeyed. Indeed, such communities might be reasonably said to have a "body of law" or *corpus juris* in the lawyer's sense.

Law in a stateless society was almost as effective but worked differently. Since there is no monolithic power system in the stateless society, agreement must be reached by consensus or else by compromise. The two contenders must be brought together in agreement, or at least concurrence, about what is to take place. The prin-

ciples on which such concurrence is based are usually
not as overt as is law in a state society, although the
principles by means of which compromises and concurrence are reached are well known and overt.

The difference between law and cultural norms can
best be seen from an examination of our own family law.
The norms of family living in modern America are fairly
well known and fairly circumscribed. The institutionaliza-
tion of families is such that these norms are fairly well
maintained. A very few of these norms are *restated* for
legal purposes: the bases for divorce, the laws against
beating children, and perhaps some others. The large
range of family activity is not in any wise made part of a
body of *law,* in the narrow sense. To assume a formal
body of law in an African stateless society is precisely the
same mistake as assuming that all of the norms of the
American family are part of the law of the land.

In order to comprehend African legal systems fully,
then, it becomes necessary to have a new theoretical
framework: one which is inclusive of both the law of a
state system and that of stateless societies. Such a framework is particularly necessary when we investigate the
ways in which the stateless societies have changed and
are changing on the demand first of the colonial governments and now of the independent governments. These
people, who are adapting to state forms on demand,
often experience severe difficulty because they see law
based on precedent as always and necessarily tyrannous.

There is seldom if ever a special body constituted in
order to hear and settle disputes in stateless societies.
Rather these disputes are settled by meetings that can
be profitably compared with the old New England town
meetings, except that in the case of the African stateless
societies, there are always two factions and the actual size

of the unit may change from case to case depending on the closeness of the relationship of the principals to the dispute.

There is, in Old English, a precise and accurate word to describe these "town meetings" or settlement of disputes by the important members of the village. This word is "moot." Well into the twelfth and thirteenth centuries Anglo-Saxon communities settled their disputes by meeting outside, under the shade of a tree, in whole communities, in order to discover correct and just solutions to disputes. Such is, in a sense, the origin of the "common law."

Courts, unlike moots, are special organs and require some sort of state organization from which they derive their power. While moots are a mode of the community, courts are special arms of politically organized states.

Moots and courts can, and in Africa often do, exist side by side within the same society. The jurisdiction of the courts may be limited to certain types of cases or to disputes of people of different villages or something of the sort. Jan Vansina has given an extremely cogent example from the Kuba of the Congo. The Kuba state has a very complex court system, the personnel of which changes with the nature of the dispute or offense; at the same time, however, many Kuba cases are settled by moots rather than by courts.

During the colonial era, and down to the present day, such stateless societies as that of the Tiv had a full-blown system of moots which ran side by side with the system of courts. Among these people it is considered to be totally immoral to call one's close kinsman before a government court. However, disputes obviously occur between close kinsmen. These disputes are settled in moots. In colonial Nigeria, for example, charges of witchcraft could not be brought before the courts. Obviously, since the court could not admit to a belief in witchcraft, only an accusation of witchcraft could be proved or disproved. Under these situations, if somebody accuses someone else of using witchcraft, that accusation becomes slander. However, for those members of the community that believe in witchcraft, the original charge could not be brought up for settlement. Therefore witchcraft disputes had, throughout the country, to be settled either in moots or in kangaroo courts.

There were devices other than courts and moots by which Africans sometimes settled disputes. Ordeals and recourse to seers and diviners were both fairly widely spread throughout the continent. An ordeal is a means for settling a dispute in the absence of any kind of evidence which can prove or disprove the charge, either because there are no witnesses or because (as in the case of witchcraft) empirical proof is impossible.

Probably no people claims that oracles and ordeals have much to do with justice, although the oracles are said to reveal the will or knowledge of the gods. However, they do settle the dispute. Ordeals range from taking oaths on shrines through the deliberate administration of poisonous substances either to animals or to human beings themselves. These substances are not necessarily lethal, and if the animal or the person does not die, the party is usually considered innocent. In some African societies, such as the Azande of the Sudan, the oracular mechanisms were checked and counterchecked through the requirement that a second oracle corroborate the first before action could be taken. Ordeals have all but disappeared from modern Euro-American courts. However, the divine sanctions which ordeals symbolize are still a part of such courts because it is still necessary for both witnesses and the principals to take oaths on entering the witness stand.

Africans sometimes resorted to contests to settle disputes. This "game" solution to a dispute is one in which the disputants either are forced to or agree to reduce the field of relevance, and determine a winner; they reopen the field and declare the winner in the game to be the winner of the real-life situation. In the early history of Roman law and during the Middle Ages in Europe, gladiatorial contests to settle disputes occupied important places in the legal repertoire.

Perhaps the most important of the sanctions, particularly in the stateless societies, was the institutionalized use of self-help. It is common throughout African stateless societies—and also in some of the states—for a man to collect his own debts by going to the farms or compound of his debtor and removing the property (a goat, for instance) that is owed to him. If he can make a case before the moot, if the debtor calls one, and both his group and that of the debtor agree that the debt is now and adequately discharged, his self-help was successful.

Some degree of self-help is either condoned or required in all legal systems. It becomes even more important in non-state organizations than it is in states because the major sanction, and the power behind it, is to be found in the right and ability of the groups concerned to carry out the decisions and compromises made by the elders.

If self-help gets out of hand it becomes, of course, akin to lawlessness—in any sort of society. The boundaries have to be fixed and the use of self-help contained if it is is to be an adequate judicial mechanism. In states, such limitations can be defined by legislation or by precedent. In non-states, self-help is controlled, but controlled somewhat differently. In our example of the man taking the goat, his own group will come to his defense if the others try to retaliate. However, if he takes the goat unreasonably and in a way that they believe the moot would not approve of—if he has a "bad case," or if he is a criminal—his kinsfolk will not risk the peace of the countryside, their hides, and their reputation for him. In such a case, two centers of judgment and power must be satisfied, and in achieving such a satisfaction, any community whose members overstep the accepted norm will find itself attacked and perhaps routed—yet such attacks seldom occur, because the moots and the good will of the two communities usually effect a settlement.

Africans in every part of the continent are running complex modern governments. The basic ideas behind the political thinking of many of their citizens, however, are still to be found in the type of situation that has been described here.

On the surface, African institutions are changing very rapidly, but the quickening ideas, molded by experience and language, have deep roots in African tradition and history. Because the deep roots of both African and European tradition tap the same prehistoric reserves, and because Africans have passed through most of the cultural revolutions which have, perhaps in other terms, also been the experience of the West, their adaptation has been fast and often successful. For all that, however, the distinct idiom in many instances remains. Whatever trouble Africans and Europeans may have in discussing matters with one another in the post-colonial world, much at least is attributable to the fact that they make different political assumptions.

Chapter Nine

AFRICAN TRADE AND MARKETS

THE BELIEF THAT AFRICANS LIVED IN A STATIC, unchanging economy—where each family provided for its own subsistence, where any market production was for strictly local markets, where the only export for sale overseas was slaves—was a sort of "sub-myth" to the myth of a savage Africa. As is always the case with myths, the fact that there were elements of truth in it gave unwarranted support to the rest of it. Between about the 1690s and the 1830s, the economically most valuable single export from sub-Saharan Africa was certainly slaves. However, commercial contact between African and European shippers began about 1480. Thus the slave trade was dominant for only about a third of the 400 years between 1480 and today.

As early as the 1660s, Senegambia alone exported as many as 150,000 cowhides in a single year. The Gold Coast exported an annual average of more than half a ton of gold. A century later, slave exports reached around 50,000 a year. Whatever we may think of the morality of the slave trade (and it has few defenders today), the commercial system necessary to acquire and transport that many slaves for sale on the coasts was far from primitive.

Long-distance trade within sub-Saharan Africa began well before the beginning of maritime contact. When the

169

Portuguese seamen first arrived on the Gulf of Guinea, they found African traders already working the routes from the Sahara fringe right down to the coast. And African long-distance trade continued to develop during the era of the slave trade. Yet, even at the height of the slave trade, long-distance caravans in Africa carried far less goods destined for export than they did goods for consumption within Africa.

By the nineteenth century, caravans from the Atlantic coast in Angola or the present-day Congo Republic reached the center of Africa, where they could encounter other caravans coming from the Indian Ocean and still others coming south from the upper Nile. When the European explorers first began to enter Africa in the late eighteenth and early nineteenth centuries, they always travelled with the help and guidance of African long-distance merchants, who often knew more about Europe than the explorers knew about Africa.

MARKETS AND MARKET PLACES

The African economy was mainly agricultural, and remains so to the present. The long-distance traders were a comparatively small group of professionals who worked the routes between markets. These markets were periodic meetings at fixed market places in most of Africa from Zaire northward. In other regions, where regular market places were less common, people nevertheless met to exchange goods on the market principle of price regulated by supply and demand.

But alongside exchanges dominated by the market principle, other exchanges did and still do take place on other bases. It is important here to distinguish between the market place and the market principle. The market place is the specific spot where buyers and sellers meet. It could be used for many purposes other than buying and selling — to meet your girlfriend, settle a legal dispute, get the latest news, or pay your respects to important elders or chiefs. Market places in Africa are almost as important politically and socially as they are economically.

The market principle is the process in which a multitude of buyers and sellers bargain together until they arrive at a price, fundamentally established by the pull and push of supply and demand for a particular commodity.

We have two tasks at hand. One is to see what goes on in market places. The other is to see how the market principle has worked or failed to work in African societies. We shall find some societies without market places; some with market places, but where few of the necessities of life pass through them; and finally some parts of the modern African economy where the role of the traditional market place dwindles, but that of the market principle dominates society as it does in Europe or America.

A market-dominated economy such as the United States — and the society that goes with it — is one in which not merely products and manufactured items but the factors of production such as land and labor enter into the same market. These markets may be more or less controlled by political authorities. The difference to be emphasized here is not a difference between free and controlled markets, but a difference that stems from the entry of land and labor into the same market on which yams, corn, cocoa, clothing, and beer are exchanged.

In a society dominated by the market principle, at least some member of every primary group must sell one of the factors of production or else the produce of his work and land (which amounts to the same thing) in order that his family may be provisioned. The opposite is usually called a "subsistence economy," which means no more than that the basic provisions of the members of the society are gained some way other than through market exchange, and that ultimately the factors of production, particularly land and labor, do not enter the market (albeit they are no less necessary to production):

The word "subsistence" is tricky in English because it means two things at once. It is associated with the word "level" on the one hand, to indicate poverty and life on the thin edge between existing and perishing—"bare existence." A subsistence economy is different; it must not be confused with subsistence level. The only link between them is the ambiguity in the word subsistence. There is no reason that a subsistence economy must always or even commonly be found to hover at the subsistence level. A subsistence economy means merely the absence of factor markets or a comprehensive political substitute for them.

Poverty, obviously, need not accompany the absence of a factor market and may, just as obviously, be overwhelming in the presence of factor markets. Indeed, given an adequate ecological adjustment and a sufficiently good tool kit, poverty cannot exist except in societies organized on a market basis. Famine may occur—but poverty in any other sense does not.

Except for hunting and gathering economies of the rapidly disappearing San and Pygmies, the subsistence level is usually far exceeded by all subsistence economies of Africa. Some places have a "hungry season," but that is different. The hungry season occurs just before the harvest: it has to do with the agricultural cycle and the difficulties of storage in a tropical climate. Even in the hungry season, people usually eat. They do not eat as much as they would like; in fact, they may regularly lose weight during it. But this period, where it occurs, usually lasts at most six or seven weeks.

In a market society, produce and the products of factories are sold on a more or less controlled market at prices more or less determined by supply and demand. The result is that the market in produce can and does limit and even control the market in factors, because of the workings of supply and demand (or a political equivalent). Such a system is to be found in many parts of the world, but it tends to be more or less important. In the modern Western economy it becomes the primary organizational principle. But even in a subsistence economy with comparatively little exchange, the scarcity or abundance of any commodity has an influence on the value attributed to it. And this influence can vary within a single economy, being important in some sectors, less important in others. Some subsistence economies have highly developed markets for export produce. Long before the colonial period, a complex network of local markets for African exports offered African farmers a price for their exports that was related, however distantly, to the work price for those commodities.

Yet land, labor, brains or ability, and capital were rarely offered on the market in traditional Africa. Capital was available in only modest amounts — a canoe, a fishing net, bellows and forge, agricultural tools, or occasionally in loans to traders. Labor could be "bought," in the sense that slaves were bought and some of their labor could be diverted to producing goods for the market. The labor of free men, however, was seldom "bought" through contract. Land was allocated in such complex and socially determined ways that it too rarely had a market price. The force of the market principle was therefore comparatively weak insofar as the basic factors of production were concerned.

The problem for understanding the traditional African rural economy is to find how goods were distributed, when not consumed directly by the producers, and how life was organized when the market principle was comparatively weak.

MARKETING AND TRADING

An important distinction can be made between marketing and trading. Marketing is the activity of a producer who takes some of his product to the market place to exchange for other products. Trade, on the other hand, is the activity where an entrepreneur buys in one market with the intention of selling in another, or in the same market at a later time. The fact that marketing and trading go hand-in-hand does not make them inseparable. If produce markets had disappeared in precolonial Africa, the society would not have perished, nor even changed its structure very much. People would have been uncomfortable; that is all. If the market principle stopped working in present-day America, on the other hand, the economy would collapse. Even farmers sell most of what they grow on the market, and buy most of what they consume. The rest of us sell our labor for a salary and buy almost everything we use.

Trading over long distance, however, has been part of the African scene for a very long time, and the older traders' traditions and practices have lived down to the present in somewhat altered form. All over the world, pre-industrial long-distance trade tended to be carried by merchants organized as a trade diaspora. One of the problems encountered in trade across cultural divisions was the vast differences in language and culture, often over quite short distances. One way to surmount this difficulty was to send out merchants to take up residence in a foreign commercial center, where, over time, they could learn the local language and come to understand the alien way of life. Once accustomed to the foreign setting, these emissaries could set themselves up to act as cross-cultural brokers, helping to smooth the way for traveling merchants from their homeland.

Thousands of different merchant communities have organized trade diasporas, going back in time to ancient Mesopotamia. The most familiar will probably be the Greeks and Phœnicians of the classical Mediterrean, or the north Germans of the Middle Ages whose trade diaspora stretched from London far into Russia and ultimately became the Hanseatic League.

In Africa, some of the oldest trade diasporas were those of North Africa, like that of the Phœnicians. When camels began to be used in the Sahara after about the fifth century A.D., North African merchants began to reach across the desert, setting up small merchant communities at the desert edge to the south. From there, other, sub-Saharan merchant communities brought in goods from the savanna and forest country, including minerals like gold or agricultural products like kola nuts. Many of these early sub-Saharan trade diasporas were originally Soninke in culture, since the Soninke were a major group near the desert edge, but their diasporas spread off to the south under a number of different ethnic names, Wangarawa, Jaahanke, or Juula (Dioula in French) among others. These diaspora communities were so specialized in commerce that the name, Juula, simply means merchant.

Later on, many other ethnic groups began to enter trade as a specialized occupation, most notably the Hausa from Northern Nigeria and the Republic of Niger, who have settled in trade enclaves within many African cities. These enclaves are now called Zongos, where Hausa is still the language of commerce. Others, mainly in the twentieth century, have become trade specialists, like Wolof-speaking Senegalese, whose commercial communities can be found scattered in the market places from their home country around Dakar, through West Africa to Brazzaville in Congo and Kinshasa in Zaire. Today, significant communities of Senegalese traders are street-corner peddlers in Paris and in New York.

In the pre-colonial past, the traders travelled in armed caravans for mutual protection, sometimes as many as a thousand men together; with their goods carried by porters, where the tse-tse fly prevented animal transport; by donkey in much of the savanna; and by camel or pack-ox near the desert edge. Today, they use trucks on the highways, telegraph and telephone for communication, and often travel by air with their trade goods as part of their baggage. Some, whose families had been members of trade diasporas for centuries, have gained a Western education and moved over into the Western-style sector of the economy as members of trading firms.

Nor did all the successful big traders of present-day Africa begin in the trade diasporas. Many worked their way into long-distance trade from a beginning in the local market. Women were the chief retail marketers in much of West Africa. They could slip more easily from marketing into trade where (as with the Yoruba) men produced most of the food. Women marketers and traders have been particularly important in buying and selling food crops, and from this base have worked their way over into the import and retail distribution of European manufactures.

Because the main point of this section is the diversity of uses to which Africans put market places, and the vast amount of fun that they have in them, it is well at the beginning to emphasize the fact that market places are primarily regarded as points to do one's marketing and trading. The amount of internal trade in various African countries that goes through the market places is tremendous, but nobody has any idea how much volume or what value of goods may actually be distributed in this way. Weights and measures are more or less absent, although in many parts of the continent standard weights and measures have appeared in the last few decades. The quart beer bottle, the standard-size cigarette tin, the standardized four-gallon kerosene tin, and an empty 30-30 shell casing are all used as measures. There are others. There are also many non-standardized units of measurement. Moreover, no formal records are kept by individual marketers. Many West African traders do keep books of one sort or another, although most do not. Marketers—even when marketers do a little bit of trading along with their marketing—never separate their marketing or their trading from their domestic activities. Obviously, acquiring any kind of quantitative ideas about the amount or the value of such goods becomes a task in data acquisition that has scarcely been tackled, let alone solved.

It is true, however, that vast quantities of local produce such as food, craft products, livestock, cloth—everything that is the staff of life and the basis for the provisioning

Market Woman Making robo, a form of "fast food" in northern
Nigerian markets.

of society—may go through these markets in parts of
West Africa and the Congo area. Yet in relatively few places
are people dependent on the markets for the basis of their
subsistence.

Markets are vital links—they are the very nodes—in the
transportation network. The famous "bush telegraph"—
the rapid spread of news by means unknown to Europeans
—works in part through the market places. Africa is a
country on the move, and it appears that it always has
been. However, the peace of the colonial era and the
improvement of roads that accompanied it meant that
market places increased in number, that the amount of
travel to and from marketing increased vastly, and there-

fore the "bush telegraph" worked with better and better efficiency.

Markets are, throughout that part of the continent to which they are indigenous, organized under political authority. Indeed, in those parts of East and South Africa to which they have been introduced, it was colonial government that introduced them. In some areas of West Africa, chiefs retained direct control over the markets and either themselves or through special deputies maintained the market place and kept the peace within it. In other areas, committees of elders, representative in whatever way was considered important to the community, took it as one of their most serious civic duties to maintain a market place so that their part of the world would be "kept on the map" and prosperity would reign.

All African market places are policed by someone. In many areas, this task has gone to the policemen of the recognized local government. In others, however, they are policed by special appointees or by the kinsmen of a chief, or by special groups designated by the elders to carry out the task. These policemen are always subject to the authority of somebody who is the headman (it may be a committee) to whom they can refer wrongdoers and disputes which occur in the market place. Disputes inevitably arise in market places, because people may cheat each other, and because they may meet their enemies and their debtors. For this reason, every ordinary African market has, some place in it, a court in session. It may be no more than a market court concerned with arguments over shortchanging, quality of goods, and petty theft. In other market places, however, the judges of the local government may set up their courts. Courts are a necessary concomitant of market places and of the type of crowds which meet in market places.

In some parts of Africa, the market authorities enforce quality control. They disallow sale of rotten meat or other unsatisfactory goods. The usual mode of treatment is *caveat emptor,* but some control is maintained, the degree varying with the personalities and power of the market officials.

Market administrators are usually rewarded. They may be paid salaries by the local government. They may, on the other hand, be allowed to make a levy on the goods sold in the market. Sometimes entry fees are demanded from marketers who intend to sell goods. The amount of the levy or entrance fee is itself subject to what the market will bear. If the levy is too high, traders and marketers will avoid such market places and establish new ones nearby. The only way to avoid such a situation is for governments to demand control and licensing of market places—a situation that was fairly widespread in colonial Africa and is found in some of the new African states.

Market places can "die," which means merely that people cease to come to them. They can also be "stolen," which means that one gains popularity at the expense of another. In short, the location of market places, their organization, and their popularity are all highly volatile and subject to quick change. Since it is to the advantage of individuals and government officials to control large popular market places (by so doing they are able to see and to influence large numbers of people), few petty tyrannies can be kept up for long.

In traditional Africa, almost all market places were associated with religious activities. That is to say, the market places were consecrated in one way or another, and to this day, most African market places have shrines associated with them. Such consecration guaranteed that supernatural sanctions would back up the political authori-

Woman dressed up for Market Day, Burkina Faso.

ties in their maintenance of peace in the market place. Such supernatural sanctions, and the shrines that were their symbols, varied with the particular religion in question. They may have been no more than a bundle of "medicine." In many areas they were specially consecrated trees. In some, there were special small huts with carved figurines in them. The purpose of these shrines was the maintenance of the market peace. It is well recognized that it is impossible, in even the best-policed market place, to be sure that all who cheat or steal or water their beer or sell bad meat will be caught by the mundane authorities. Therefore, it is best to reinforce their vigilance with supernatural sanctions.

Finally, markets are fun. Each displays an element of the fair or the carnival. In West Africa and the Congo they are major centers of entertainment. Dancers come to the market and display their skill. Work parties, wedding parties, christening parties, and spur-of-the-moment parties come to the market to dance and sing and to announce their good news to enlarged audiences.

In all these regards African market places are reminiscent of those in Europe during the Middle Ages and indeed up into the eighteenth century. Markets in Europe were also fairs that were held in the shadow of the church and were policed by the bishop and the market master and their officials. They were religious centers as well as important centers of trade and distribution. Market places may be extremely important institutions in almost every phase of human activity. Yet for all that, the fact remains that their *raison d'être* is channeling trade and providing an outlet for the marketing of subsistence farmers.

SYSTEMS OF MARKET PLACES

Different market places specialize in different goods and in different activities. One market is a good place to buy X and sell Y. The next one is a good place to buy Y and sell Z. The next one may be well known for its beer drink, and the one after that for its wise counselors and judges. Such specialization, when combined with another fact—that markets do not meet every day—leads to two vital points about the marketing system of africa, particularly West Africa and the Congo Basin. First of all, every community is at the center of a group of markets which meets every fourth, fifth, or seventh day, depending on the area. There is, therefore, an association of market places with time as well as with special products. In a neighborhood with markets that meet every five days, each community is likely to be either at or near the center of a cycle or a ring of five markets, each of which meets one day of the five-day "market week" that results. These market neighborhoods, or rings, overlap in a chain-mail fashion, and spread across the countryside. Such overlapping rings, with a few gaps, run from Dakar almost to the Nile, and south well into the Congo Basin.

The other major characteristic of the market system is that goods can move through market places and traverse very much greater distances than people themselves. Every different African product that goes through market places follows a route determined by specialization of market places. A large number of "middlemen" add to the price, but the markup is amazingly small, considering the number of intermediary links that may separate a producer from a consumer.

Market places, thus, provide another map, based on a

different institution, by means of which space, time, and social structure are coordinated. This trade map or market map permeates different cultures and crosses national and language barriers. If a market place is commonly used by several ethnic groups, the consecrated shrines and the ritual that surrounds them contain the elements from each religion which make it workable in all the cultures. There may be, indeed, very highly original rituals consciously created and especially performed in order to get in the vital elements from several religious systems. Violence can still occur, however. Today weapons are forbidden—and usually were so even before colonial governments made the practice general. Moreover, throughout the indigenous market area of Africa, people sit in the position in the market place closest to the path leading to their homes—this is particularly true of women marketers. Such seating arrangements keep the escape routes open. Yet, market places are, at the same time, often legal sanctuaries, because of their position of political neutrality and their consecrated shrines.

THE SPREAD OF THE MARKET PRINCIPLE

One of the first reactions to colonial control was the vast expansion in the number of market places in Africa, and of the goods that went through them. Only later did the market places themselves begin to dwindle as their task was taken over by modern transport systems and expanding firms and thousands of entrepreneurs, some small-scale, some handling large volume.

In the process of the enlargement of the importance of market places, the importance of the market principle also became magnified. The "market" in both its senses was spreading.

Dhows loading for the Voyage from Mombasa to the Persian Gulf.

To Westerners, money, trade, and market are more or less inseparable. Rather, they need not be separated to be understood. European governments therefore encouraged the growth of market places, and by introducing coinage and demanding that taxes be paid in it (and abetting importation of goods that could be bought with it), they actively hastened the enlargement of the social scope for the market principle.

Money is probably the most important single item in changing an economy. A monetized economy is, by that very fact, different from a non-monetized economy. Money is a cultural trait that has been discovered several times in the history of the world, including several places in Africa. However, there is money and money. Money is said by economists to do at least three things: (1) it is a method for evaluating and comparing goods of different kinds; (2) it is a means of payment; (3) it is a means for facilitating exchange. If the authority is old enough, money may also be said to be a means of storing wealth.

The three uses of money must not be confused simply because coinage—a single cultural item—carries out the three tasks in our own society. Money is used in the West to pay fines (while crimes cannot be evaluated) and money is used to pay taxes (which is only by the furthest stretch of analogy an exchange). We have a general purpose money, but we must not therefore assume that a money used for one of these purposes in other cultures is general purpose money.

Africa had some examples of general purpose money— cowrie shells in a few places in West Africa and the Congo Basin, and again on the East Coast where Indian rupees, Spanish and American and Austrian, "Maria-Theresa," dollars all circulated long before the colonial period began. Throughout West Africa, the most common kind of currency for ordinary marketing was cloth of particular styles and qualities. Many, if not most African societies had other forms of currency that could be used for only one purpose. These are called "special purpose money." Metal "hoes" in Guinea and Liberia were used principally for paying bride-wealth, while ordinary food in the market place required other forms of currency. Western societies have had special purpose currencies in the recent past. During the Second World War, people had the general-purpose money they earned, but they had to have ration coupons as well to buy gasoline, sugar, shoes, and some other items. In this way, the government could assure itself that gasoline went mainly to those with a need to drive, or that food and other scarce items were shared equally. In much the same way, special purpose currencies control the distribution of particular goods— chiefly brides.

Other, social factors also lie behind these specialized monetary systems. Three, or perhaps more, economic principles can serve to organize exchange: they are the market principle, the principle of reciprocity, and the principle of redistribution. Taking the American economy as a model, we can think quite correctly that we live in a market economy. Most of the transactions that take place are transactions according to market principles of price determined by supply and demand, with more or less government "interference." However, we pay taxes, which is a form of redistribution: wealth moves toward a political center and is redistributed from it.

Redistribution may be (but in our own case is not) the dominant mode of institutionalizing an economy. In some African societies until quite recently, much of the allocation of goods took place within a pattern of redistribution. Large family groups or even whole societies paid much of their produce to the family head or higher authority, who then redistributed it according to political principals.

Sometimes in traditional Africa, a gift that was expected to be reciprocated by gifts or favors was given in a particular ritual manner. On the Sengambia coast, for example, traders made ritual gifts that included the widest possible variety of goods; and such gifts were sometimes called "one of everything," meaning everything under the sun, though in practice it simply meant one of every kind of trade good. Such gifts were designed to reassure opposing traders of one's good intent. When it came to actual exchange of commodities, however, it was hard bargaining with supply and demand clearly the prime concern. And of course, both sides considered the value and cost of the preliminary gifts as part of their profits and loss account.

The other allocative principle is reciprocity. Mid-twentieth-century Americans have a sort of vestigial reciprocity, confused easily with market because we acquire on the market most of the goods that enter the institutions of reciprocal allocation. Gifts we give at Christmas are usually bought—yet, even there, it was until very recently considered more genteel to make your own Christmas cards and to put personal work and attention into the gifts one gave—only today have we come to prize instead the thoughtfulness and individualization that go into buying a gift to suit the personality of the recipient. It is still bad taste to compute market price on the gifts that are exchanged.

In the American economy today, the market is central; redistribution has an important part, but is purposely underplayed. In pre-colonial Africa, the emphasis was different. Redistribution and reciprocity were supposed to be more important. Goods were often supposed to be sold at prices that changed very little over time; they had a semi-official exchange value imbedded in tradition. One ox equalled ten cloths of a certain type; so many oxen were the proper bride price; so many measures of millet were equal to a measure of milk. In fact, goods rarely changed hands at these traditional values, simply because people knew that an ox or a measure of millet was scarce or plentiful at that time. The market principle thus slipped in by the back door, so that, when millet was scarce a half-measure would "count" as a whole. When it was plentiful, perhaps two measures were necessary to "count" as one.

Through the past century, the market economy has gradually triumphed, first through convenient fictions, then more and more openly through the spread of general-purpose money. Though special-purpose moneys continued to be used for such payments as bridewealth, it became increasingly easy to transfer from one kind of money to another—like buying ration coupons on the black market in wartime. Finally, even that fiction has disappeared and most bride-wealth passes openly in the form of general-purpose money—bank-notes and coins issued by the African governments. But the spread of the market principle into new spheres, here as in other aspects of life, has created tremendous moral problems that are not entirely resolved.

In rural Africa, the noisy, colorful market place is a growing phenomenon. In urban centers, open market places of the old style still function as vital institutions, operating on the market principle. Western-style firms are also present alongside them—dealing in manufactures, imports, exports, and retail sales. The market place and the supermarket exist side by side.

Chapter Ten

AFRICAN RELIGION

THE MYTHS IN THE WEST CONCERNING AFRICAN RELI-gion so distort the facts, let alone the ideas that lie behind the facts, that it becomes difficult to present these ideas without opening oneself to the charge of being a "see no evil" optimist. Yet the facts have to be stated, at the same time that one declares oneself not to be a do-gooder setting out to erase the differences among people in the name of a sentimental reinterpretation of the doctrine of the psychic unity of mankind.

All African religions are monotheistic in the sense that there is a single High God, who is said to be the creator of the world and of mankind, and a central source of order and of whatever sense is to be found. Many African religions are also polytheistic in that either pantheons of gods or large numbers of spirits or ancestors or some other kind of divinities may stand between man and the ultimate God.

African religions also tend to have a precise, one-to-one association with a particular form of social group. In this characteristic they are unlike the international religions, which are supple enough to subserve many forms of social structure. African religion and African society are different ways of viewing the same universe, for God and the spirits are, even to the skeptical, members of the same society as enfolds living human beings.

191

The Imam, leader in Friday prayer, at an Urban mosque in Ivory Coast.

Prayer and sacrifice are to be found in all the religions on the continent. Prayers, however, are likely to be generalized requests for health and well-being, and to include statements of innocence of any evil intention. Sacrifices are used not so much for purposes of cleansing (although such may be dominant, as in Kikuyu religion) as to provide paths of communication between the human beings and divinity. To oversimplify, it can be said that in all parts of the continent, life is the supreme value, and that sacrifice takes life (usually goats or chickens) as a means of getting in touch with the source of life and enhancing human life.

Perhaps the most characteristic quality of African religion is that there are many strings to the bow: the late S. F. Nadel, an anthropologist with wide experience in Africa, was the first to point out (for Nupe religion) that for each purpose to be achieved there were several ritual and moral ways of doing it. African religion does not in most places have undeniable orthodoxy (the exceptions are those such as Dahomey in which an established priesthood exists). Therefore it has no heterodoxy. It must be understood rather as a set of goals, a dogma of the nature of God and man, and a more or less experimental (and therefore constantly and rapidly changing) set of rituals for achieving those goals within that conceptual framework of dogma. To study African religion, therefore, means to study the ritual and the stated dogma behind it, and the goals to be achieved by it.

Ritual occupies an important place in Africa. Passage through the life cycle tends to be marked with religious ritual—at least, there is the idea that it should be, and if a man gets ill the reason may be found in the fact that a vital rite was omitted. Christenings, initiations, weddings, burials—moreover, the seasons and the annual schedule—

are usually marked by religious rites. The world must be constantly renewed by the ritual activities of people, so that humanity may prosper as the world prospers. Most importantly, perhaps, ritual occurs in association with medicine as means of curing the infirm and postponing death.

Africans have, however, a tendency to neglect ritual until it is demanded by the divinities—the demands take the form, they say, of illness or crop failure among the living members of the societies. The immediate reaction to misfortune is always to ask "Why?" and to consult a diviner about those aspects which are beyond the reach of the human senses, then to repair the ritual breach and treat the difficulty.

Perhaps most impressive of all to a European visitor is the casualness of African religious activities. This casualness does not mean that Africans do not take their religions seriously, but only that they do not consider the divinities either prudish or unsolicitous.

A RUBRIC FOR AFRICAN RELIGION

The absence of orthodoxy in African religion means that there are many "literary" versions of its substantiating myth to be collected from any single society, and that the "truth" must be extracted from the common motifs of the many versions. In Dahomey, priests can give fairly congruent versions of views concerning the nature of man and divinity and the establishment of the social and divine order. In stateless societies such as the Tiv, every man is his own expert—in religious matters as in everything else. What specialists there are maintain their position by social criteria and not by priestly ones, even as they use ritual knowledge for political ends.

Underneath the wild diversity of African religious practice runs a common set of themes and occurrences which an investigator can pick out and turn into a story. He must, as he does so, warn his readers that if they read such a story as a connected version of African statements, they will be wrong. Rather, a story is the most economical means to interrelate beliefs and practices. Unlike the myths that we have tried so far to expose—untrue but widely stated—this story is true but never stated.

In the beginning, the story behind African religion might run, God created the Heavens and the Earth. And he created them without regard for good and evil. They existed and, like God himself, were morally neutral. God, having accomplished his task, withdrew. The extent of his withdrawal varies from one society to the next—from the truly "otiose" or removed God, who is not available to human beings, to a God almost as personalized as the Judaeo-Christian divinity. In all places, however, the created universe was a mechanically or organically perfect system (both analogies misinterpret the African view to some extent, but allow Westerners to see the interconnectedness in it). It lacked only one thing: energy (again, to use a non-African metaphor). The power had to be supplied by the human creatures and their ancestors and the lower spirits that God had created. Human effort and spiritual energy (which often had to be primed by human effort) were the driving forces.

The nature of the beings that lie between men and God is everywhere said to be unknown, but everywhere described by local people. There are usually at least two levels in the hierarchy—in the "channels," to use a bureaucratic analogy. One is the ancestors, the other is a set of aspects of God or more straightforward, personalized godlings. The will of God (which may be fixed, and therefore unwilled in any specific instance) is made known down through the channels; it is satisfied by ritual, sacrifice, and the protestations of prayer, which go up through the same channels.

Good and evil enter such a system by two possible routes, and African religions may use either or both: the evil is inherent in human selfishness, which leads men to pervert the ritual that is the means for supplying the force. This (one might almost say "Protestant") notion is commonly found among peoples who live in stateless societies; here it is human selfishness in its individual manifestations that creates misfortune and causes death. Man's weakness and selfishness throw a spanner into the works.

The other source of evil is the "joker," played wild. The joker is a widespread religious phenomenon—the Judaeo-Christian devil is, in fact, a joker who perverts all the rules and hence accounts for evil. Legba of Dahomean religion can be seen as the archetype of the joker whose ineptitudes, carelessness, and malice have allowed misfortune, death, and the threat of dissolution of society to enter the firmament. "Fate," as the joker is often called, must be invoked to explain catastrophe in the absence of human selfishness and weakness.

The task of man is, through worship and sacrifice, to hold up his end of the process by supplying the motive force for the universe. Even more important, it is up to man through right and generous living to avoid creating the antisocial and anticosmic situations that bring about disaster. Whoever says that African religion has no moral content (and it has often been said) does not know an African religion—or else he is saying that African religion does not much concern itself with the sexual conduct of human beings and does not set forth its moral precepts as ten imperatives.

If it is charged that this treatment is a myth for African religion the defense is that the line between myth and theory is still vague in the study of comparative religion. A myth organizes data as narrative in order to condense mountains of facts or beliefs into recognizable form; a theory is not a story, but does the same thing. Myths and theories are also subject to different canons of proof: theories must stand up to experiment and ratiocination. Myths must stand up to the abrasions of social life. In that sense, this organization of the data is a theory—it allows the exposition of the concepts. But it cannot be gathered, in this form, from any informant.

DOGMA

Like most religious practitioners, Africans start at the opposite end of the chain of events from theologians or social scientists. They begin with the situation that calls for explanation and perhaps intervention between God and his emissaries. In Africa, that situation is most commonly individual or community misfortune: disease or sterility, misgovernment or plague.

Twentieth-century Europeans often fail to remember that it is only about three hundred years ago that William Harvey discovered the circulation of the blood, and that scarcely a century has passed since bacteria were discovered to be the carriers of some diseases; that only a few decades have passed since we discovered viruses, and only a few years since we discovered the first hints about the etiology of diseases created by chromosomal malformation or the immune system. Scientific information of this sort filters, via the press and the educational system, so rapidly into the general knowledge of the educated public that it becomes difficult to appreciate ideas about the nature of disease and its causation held by peoples who lack such scientific knowledge. Science has, if we may put it so, mainly "dominant genes," and the cultural gene loss that accompanies the achievement of scientific progress is surely as vast as the gene loss involved in the hybridization of corn.

Most traditional African religions state the opinion that were it not for the workings of the forces of evil, human beings would live forever in health and happiness. Therefore, when disease and misery strike, the source must be rooted out. That source contains two elements: there is, on the one hand, the cause of the difficulty—Africans, within their knowledge, are as sensible about cause as anyone else, and most of them know that some diseases are communicable, and that droughts appear in recurring cycles. Cause in this sense, however, leaves certain questions unanswered—all the "why" questions. Therefore, misfortune must have not only a cause but it must have a source of motivation (like the running of the world itself must have motive energy).

Therefore the very fact that misfortune strikes is in itself an indication that all is not well in the world and in the cosmos. The cause and motivation must be discovered. It is possible from a Western point of view to realize that motivation cannot be determined by what we would consider to be rational means. Westerners have, in fact, been rigorously trained not to ask "why" questions about misfortune. When a doctor tells us that we have a rare disease we do not immediately say "Why me?"—at least we do not say it to the doctor. We have become a statistic, for better or for worse. It is, however, exactly the "Why me?" question that Africans ask, and to which they seek an answer. In answer, they link social problems to divine action. In so doing, they air and often solve the social problems in the course of seeking to counter the divine manifestations.

When misfortune strikes, the first thing one must do is go to a diviner to discover the device which was used to bring it about and perhaps also to discern the author of it. That author may be a spirit to whom insufficient attention has been paid. It may be an ancestor who is punishing a descendant—perhaps an innocent one—for social, moral, or spiritual shortcomings of the group of his descendants. Or it may, indeed, be a "witch," who is a human author of evil, venting his anger, his envy, or his selfishness.

African diviners use many modes of carrying out their task. They may throw palm nuts and read answers to their queries in the juxtaposition of the fallen kernels. They may toss chains of snake bones. They may rub carved oracle boards together. They may become possessed, and receive their answers through a spiritual intermediary. They may administer to chickens a poison that is sometimes lethal and sometimes not, and then judge by the results. They may examine the entrails of sacrificed beasts. In short, when one is seeking to establish a connection which is in scientific fact a *non sequitur,* any means save a scientific one can be brought into play.

Divination in African religion is vital because it tells priests, patients, and the entire community what ritual they must perform. Successful diviners are highly intelligent, and often high-strung men or (occasionally) women. They are often also physically handicapped. Divination is one of the specialties most likely to attract the person with an intellectual bent. Diviners must have an excellent intuitive knowledge of the societies in which they live—and

often the knowledge is not merely intuitive but can be
made explicit, so that diviners sometimes make excellent
informants for anthropologists. They must also be men
of courage. It is they who are putting their fingers on, and
bringing into the open, the inadequacies and the sore spots
in day-to-day living. Unless they are strong and forceful,
they can be cowed. Many diviners who complete their
training never practice, specifically because they cannot
stand the heat in the kitchen.

Once divination has been carried out, two steps remain.
One of these is ritual, the other medical—or in the case
of community misfortune, legal. Indigenous African practice was first to carry out the ritual so that the motivation
for the misfortune could be counteracted. Only then could
medical curing be undertaken, for to do so before ritual
counteraction of the motive force would be fruitless.

RITUAL

All African ritual—perhaps, indeed, all ritual—involves
putting a person, or the representatives of a community,
into touch with God or his representatives, in order that
communication can be made. The person must then also
be safely returned from the state of sacred contact. There
are two main components of most African rituals: sacrifice and prayer. There are many lesser elements: magical
gesture, a social demand that ritual must be carried out
by certain people in the presence of certain other people;
prayers must be supported by communities—the congregation—and the sacrifices must be consumed by the
beneficiaries, past and present, of such ritual.

Most sacrifices in African religion involve the taking
of life—there are a few offerings of food, tobacco, or kola

nuts that are of a different nature and are sometimes called sacrifice by Westerners. For major purposes, however, sacrifice takes life. The common sacrificial animal is the chicken, although every kind of domesticated animal that one can think of has probably been sacrificed. In West Africa, and indeed throughout most of the continent, the blood of the sacrificed animals is smeared onto the beneficiary of the sacrifice and onto the emblems of divinity, whatever they may be. There are, however, some areas in East Africa in which the cheam of cattle or goats—that substance contained in their first stomach—replaces blood. The point is that the taking of life and the smearing of the symbol of life onto the person and the divine emblems establishes a contact between the two. While thus exposed, one is in a state of extreme jeopardy. However, only through such exposure is curing and reparation possible.

Either as a part of the ritual, or at the completion of the ritual, the sacrificial animal is eaten. It is cooked and consumed by the congregation of the persons who have benefited from the specific ritual in question. The ingestion of the ritual animal redoubles the solidarity of the community, and also provides symbols of status.

A good deal of nonsense has been written about human sacrifice in Africa. Human sacrifice was witnessed and reported by European travelers in several parts of the continent during the nineteenth century; it has occurred secretly (occasionally exposed by government police and courts) on a small scale into the twentieth. Human sacrifice is, in almost all cases (but there may have been a few exceptions), an act of desperation: since human life is the dearest life, it is therefore the most powerful when taken in sacrifice. The idea of human sacrifice is not unknown in modern international religions—it is merely that most of them have devised symbolic means by which the sacrifice, once made, can have permanent effect and need never be repeated. Africans too have devised many means of maintaining the idiom of human sacrifice while not actually carrying it out. One is outright symbolic association of an animal (commonly the dog) with the human being; another is to treat the corpses of those that died natural deaths in such a way that they count for sacrifices and hence for the greatest good of the community.

Although there are vast quantities of texts of prayers from African religious services preserved in the literature, there has not been as yet any extensive and systematic examination of them. Only very broad generalizations can be made. They often protest the innocence from evil of all those present, particularly the ritual participants; often such protests involve oaths—"May I die if . . ." or some equivalent form. The request is usually uttered in very broad terms: for health, welfare, and fertility of entire communities. There are also private prayers in African religion, but it is difficult to say whether the general opinion that they are of considerably lesser importance than the prayers uttered in public ritual is the actual case, or whether it is just that the public prayers are overwhelmingly easier to observe and discuss.

WITCHCRAFT: THE PARASITE OF RELIGION

Witchcraft has to a greater or lesser extent been a parasite on religion in widely scattered areas of the world for the simple reason that it answers many of the same questions about misfortune that religious dogma sets out to answer. There are deep psychic bases for setting the cause of one's troubles outside one's self—the defense mechanism called "projection." Western history is rife with witchcraft: accusations, trials, and executions of people who were necessarily innocent of the charges made against them for the simple reason that there were no human means to encompass such acts. African history displays the same phenomenon; the same subject/object confusion, the same charges, trials, and executions. Witch hunts go in waves, whether in Calvin's Geneva, seventeenth-century Massachusetts, or Zaire today.

Most telling of all, witchcraft is a faulty logical device. Its fault lies in its premise. The premise is that human disease and death can be caused by the ill will of other human beings. Often a vast lore surrounds the necessarily secret (because they are non-existent) devices by means of which malice is converted into misfortune. It may be the "Evil Eye," so that even a glance can be lethal. There may be mysterious ways of introducing foreign substances beneath the surface of the skin. "Black magic," even Black Masses, may be said or performed in order that good can by inversion be turned to evil. In this realm of imaginative activity there can be no limit on the ways in which people think that evil can be done. Somebody, evil through and through, can always invent a new one.

Witchcraft under some conditions has some positive benefits, although such a view can be quickly overworked. It is a means in most places by which the tensions in families and within communities can be brought into the open and relieved. It is nevertheless also true that witchcraft is usually more upsetting than it is soothing to a community. Africans are not, however, constantly afraid of witches, nor do they lead their lives in terror of black magic, as some nineteenth-century writers would have us believe. To a community that believes in it, the occurrence of witchcraft is rather like an accident rate to a community that uses automobiles. One deplores both accident rate and witchcraft, but learns to live with it and is not really convinced that it will strike one's self, so long as one conducts one's own affairs sensibly, morally, and with caution.

It takes a very high degree of education and training to stamp out witchcraft from a community which has known it. It also takes good government and good welfare. The reason is that witchcraft is one of the most suitable answers to the question "Why me?" "Those nasty people" have brought about my misfortune. The world is always full of nasty people and misfortunes. The *non sequitur* is apparent only to the most sophisticated and to those who lack a dogmatic faith that evil spirits may indeed possess persons and turn them into their own evil instruments.

ISLAM AND CHRISTIANITY

Christianity has impinged on Africa for centuries. Ethiopia is largely Christian, and has been so for centuries. The Coptic Church there and in Egypt is one of the basic forms of Christianity. Christianity in northeast Africa, however, has lost ground to Islam, which has spread widely across the Sudanic lands and down the eastern coast of the continent. Many African nations today regard themselves as Muslim; and most others regard themselves as Christian.

Islam and Christianity, although in one sense they have divided the continent between them, in another sense are both only marginally in control. It is the opinion of both Muslims and Christians that both religions will continue to spread in Africa during the coming decades. They are probably right. Many Muslims and some Christians believe that Islam demands less culture change of African converts than Christianity does—that it will therefore expand more rapidly in future. On the other hand, Christianity is offered in present-day Africa in many shades of deviation from the

Muslim Women in Lamu, Kenya, wearing the traditional buibui.

original missionary teaching. The immensely popular Aladura or "praying churches" of Nigeria are evidence of the vitality of new religion mixing the older African beliefs with the Christian message.

Christianity, however, has a pronounced lead in another respect: it is the Christians who created, manned, and financed most of the schools in Africa. Therefore the elites have, with a few exceptions, been educated primarily in Christian schools. Thus, in much of the continent, the new national leaders profess Christianity.

One thing can be certain. With development and industrialization, African religions will dwindle in importance. It is unlikely, however, that they will disappear for many decades to come. The reason is that they are both tough-minded and have been found to work well in the social situations of small groups; they also answer that nagging question, "Why me?" Christians and Muslims fall back on a doctrine of the will of God, or else back on the explanations garnered from traditional religions.

On most other points, however, there is an amazingly close overlap between the basic ideas of Islam and Christianity, and of the African religions. Neither Islam nor Christianity is foreign in its essence to African religious ideas. And once they are stripped of some of their specific modes of expression, African religious ideas are not foreign to the Christian or the Muslim either.

It is impossible to overemphasize the influence that Christian missionaries have had in Africa. It should at the same time be pointed out and recognized that much of their influence was of a cultural nature rather than merely of a theological nature. They have indeed taught new theologies, but they have also taught literacy, new ways of expressing basic theological notions, new moral precepts, and the principles of bureaucracy. Christianity and Islam both bring the morality of the individual into the religion in a way that is not done in African religion itself, and that has in the past often led Christian and Muslim observers to say that African religion had no moral dimension. The great debt that Africa owes to missionaries is that in a situation in which the forces of trade, colonial government, and the missions themselves were creating cultural havoc, it was only the missions that began to rebuild, and gave them a chance to rebuild. Whatever any individual Westerner may think of the missionary edifice, every African knows that it is to missionaries that they owe the beginning of the African educational system.

Part Three

AFRICAN HISTORY

Chapter Eleven

THE PEOPLING OF AFRICA

AFRICA, FOR ALL THAT IT WAS THE LAST CONTINENT to be "explored"—which means that it remained longest unknown to modern Western civilization—has nevertheless yielded the oldest "human" remains and artifacts yet discovered. According to our present information, the earliest anthropoid forms that could have begun the systematic invention of culture are indisputably associated with Africa.

To say that Africa is the "home" of mankind does not mean, however, that Africans as we know them today were the first human beings—indeed, it seems likely that today's Africans are all recent immigrants.

WHEN IS A MAN A MAN?

In any discussion of early man, the knotty question always emerges early: when is a man a man? In the apt phrase of Professor Raymond Dart, the earliest culture-creating anthropoid forms were "trembling on the verge of humanity." The question becomes: when did they topple over?

The question is usually answered on the basis of behavior rather than of the anatomy and physiology of the creature's body. That is to say, the closer we come to hu-

211

man beings, the more we must distinguish by acts and capabilities and the less important does the physical aspect of the creature emerge. For many decades, anthropologists defined mankind as a tool-making animal, leaving the assumption that every ape that could make a tool was human—and the false derivative that since apes were not human they could not make tools. If such a definition is maintained, both chimpanzees and gorillas are today "trembling on the verge of humanity," for both of them make tools of a crude sort. A tool is any creation, external to the physical body, that is made in order to accomplish something else. Elephants break off branches of trees in order to swish flies, but the branch is usually not considered to be a tool, for it is not worked specifically (although it is obvious that such a position can rapidly deteriorate into a quibble). Chimpanzees do alter the shape of the proto-tools that they create. In short, the best that can be said of human beings is that they have by far the most effective culture of any animal, but it is futile to try to define them on the basis of being culture-producing and using animals, and then fighting off all the evidence of other creatures that use tools.

Mankind shares a great many physical characteristics with the great apes, as well as the more general ones with all of the mammals or all of the animal world, and ultimately all the world of the living. The major blood types found among human beings are also found in the four great apes—gorilla, chimpanzee, orangutan, and gibbon. The body musculature is largely the same—the differences arise from such distinctive human features as the head being balanced differently on the spine and so needing fewer heavy muscles to hold it up, and the fact that the bipedel locomotion has led to musculature development in the lower back, the legs, and the knot of muscle in the buttocks which none of the great apes share with man. The question emerges: what combination of cultural factors and physical capacities—and remember, that at one level the ability to create and use culture is a physical capacity—defines a beast as a man?

The argument rages, and it is this argument that lies behind the difficulty in understanding the problems of early people. When we ask "Were they human?" we usually mean "Were they like us?" And to answer that question demands extensive examination of the degree of self-knowledge and even of narcissism in the human outlook. It also brings up another problem: the only remains of early man that have ever been found are bone. When, in the course of reconstruction, the flesh and the external appearance is guessed at (and it is never anything but a more or less educated guess), the early man must be given features that resemble in one way or another at least some aspects of the presently existing races. What was the color of Java man? What was the hair texture? We do not know.

The only answer to these riddles is that we must begin to think of ourselves as part of a continuum of the living; we must also realize that the races we know are ephemeral, probably recent, and change more rapidly than do species. We must also recognize the narcissism inherent in whatever reconstructions we make. Early people may be cast in the image of the people we most admire (usually ourselves) so that we can claim that our admired type is the oldest and the original; they may, just as readily, be cast in the image of the people we least admire, in order that we can say that "we" (whoever we may be) have evolved away from the disadmired type.

What is true, however, is that mankind and the culture by which they live evolved together. The development of one cannot be considered in the absence of the other. Man did not evolve a large brain and then discover culture, as the counterfeiter of the Piltdown "man" hoax would have had us believe. Neither did pre-man first discover culture and then evolve because of the benefits it conferred. Rather, the development of culture and the evolutionary changes in the beast counteraffected one another. Man and culture are indistinguishable historically—the distinction is valid only as a simplifying device for purposes of scientific study.

APES AND HOMINIDS IN MIOCENE AFRICA

The Hominidae form a family of living and fossil forms that resemble modern man more than they do the other primates, monkeys or apes. The distinctions among the three—man, ape, and monkey—are manifold, but scientifically the classification is usually based on their mode of locomotion. Only the hominids are totally two-footed, leaving the arms and hands free.

The study of early man in Africa has developed rapidly in recent decades. Today, the origins of man in Africa are as well established as any conclusion paleontology can reach. The dating for early man is also as secure as any comparable dating anywhere else in the world. While radio-carbon techniques, measuring the passage of time by change in an isotope of carbon, are suitable for more recent dates, the origins of humankind lie too far back for that. Instead, another radiometric technique is available using isotopes of potassium and argon. This makes it possible to date the approximate time at which a particular volcanic formation was laid down. Evidence of this kind can be checked against paleomagnetic evidence.

The earth's magnetic field shifts through time, but rock layer's magnetism will reflect the magnetic fields that were present when it was deposited. The differences between present and past magnetism can show the passage of time. Finally, radiometric and magnetic evidence can be checked by chemistry. Simultaneous volcanic deposits in East Africa show a marked "chemical fingerprint" that differentiates them from other deposits laid down at other times. In this way, reliable dates established by magnetic and radiometric evidence can extend to other places where the combined evidence is not as good. These kinds of evidence in turn correlate with the presence of certain rapidly-evolving mammalian remains, especially those of pigs. It is thus possible to translate the fossil remains of pigs into the passage of time.

When a field changes as rapidly as this one, even terminology sometimes changes. The relevant geological ages here are the Pliocene, between about 5 and 1.9 million years ago, and the Pleistocene, now considered to begin about 1.9 million years ago. The earliest of the hominids so far discovered, however, lie in the early Pliocene. Skeletal material discovered in both Tanzania and in Ethiopia attest to the presence of a relatively small-brained hominid who walked on two feet and lived between about 4 million and 3 million years ago. The Ethiopian version of this species has been called *Australopithecus afarensis* (southern ape from Afar). Other authorities believe that *A. afarensis* is actually a sub-type of a more widely scattered species, *Australopithecus africanus,* but the significant fact is that at least one human-like species had come into existence at this distant time.

Other hominids soon evolved — if we accept "soon" as

a measure of time on the geological scale—either
separately or as modified descendents from *A. africanus.*
Between about 3 million and 2 million years ago, two new
species of australopithecines appeared, *A. boisei* and *A.
robustus,* along with a larger-brained species called
Homo habilis, and the first securely dated, manufactured
stone tools. It is unfortunate that this period of time is
one of the least known in East African prehistory.
Several theories exist as to the relationships between these
early hominids and their tools, but paleontologists provide no consensus about which may be descended from
the other.

Still another uncertainty is which of these species was
responsible for fashioning the first stone tools.
(Whatever tools they may have made from wood or other
perishable materials are, of course, lost.) From what we
know about the present behavior of chimpanzees, it
seems clear that all the species of hominids were capable
of using tools. The question of manufactured tools is
more problematic. Flaking stones to produce an edged
tool is clearly a manufacture. Battering stones or
breaking them to make them smaller is not very different
from the practice of elephants today, who break off a
branch from trees to use against insects. The earliest use
of controlled fire is still more puzzling. It might well have
been used at very early periods, but tropical climates are
unlikely to preserve evidence of such use over periods as
long as a million years.

We know very little about the territorial limits of these
various early hominids. Our fossil and archaeological
evidence comes from a series of sites along the rift valley
that emerges from the base of the Red Sea and runs
southward through Ethiopia, Kenya, Tanzania, and on
into Malawi. In South Africa, the remains of hominids

and their tools are confined to limestone caves. But this fact doesn't mean that early hominids preferred rift valleys or caves. Geology simply doesn't provide good evidence elsewhere. Without the rift valley and the caves, we would have no evidence at all—just as we have no evidence at all from parts of Africa where early hominids may perhaps have lived without leaving a trace.

EARLY MAN

The picture clears somewhat about a million and a half years ago. A new hominid appeared on the scene, *Homo erectus*. The new species had a considerably larger brain than its predecessors. Some authorities consider it to have been the first "real" human, though not yet the same as our present species, *Homo sapiens*. *Homo erectus* not merely joined the existing hominid types; it replaced them, including its presumed immediate ancestor *Homo habilis*. The australopithecines also disappeared, though *A. boisei* lasted till about one million years ago. Finally, about 300,000 years ago, early varieties of *Homo sapiens* appeared, also in Africa. This species in its turn soon replaced *Homo erectus*, not only in Africa but everywhere in the world.

Well before this time, the hominids had begun to move out of Africa. Remains of *Homo erectus,* known as "Peking Man" and "Java Man" have been discovered in both China and Indonesia, dated to about 700,000 years ago. At roughly the same time, *Homo erectus* seems to have moved into Europe as well, where his characteristic tools have been discovered in central France, dated to about 800,000 years ago. Similar discoveries have been made in southern Italy. The earliest skeletal remains in central Europe, however, are those of Heidelberg man, dated to about 500,000 years ago.

This combination of evidence leads to a secure conclusion that *Homo erectus* began its migration from Africa about a million years ago. Recently, however, new evidence has emerged suggesting that the migrations might have taken place even earlier. Stone tools found on the shore of the Sea of Galilee are datable to about 1.3 million years ago. As usual with archaeological finds, this implies a movement out of Africa somewhat earlier, since the likelihood that archaeologists will find the very earliest evidence is only slight. Other finds of tools in Pakistan, indeed, can be dated, a little less securely, to about two million years ago. The mere fact of an earlier date, two million instead of one million years, is hardly important at this distance in time. What counts, however, is the evidence that *Homo erectus* was more able, inventive, and adaptable to different environments than many had previously thought him to be.

The earliest fossil remains we have of *Homo sapiens* are from Swanscombe in England and Steinheim in Germany. However, this population disappeared in Europe during the next glaciation, and after it was replaced with a population of the sort known as Neanderthal man. The Neanderthal population in turn disappeared in Europe after the last glaciation—from thirty-five thousand to fifty thousand years ago—and has been entirely replaced throughout the world by a population of modern type.

STONE AGE CULTURES IN AFRICA

After the first stone tools appeared about 2.5 million years ago, a new style of tool manufacture appeared featuring hand axes, cleavers, and flaked scrapers. These belong to a type conventionally called "Acheulian" after the town of St. Acheul in France, where they were first identified. They are not, however, of European origin. The earliest examples begin to appear in East Africa about a million and a half years ago. From there, their use spread not only to most parts of Africa but to other parts of the Afro-Eurasian land mass from Britain and Spain on the west through Asia as far as India. The area over which these tools were used is unusually wide for a tool assemblage of this kind, and its existence in time is even more remarkable, lasting about a million years, with some instances of continued manufacture as late as 100,000 years ago.

Except for the existence of these characteristic tools, very little is known about the people who made and used them. The length of time they were used, however, means that a great deal of human development and diversification of language and culture certainly took place. The earliest Acheulian tools occur while *Homo habilis* and *A. boisei* were still around, but they are more clearly associated with *Homo erectus*. The time-span for Acheulian is so long that it extends from the later centuries of *Homo habilis* to the earliest period for *Homo sapiens*. At least in southern Africa, a variety called *H. sapiens rhodesiensis* was present late in the Acheulian period, and continued to be the most important human type in the Middle Stone Age that followed in southern Africa.

The latter half of the Acheulian was a time of great migratory movements. As always, as time passes and culture develops, the rate of cultural development speeds up, and the distribution and migration of people increases, and therefore local varieties proliferate. Apparently most of Africa was suitable for human habitation during the second and third glacial periods.

The Acheulian populations were, however, confined to the savanna or bushland; the move into the permanent forest zone was much later. Most of the Acheulian sites in Africa would seem to date from about 150,000 years ago; they extend from Casablanca to the Horn, and from Egypt to the Cape.

Homo erectus and its culture are associated with the hunting of large mammals. Stoneworking has become highly sophisticated. Besides the hand axes there were "cleavers" that were apparently used as adzes to work wood, balls of stone that may have been used as bolas, and apparently some stones that could have been used as spear points, as well as chopping tools. Variation by geographical area appears for the first time in the culture pattern. Although the size of many campsites remains small, some now show a slight increase in area, indicating that the size of the groups is getting somewhat bigger. Acheulian culture is also, of course, to be found in Europe and throughout much of the Middle East.

During Acheulian times, fire became a regular part of mankind's tool kit in Africa. With fire and an improved tool kit, people could penetrate the forest regions. Here the old types of tool, the hand ax and the cleaver, disappeared, and smaller tools are found, believed to have been associated with woodworking. This forest culture is known as Sangoan.

Given the use of fire, people could eject other animals and occupy caves and rock shelters. Because of their acquisition of efficient means of carrying things, they were also able to stay in one place longer. As efficiency in food-getting increased, the size of the band also increased.

Acheulian culture disappeared from North Africa about the time that the desert began to encroach as a result of climatic change, and in Cyrenaica and Morocco there are new cultures that look like general Mediterranean flake cultures. They are known as Levallois-Mousterian, and in places where the physical type associated with them is known, it is Neanderthal or *Homo sapiens Neanderthalensis*. We do not know whether Neanderthal man was intrusive into Africa, or originated in Africa, but it seems more likely that both he and the Mousterian-type culture originated elsewhere and moved into Africa. From this time on the Cultural remains of the northern edges and the southern edges of the Sahara are different. Levallois-Mousterian is approximately contemporary with the Sangoan of the savannas, south of the Sahara. Most authorities believe that *H. sapiens neanderthalensis* became dominant north of the Sahara, while *H. sapiens rhodesiensis* was the most important type in the south. People of a fully modern type, *Homo sapiens sapiens* began to appear in southern Africa about 100,000 years ago, and human skeletons begin to be really numerous beginning about 20,000 years ago. From that time onward, we can begin thinking of people in Africa as the distant ancestors of present-day populations, though the great extent of mixing between originally-diverse populations has made it impossible to follow the movement of populations in any but the most generalized ways.

At the end of the Pleistocene, about 8000 B.C., the climate (which had been cool) began to change. Two Caucasoid immigrations took place, one of the tall, modern type called Cro-Magnon man, the other probably of a Mediterranean racial type, each bringing a specific type of culture into northern Africa, extending up the Nile. The result was such cultural items as tanged projectile points appearing in the Congo Basin in association with Middle Stone Age cultures, and new forms of tools appeared in South Africa and Rhodesia. As recently as about 2500 B.C. the Sahara was still moist enough that both Mediterranean and Negroid populations were moving about in it. In that period, fishing and the use of water resources became increasingly more important.

The Khoisan physical type made its appearance toward the end of the Pleistocene; the other modern types have their earliest fossils associated with the Middle and Late Stone Age.

The Late Stone Age was a period of great adaptive specialization, and a large number of different cultures can, by this time, be found throughout the continent. Savanna cultures are quite different from those of the forest and those of the Rift Valley are different from either.

Neolithic or New Stone Age culture, marked by complexity and reduced size of the stone weapons, spread throughout the Sahara by 3000 B.C., but did not proceed south of the Sahara; it never did replace Middle Stone Age food gathering as a way of life. The security of the hunting-and-gathering way of life was not threatened farther south as it was in the north, with desiccation and other changes, and there was no pressure demanding the changes toward agriculture and stockkeeping. After 2500 B.C., when the Sahara was getting drier and drier, many of the Neolithic populations were forced south, and new food crops had to be developed: rice in Guinea, sorghum in the Sudan, and the indigenous grains called teff and eleusine in parts of Ethiopia. It may have been in this time that the domestication of indigenous African yams occurred.

It was long considered, and has been corrected only in the last half century, that mankind was created in, or first evolved in, Asia, spreading from there to people the rest of the world. Most of the major civilizations of the world were committed to that view either because they themselves were located in Asia or because their myths of origin made that assumption feasible and comfortable. During the millennia before archaeology, and during the centuries in which Africa had disappeared from the purview of Europe, such seemed a sensible belief.

Now, however, it is agreed by all authorities that the earliest human types and the earliest culture both appear in Africa. It would seem that culture-bearing human beings emigrated from Africa and filled up the rest of the world, moving back and forth into and out of Africa until present times.

Chapter Twelve

FARMS AND IRON

THERE HAVE BEEN MANY OCCASIONS IN THE HISTORY of human development when cultural steps were taken from which there was no return: steps which were so intrinsically simple and which so simplified the processes of living that to go without them thereafter would be quite literally unthinkable. Tool manufacture is such a step. Once the idea of a tool is present, men will make tools—particular techniques may be lost, and whole cultures may wither, but tools will be made, and the general direction of development will be toward efficiency. The discovery of use of fire is another such irreversible revolution. The comforts it provides—both for heating and for cooking—are so apparent and the idea so simple that men will put vast ingenuity into acquiring and maintaining a fire. To revert to fireless living would be quite literally unthinkable.

It is just such shatteringly simplifying discoveries as these that make cultural evolution more than merely a faulty analogy to biological evolution (which it nevertheless remains). We are accustomed to thinking of evolution in terms of complication—going from the simple to the complex. In one sense—particularly if we examine the technological development of humankind—such a position is a true one. But there is another sense which allows us to see that the constant complications are possible only

225

concomitantly with vast simplification. It is easier to live with fire than without it. The increasing complexity brought about by cultural evolution is material and usually superficial; underneath the complexity lies a growing simplicity.

Although the use of stone tools and the use of fire are in the distant background of African history, as of all human history, two other simplifying discoveries bring us to the borderland where history and pre-history meet. They are first the discovery of agriculture and animal husbandry, which made vast new amounts of energy available to men, and second the discovery of metallurgy, which made energy more efficiently usable.

THE AGRICULTURAL REVOLUTION

So far as present-day archaeologists are aware, fixed agriculture and urban living developed together in the Middle East about 10,000 B.C. In most parts of the world, societies which depend on hunting and gathering for their subsistence are necessarily limited to a few hundred people and must necessarily range over a wide enough area that fixed villages or other dwellings are impractical. Almost the only exception to this generalization is to be found in fishing communities: quite large villages of fishermen may grow up and be permanent over long periods of time. We shall see that fishing industries probably had as great an effect in Africa as they have had elsewhere on the history of the expansion and spread of culture.

The shift from hunting to agriculture was revolutionary in the long range of human history, but it may not have taken place as rapidly as the word "revolution" implies. Cultivation may have been practiced

Cultivation in Burkina Faso.

before total settlement, as it is by some bands of nomads today—catch crops that need little care. Extensive cultivation, however, demands close attention and ultimately settled existence. It both demands and allows much larger populations, and it is safe to say that the world's first major "population explosion" occurred during these millennia.

Both the idea of horticulture and the crops to be grown spread slowly from this base. Cultivation brought new securities—and new insecurities; the increasing population further increased the rate of speed at which techniques and new cultigens were discovered and adopted.

Nevertheless, by about 5000 B.C. agricultural technology began to remake the society of the Nile valley in Egypt, and that technology clearly came from the Middle East. The crops and animals—wheat and barley, sheep and goats—were the same in the two places. What happened in Egypt is that a strong Asian influence was stamped upon a basically African culture, giving rise to Egyptian civilization. A warning must be issued: "African culture" has nothing to do with the race of the people who practiced it. It has rather to do with forms of social organization, economy, polity, religion, and the like. As we learn more and more about the cultures and civilizations of Africa, we realize that by these criteria Egypt lay culturally as well as geographically between Africa and Asia. Egyptian religion can be best understood by reference to African religion; many other aspects of Egyptian history and polity are illuminated by African ethnography. It has been stylish in the past to assume that all these social and cultural forms were invented in Egypt and spread to other parts of Africa. Today we know that such was an oversimplification: Egypt was basically an

African culture, with intrusions of Asian culture. And the swing of cultural influence could go the other way as well. The ancient Egyptian language belongs to the Afro-Asiatic group, whose earliest origins were in Africa to the southeast of Egypt proper, but some languages of that group also spread into Asia, as the Semitic languages did. But again, this export of one aspect of African culture had nothing to do with the race of the people who practiced it.

In order to see the picture most clearly, it is necessary to go back several millennia. Some twelve thousand years ago the Sahara was habitable, but dry—not so dry as today, but drier than a wet phase that came later. People hunted across the territory that was later to become Egypt.

The Sahara subsequently went through a wet phase, when people encroached upon it from both north and south. In the wet phase of the Sahara, the hunting-and-gathering subsistence economies seemed to include considerable fishing, which, as we have seen, can support comparatively large populations. It would also seem that the situation at this time allowed a very considerable gene flow through large areas and diverse populations.

Then, some six or seven thousand years ago, the desiccation of the Sahara began again, which was eventually to bring it to the state that we know it today. With progressive drought, people withdrew from the desert in both directions. With progressive withdrawal, the gene pools, as well as the "culture pools" (if the analogy be permitted), became smaller.

It seems likely that the peoples who left the Sahara and went north were swallowed up into the greater populations of the Mediterranean. Those who went south encountered a far different fate: to say that the Negro race "developed" at this period would almost surely be a misstatement, yet in the new situation the physical traits that today are considered to be characteristically Negroid were undoubtedly intensified in a relatively small, inbreeding population in the sudanic areas south of the growing Sahara.

Not only genes, but culture as well, spread to both the north and the south of the Sahara. Only by some such theory can the genetic similarity of Europeans to Africans as well as their manifest differences be accounted for.

It is difficult for modern man, that most numerous of beasts, to accustom himself to the idea that a few thousand years ago men were rare animals. The gene pools were undoubtedly small—small enough that a race could be consolidated in comparatively few generations and then, through social practices and limitations, spread throughout a continent, multiplying rapidly.

The story can be summed up this way: As men withdrew from the Sahara to the south, and continued to live in fishing communities, they brought with them the genes of the Sahara population, and consolidated them into a racial "type." They also carried with them the cultural background that underlies both Europe and Africa and is at the basis of what has been called the "Old World Culture Area." The story is given verisimilitude by the fact that Negroes are, relatively, such a scarce people compared with either caucasoids or Mongoloids. It is possible that, under favorable conditions, that number could have been reached in only a few thousand years from an extremely small original population.

The Negroes spread in Africa presumably as fishermen. The agricultural revolution reached them in two waves, both depending on the finding of satisfactory crops for the areas in which they lived. Near Eastern grain crops do not thrive in the sudanic areas of Africa, and they will not grow at all in the forested regions. The first phase of the agricultural revolution in Africa south of the Sahara came with the domestication and spread of millets and sorghums and a species of rice. *Oryza glaberrima,* or African rice, was first domesticated in the western sudan and developed there independently of Asian rice (*O. sativa*). The second phase came with the introduction of root crops and bananas that could thrive in the forest. Some of the crops that are basic to African agriculture today were either developed from indigenous roots or came from Southeast Asia, long after agriculture had been established in the sudan. Others came still later—indeed since the fifteenth century A.D.—from the Americas, including maize, manioc, and peanuts. The result was to give African farmers the ability to support increasingly dense populations over a very long period of time. In this sense the agricultural "revolution" was not a rapid process. The first advances south of the Sahara were almost certainly made before 3000 B.C., but the latest, depending on the inland diffusion of American crops, introduced here and there on the coast during the sixteenth century, reached more isolated areas only in the eighteenth or even the nineteenth century.

Many unanswered questions remain, and pre-historians of Africa are undecided how the agricultural revolution actually reached the Negro population of Africa. Most agree, however, that one early center was in the western sudan, while another was the Ethiopian highlands. Ethiopia and the "horn" of Africa have always been a little separate from the rest of sub-Saharan Africa. They have close cultural and botanical ties to the neighboring highlands of southern Arabia. Some crops that originated in Ethiopia diffused very slowly to other parts of Africa. Coffee—the name comes from the Ethiopian province of

Kaffa—spread to many parts of Asia before it reached some parts of Africa that now depend on it as an export crop. Other African crops also diffused outward to the rest of the world. Sesame, which originated in the western sudan, had reached the Middle East before 2000 B.C.

The question of crop diffusion is further complicated by a process anthropologists call "stimulus diffusion." That is, the *idea* of planting crops may have entered sub-Saharan Africa from the outside, while the development of crops appropriate to a particular region had to wait for the domestication of species that could thrive there. The picture that begins to emerge is therefore one of many crosscurrents, not a simple introduction of agriculture as a ready-made system of food production.

Yet, at a slightly more abstract level, a general picture can be drawn. We know that the idea of metalworking went from Southwest Asia into Africa, both north and south of the Sahara. The idea of agriculture may well have followed a similar course, even though the use of individual crops followed a more complex pattern. The millets, for example, appear to have been domesticated in the western sudan, and afterward to have diffused eastward to the Nile Valley and on into Asia, while the idea of agriculture may well have moved in the opposite direction. Further botanical and archaeological research will undoubtedly provide a more complete answer.

Meanwhile, within the whole picture, the point has little importance. What is obvious is that fishing and hunting communities of prehistoric sub-Saharan Africa could grow very rapidly when they got agriculture. They could grow still more rapidly as they found or imported crops better suited to their environment. And that undoubtedly did occur. People of predominantly Negro type first filled the savannas of the sudanic belt just south of the Sahara.

Some undoubtedly moved into the forests as fishermen and hunters, even before the coming of agriculture. As the range of crops increased and techniques improved, they moved in still greater numbers into and across the forest until they ultimately came to occupy most of Africa.

THE COMING OF THE IRON AGE

The spread of peoples of sudanic origin into and beyond the forest is not only associated with early agriculture. Archaeological evidence indicates that iron smelting and the manufacture of tools moved south with much the same timing as agriculture itself. But the two did not necessarily move together, and the beginning of the Iron Age was, in most places, a slow process, passing through several stages of improving techniques.

The use of iron was probably discovered in several parts of the world, since meteors contain usable iron that can be fashioned into tools or decorations. Iron smelting from the terrestrial iron ore, on the other hand, requires special furnaces. Iron smelting may have been invented only once, in Anatolia, where a few iron objects have turned up that seem to date from about 2000 B.C. By that time, the Middle East was already about a thousand years into the Bronze Age. Bronze was satisfactory for many purposes, and at first iron remained rare and expensive. It was only about the eleventh century B.C. that iron became common enough to replace bronze tools in ordinary use. This improvement in techniques for manufacturing iron marks the real beginning of the Iron Age.

The secret to producing relatively malleable, low-carbon wrought iron—or steel which is both malleable and will hold an edge—was to heat charcoal and iron ore together in the confined space of a furnace, but at

Smiths in Burkina Faso making a hoe blade.

temperature well below the melting point of iron. Combustion with oxygen gave off carbon monoxide, which then picked up a second molecule from the ferrous oxide of the iron ore to leave comparatively impure but perfectly usable iron, as the carbon monoxide became carbon dioxide. The process was time-consuming and produced only a little iron with each smelt, but the product was much superior to the brittle high-carbon pig iron the Chinese and Europeans finally learned to produce in large quantities with blast furnaces—but that did not take place until well into the Christian era.

Iron technology diffused as rapidly into sub-Saharan Africa as it did into Europe. It reached Italy about 750 B.C. and central Europe about 650 B.C. By 800 B.C. it had already reached southern Arabia and Carthage in North Africa. From there it diffused into sub-Saharan Africa— across the Red Sea to Ethiopia, across the Sahara to West Africa, and perhaps by other routes as well. By 600 to 700 B.C. it had already reached present-day Nigeria and Rwanda and Burundi in Central Africa. Spread from these centers into other parts of Africa was so complex it is hard to trace with precision. Archaeologists find, however, that iron working did not diffuse alone. Its remains are found with an assortment of tools and other evidence. They often divide evidence into two groups, an Early Iron Age Industrial Complex and a second for the Later Iron Age, which was considerably more sophisticated technologically.

As in other parts of the world, metallurgy improved by borrowing inventions made elsewhere and by local inventions that spread abroad—just as agriculture changed and improved with new techniques and new crops. But the coming of farms and iron to Africa followed a different pattern from that of the Mediterranean world, where farming was practiced for several millennia before the Bronze Age, and bronze was known for centuries before iron. For all practical purposes, Africa skipped the Bronze Age altogether, and the time lag between the first farming and the first iron work was much shorter everywhere south of the Sahara. To the south of the equatorial forest, they may have come nearly at the same time.

THE EXPANSION OF BANTU-SPEAKING PEOPLES

Who carried iron and agriculture from the fringes of the Sahara to most of Africa? It now seems clear that some of the carriers were Negro peoples who came originally from northeastern Nigeria. They spoke a language related to the present-day Bantu languages in much the same way Latin is related to the present Romance languages like French or Italian. Bantu languages are now spoken throughout Africa south of a line that can be drawn from the base of the West African bulge across to Kenya. They are so closely related, they must have been a single language only a very few thousand years ago. Furthermore, the Bantu language family belongs to a larger group of language families, all of them found today in northern or eastern Nigeria. This suggests that people who spoke the original Bantu language must have left northeastern Nigeria and spread quite rapidly through most of central and southern Africa.

Almost all linguists and historians accept this hypothesis as the best explanation for the spread of Bantu languages. But there agreement ends. Some authorities go further, linking the languages, the people who spoke them, ironworking, and agriculture to a single movement. Fol-

lowing this hypothesis, the original speakers of proto-
Bantu expanded into central and southern Africa because
they had iron weapons to conquer the aboriginal hunters
and fishermen they found there, and because they had
agriculture to support a growing population on the new
land.

Unfortunately, present evidence will not support such
an elaborate hypothesis. A language, or farming, or iron
metallurgy are all culture traits. They can be learned and
passed from one people to another, and each can be
passed on independently of the others. We know that
Bantu languages were passed to new people; the Pygmies of the Congo forest and the Tutsi of Rwanda and
Burundi are a different physical type from the people of
the Bantu homeland, yet today they speak Bantu languages. This kind of transmission to others was even
more likely to happen with useful techniques like ironworking and agriculture. What we actually know, then, is
that Negroid people moved into Africa south of the forest
zone over a period of one to two millennia. At nearly the
same time, a new language, metallurgy, and agriculture
moved into the same region.

We can also assume from our meager evidence (and
what we know of human history elsewhere) that these
movements must have been related in a very complex
combination of currents and countercurrents. We know,
for example, that some techniques for working iron diffused inland from the East African coast, but the original
knowledge of how to work iron may well have come by
some other route. We also know that certain styles or
inventions could spread widely from their place of origin.
Some of these can be traced; peculiar forms of flanged
iron bells (and the techniques for making them) diffused

from the Niger Valley in Nigeria to central Africa on two separate occasions long after the dispersal of the Bantu-speaking peoples and their languages.

Some of the crops that were important in Bantu-speaking Africa were probably domesticated on the forest fringes in West Africa. Others, with somewhat greater certainty, originated in Southeast Asia. They were probably brought across the Indian Ocean in the early centuries of Indian Ocean maritime trade—just as people from Indonesia came to settle on the island of Madagascar, where their descendants still speak a language related to Indonesian. But there is no evidence that people from Southeast Asia actually settled on the African mainland. It is possible that the Asian crops diffused across Africa north of the forest and were then picked up by the Bantu-speaking peoples and carried southward. It is equally possible that the Bantu-speakers simply began using these crops in their new homes, having found them in use by others when they arrived.

Whatever the diffusion pattern of the Southeast Asian crops, the use of cattle came into sub-Saharan Africa in still another way. Cattle and cattle keeping (but not the custom of milking them) apparently came from the Middle East at a very early time. In West Africa, they appear along with the early development of agriculture. Because of tsetse fly in the equatorial forest, they could hardly have been brought directly from West Africa to the southern savanna. They apparently diffused southward down the ridge of highlands in east-central Africa and from there into the southern savanna. The names for cattle in various eastern and central African languages suggest that they were already in use before the introduction of Bantu languages, but the practice of milking came after the Bantu languages were already spoken to the south and west of present-day Tanzania.

Cattle were a very important supplement for the diet of a farming population, but they could be even more important in regions too arid for agriculture. Cattle can live where crops cannot grow, as long as they have a source of drinking water and plenty of land. After the best land was already occupied, specialized communities that wandered with their cattle in search of grazing land began to develop on the fringes of the agricultural world. Little is known of their earliest history in Africa, but they were present long before the Christian era in steppe and desert country that stretched from the horn of Africa, around the Ethiopian highlands, and westward to the Atlantic.

Then, about the time of Christ, camels were introduced from Asia. They spread very rapidly along the southern fringes of the Sahara, introducing still another fundamental change in the pattern of African history. From the sub-Saharan fringe of the desert, they diffused northward to North Africa, where they soon became the dominant form of overland transportation. Camels do not do well in humid climates, but, in arid and semi-arid climates, they are the most efficient form of overland transportation humans have discovered. They can carry far more than mules or pack oxen, more rapidly, and over longer distances without water. The labor cost for their human attendants is lower than it is for any other pack animals. They also fit into an ecological niche that was barely occupied, being able to find food in regions with rainfall as low as 5 inches a year. The Romans had developed a complex system of paved roads in North Africa, as elsewhere in their empire. With the introduction of the camel, the high capital cost of road construction was no longer necessary. The pack animals could follow unpaved tracks just as well.

After about 500 A.D., when camels became familiar in North Africa, their use intersected with another import from southwest Asia. The date palm had been domesticated in Mesopotamia several millennia earlier, and it had gradually spread along the desert fringes toward the west. Dates need a peculiar environment, with little rainfall, but with irrigation water available to their roots. In proper conditions, they could produce more food per acre than almost any other crop, but dates are too rich in sugar to be a staple food crop for human populations. Their value was greatest when they could be traded to others in return for grains, meat, and milk products. For camels, the dry pasture near date-growing oases was ideal. This means that transport could be made available to carry away the dates in exchange for other products.

From this beginning, the combination of oasis and desert suited to dates and camels made possible the creation of long-distance trade networks that could reach southward across the Sahara. After about 800 A.D., the Sahara was no longer a barrier to sub-Saharan contact with the outer world; camels provided cheap transport between the two shores, just as the seaways provided cheaper transport than inland caravans in most other societies.

Because they could live longer away from sources of drinking water than cattle could, camels increased the range of pastoral nomadism and increased the numbers of nomads that could support themselves beyond the frontiers of agriculture. In the process, they shifted the balance in an ancient conflict between people who lived a settled village life and those who were locked into a pattern of continuous or periodic movement in search of fresh grazing land.

It should be clear by now that "traditional" Africa was far from static. In the longer run of history, no society can fail to change over time, but some kinds of societies change more rapidly than others. We know of two decisive breaks in the rate of change in human history. One was the coming of agriculture with its increased population density. Human contacts became more frequent and new technologies could diffuse more rapidly from one part of the world to another. The second acceleration in the rate of historical change came with the industrial age, which began for Western civilization at the end of the eighteenth and the beginning of the nineteenth century. Africa is only now beginning to enter that phase.

For Africa, the first acceleration, the "agricultural revolution," had begun in some regions as early as 3000 B.C. and was complete for virtually the entire continent by A.D. 1000. As this happened, Africa not only began to change more rapidly than ever; it also moved into ever closer contact with the main phases of history in the Afro-Eurasian land mass as a whole.

Chapter Thirteen

AFRICA IN WORLD HISTORY

THE POSITION OF SUB-SAHARAN AFRICA COMPARED TO other world civilizations is one of the most sensitive historical problems of the present day. The fact that Africans were brought to the New World as slaves and the fact that African societies were conquered by the Europeans and dominated by them for half a century seemed at one time to imply some degree of African inferiority to Western culture. In an era when racism and ethnocentric history were accepted (consciously or unconsciously), African cultural and intellectual inferiority were unquestioned assumptions. These attitudes were spelled out in elaborate theoretical works, and they permeated the whole fabric of historical and anthropological "knowledge." As modern Africa emerged from the colonial era, and Afro-Americans demanded an equal share in their own society, historians of all races and nationalities began to readjust their view of Africa and its place in world history.

The racism and cultural arrogance of the old view are now discredited in respectable intellectual circles, even though some of the interpretations that grew out of them are still in the textbooks. Some stubborn facts also remain: in recent history, Africa *did* appear to lag behind European civilization; Africans *were* brought to the New World as slaves; and Africa *was* conquered by the Europeans at the end of the last century. Given the extensive

racism that still exists in the popular culture of Europe
and America, these facts are still sometimes used to support the old and discredited view of Africa. At the same
time, African and Afro-American historians have been
tempted to overreact with exaggerated claims that great
civilizations existed in the African past. The problem is to
assess the true nature and meaning of any "lag" in African
development and any such assessment is doubly difficult
because it carries strong political and emotional implications that stretch out in every direction.

CULTURE AND VALUE JUDGMENTS

One basic problem is that of making rational judgments about the comparative quality of different human
cultures. Scholars once talked in terms of "high" cultures
and "low" cultures, but these judgments were based on
Western values. Many aspects of culture cannot be judged
rationally outside the context of a particular culture or
style. Western music critics may agree in believing that
one eighteenth-century string quartet sounds better than
another one does, but the judgment is made within the
framework of a particular style and by men who share
present-day musical culture. (And even within this framework, the only "proof" of the superiority of one composition over the other is the consensus of trained judges.)
Once the framework of common style and common culture is left behind, judgment is still more difficult. A
particular piece of African music may sound "better" or
"worse" than a particular Western composition, but there
is no way of convincing someone else of the "fact" by
rational argument. Even though a symphony orchestra
may have more players and a more complex score than

an African ensemble has, this is merely a matter of technology without any necessary bearing on the sound produced. Similar considerations apply to the whole range of possible aesthetic judgments.

In other matters, such as ethics and morality, many cultures share certain ideas about right and wrong. Needless killing of human beings is generally considered to be wrong, but the key word is "needless." A few African societies used to practice human sacrifice, because they believed it was necessary to the well-being of society as a whole. In the West, criminals are executed for the same reason. Even if the ethical standard is universal, the interpretation is often culture-bound.

A few aspects of culture, however, may be subject to rational judgment. Technology is one of these. A technique is a *means* of doing something, and its value can be measured by its effectiveness in serving the desired end. An iron ax is demonstrably better than a stone ax—though some cultures may still prefer stone axes for ethical or aesthetic reasons. A phonetic alphabet is demonstrably more efficient than a system of ideographs, but aesthetic considerations make Chinese ideographs endure. In technology, then—and perhaps in that field alone—it is possible to make estimates of the degree of advancement of particular cultures at particular times, keeping in mind that such judgments apply only to technology and not to the whole culture.

COMPARATIVE TECHNOLOGICAL PROGRESS

Taking only technology into account, it is clear that Africa of the nineteenth century—the period of its major confrontation with the West—was the weaker of the two societies. In the longer run of history, however, it is equally clear that northwestern Europe has not always been ahead. In the first millennium before Christ, the western Sudan and northwestern Europe were nearly on a par. Both had taken over iron and agriculture from the Middle East; neither had yet moved on to evolve an urban civilization. The differences that stood out in the nineteenth and twentieth centuries were therefore the product of historical change over the past twenty-five hundred years or so. During those centuries, Europe developed the most efficient technology in the world, while Africa changed more slowly. It was a dual process requiring a dual explanation—partly in African history and partly in European. In fact, the explanation has to be sought in a broader view of world history, since the rise of barbarian Europe to world dominance was a process that involved the whole of the Afro-Eurasian land mass.

From this perspective, it is clear that neither Europeans nor Africans invented civilization. The combination of metallurgy, writing, agriculture, and cities first developed in only a few places, thousands of miles apart—lower Egypt and the eastern Mediterranean, the Indus Valley, Mesopotamia, and the north Chinese river valleys. In each case the technological base was similar, but early development led them down divergent paths. By about 1000 B.C., all of these small foci of technological progress were in indirect communication with one another; an invention or discovery in any one of them could be borrowed sooner or later by the others. As communication improved, the range of mutual borrowing and the rate of technological progress increased.

In the millennium before Christ, each of these foci of civilization began to expand. The east Mediterranean center spread westward, taking in the whole of the Mediterranean basin and parts of Europe north of the Alps. By the time of Christ, the Roman Empire had organized the culture area politically. Indian Ocean trade and land routes across central Asia to China gave a new intensity to its contacts with the other centers. These culture areas had also expanded, each in its own neighborhood. By this period, the Afro-Eurasian land mass was divided into two distinct technological zones. One was the region of intercommunication and relatively developed technology. The second was more isolated, a zone of fringe communication with the major centers, where development was often held up by difficult environments.

Both sub-Saharan Africa and northwestern Europe were part of this underdeveloped world of the pre-Christian era, but the Alps created a small barrier compared to the Sahara. As Roman civilization spread through Roman conquest, part of northwestern Europe joined the intercommunicating zone, at least for a few centuries. The fall of the Western Roman Empire in the fifth century ended northwestern Europe's full membership in the "civilized world"; but Byzantium and the Islamic world south of the Mediterranean remained in the core zone, and northwest Europe was close enough to be able to pull itself back over the horizon of literacy, city life, and direct communication with the outside world. Between the tenth century and the thirteenth, Europe rebuilt its civilization through the mediation of Byzantium and Islamic civilization and reentered the intercommunicating zone. Overland trade linked the Baltic and North seas to the Mediterranean, and seaborne traders ventured regularly into the Atlantic. The sudan, on the other hand, remained cut off behind the barrier of the Sahara.

Or, so it was until about 800 A.D. Earlier, people and

ideas and techniques had made their way across, but only with difficulty. If any regular Roman trade with sub-Saharan lands had existed, it left no record, though iron work and agriculture were already spreading onward toward the southern tip of the continent. A series of states came into existence along the frontier between savanna and desert. Some of these predated the Iron Age itself. The kingdom of Kush had been in existence since the end of the second millennium B.C. Others came much later. In about the first century A.D., settlers from Arabia founded the kingdom of Axum in the Ethiopian highlands, which later conquered part of southern Arabia as well. In about A.D. 350, Axum invaded the Nilotic Sudan to the west and destroyed the city of Meroë. With that, the kingdom of Kush disappeared from history, but sedentary civilization continued on the upper Nile. Kush was succeeded by a group of Nubian states, con-temporaries of the Roman Empire. Before the year A.D. 600, both the Nubian states and Axum responded to their contacts with Rome; both were converted to the Mono-physite variety of Christianity by missionaries from Roman Egypt.

Meanwhile, and further west, other new states emerged in response to the new camel traffic. Takrūr or Futa Toro came into existence along the middle valley of the Senegal River. Between the Senegal and the Niger bend, the Soninke state of Ghana was also founded before A.D. 600. Still another center of state formation was found in the basin of Lake Chad in the central Sudan, and we can assume that still other states probably existed, even though we lack direct evidence.

Unlike Axum and Kush, where contact with the north was easier by way of the Nile or the Red Sea, state for-mation in the central and western sudan owed comparatively little to its fragile communication with the Roman world. In the western sudan political organization had long taken the form of more or less self-sufficient villages, politically independent of one another. In many parts of West Africa, this pattern lasted until the end of the nineteenth century. In the absence of dangerous enemies or extensive trade, these small units were probably considered preferable to the economic drain of tribute payments to a distant capital. But the growth of trade, the need to protect the trade routes and organize markets made a larger political unit necessary. The earliest states all appeared on the desert-savanna frontier, where differences in ecology favored exchange—salt from the desert and animals from the steppe against millet from the savanna. It is possible, in fact, that local trade of this kind had led to state formation long before extensive trade across the Sahara made the existence of those states known to the Mediterranean world.

NOMADS AND SEDENTARIES

Still another reason why people living on the savanna side of the desert-savanna fringe needed a large political unit was the danger of their location. In the steppe to the north, too dry for farming, were the nomadic pastoralists —Berber, Tuareg, and others. The very fact that they had to move in search of pasture gave them a military advantage. They could concentrate their forces for raids against their richer sedentary neighbors. If the sedentary peoples failed to organize large populations and large territories for mutual defense, they might become tribute-paying dependents of the nomads. The result, for later times in the full light of historical knowledge, was the seesaw of nomadic-sedentary conflict. Well-organized sedentary states not only could protect their desert frontier; they were also able to reach out and control the desert trade routes themselves. Less well-organized peoples living on the fringes and in the oases of the Sahara became tributaries.

This ancient opposition between nomadic and sedentary peoples was not peculiar to the Sahara and its fringes. It was a regular and constant part of human experience in similar environments over very long periods of time—from the emergence of pastoral nomads to the Industrial Revolution. The recurrence of similar patterns of events is sometimes called a "style of history." A "style" of this kind falls short of the necessity required of a scientific "law," but it is a useful concept. Even though all the variables cannot be taken into account, the degree of observed regularity is great enough to permit generalization; and generalization about "styles" of history is a convenient analytical device for understanding how human societies change through time.

This particular style of nomadic-sedentary relations was common to much of the Afro-Eurasian land mass. The Sahara is simply the western end of a wide belt of arid and semi-arid lands stretching eastward from the Atlantic coast in Mauritania, across Africa, across the Red Sea to Arabia, on beyond the Persian Gulf into central Asia, finally across the Gobi Desert and along the northwest frontier of China to reach the Pacific at the Sea of Okhotsk. From the beginning of recorded history, a pattern of nomadic raids into sedentary territory is apparent from the Great Wall frontier of China to the steppe frontier of eastern Europe, from the northeast frontier of India to the northern and southern frontiers of the Sahara.

Historical recognition of the nomadic-sedentary conflict

is almost as ancient as the conflict itself. In the book of Genesis, it was the mythic origin of violence and murder within the human family. "Abel was a keeper of sheep, and Cain a tiller of the ground." The Lord preferred Abel's offering to that of Cain, and his ecological preference led to murder. Much later, in fourteenth-century Tunisia, Ibn Khaldun, one of the founders of analytical history, used the nomad-sedentary conflict as the theme of his greatest work, the *Muqaddimah,* which analyzed the rise and fall of Islamic dynasties. Still more recently, Owen Lattimore's investigations of ecological tensions along the northwest frontier of China have added still more to our knowledge of historical patterns along the frontier between the desert and the sown.

In Lattimore's terms, the struggle between nomads and sedentary farmers was a struggle for land that was marginal to either form of occupation. Nomads were not content with land that could be used *only* for grazing. In Lattimore's aphorism, "The pure nomad is a poor nomad." The nomadic ecology could be far more productive if it could be linked to better land, which sedentary farmers could have used equally—or if it could be linked to the agricultural wealth of desert oases easily dominated by nomadic military power. Nomads therefore could be expected to use their advantage in mobility in order to seize control of the oases and the marginal lands.

These same marginal lands and oases were equally important to the sedentary society. Its strength, countering the mobility of the nomads, was its wealth based on the higher yields of sedentary agriculture and greater density of population. But this wealth also had to be organized for frontier defense. Farmers were tied down to their fields, immovable capital, and stores of grain. If these were to be defended, the nomads had to be stopped before they could concentrate for a raid. This in turn required elaborate preparations, which could go as far as building a permanent military line like the Great Wall of China. At the very least, the marginal lands had to be brought under control. The desert oases were also important as strongholds for sedentary control over the steppe. The key was political organization. When a sedentary state was strong and united, it could mobilize its wealth for frontier defense. If organization broke down, it was open to nomadic attack. The oases and marginal lands often went first; larger raids could then penetrate into the heart of sedentary territory.

The nature and outcome of these raids depended on nomadic leadership and intentions. When they were led by men who were fully integrated into the nomadic culture, the raids were destructive and little more. Their aim was simply to seize the accumulated wealth of the sedentary society or to exact tribute, and they rarely led to a permanent military occupation that might tap the sedentary sources of wealth on a long-term basis. From time to time, however, nomadic leaders were able to seize control of the sedentary state and set themselves up as a new dynasty. To do this required a special kind of leadership that was culturally marginal—men who knew enough of nomadic life to gain a nomadic following, yet who also understood the structure and norms of the sedentary state. They could then try to seize control of the state, not destroy it. As leaders of this kind assimilated the sedentary way of life, they might carry some of their original following with them as subordinate officials. Those who failed to make the adjustment drifted back into the desert. The new dynasty would then find itself in the same position as its predecessors, confronted by a nomad threat. If it could profit by its newness to make a clean sweep of administrative inefficiency, it would again seize the marginal lands and drive the nomads back into the least favorable environment to await a new weakening of the frontier, a chance to seize the marginal lands, and the opportunity to begin the process all over again under new leadership.

Needless to say, a simplistic model of this kind is not intended to be interpreted as an accurate description of specific events, much less a "law of history." But it can serve as a useful description of a style of history over a very long span of centuries—until the Industrial Revolution finally gave sedentary powers the ability to dominate the desert once and for all.

THE RISE OF ISLAM

The rise of Islam in nearby Arabia was immensely important for the future of Africa, and the new religious message was spread in circumstances that took on the historical style of nomadic-sedentary conflict. By A.D. 600, the Western Roman Empire had fallen to barbarian infiltration and invasion. The Eastern or Byzantine portion was still strong in the Balkan peninsula and Anatolia, and it still controlled Egypt and Syria. At this period it was also changing internally, becoming less universal and Roman in character and more narrowly Greek. These changes affected the loyalty of the Egyptian and Syrian provinces, which followed the Monophysite version of Christianity in opposition to the established Orthodox Church of Constantinople. Byzantine rule came to look more and more like a form of foreign domination combined with religious persecution. Byzantium's neighbor to the east was the Sassanian Empire in Persia and Mesopotamia. It too was

weakened by religious controversy, and both empires had
been weakened by a long series of Byzantine-Sassanian
wars.

In the Arabian Desert to the south of these sedentary
empires lived bedouin nomads, divided among themselves
and worshiping many different local gods, although both
Jewish and Christian influences were also present. Along
the Red Sea coast, however, a number of trading towns
like Mecca and Medina were in closer touch with the
currents of sedentary civilization to the north. Here then
was a setting in which culturally marginal men from the
trading towns had enough contact with the nomads to
establish their leadership, and also understood sedentary
civilization well enough to lead a dynasty-founding invasion of the decrepit empires that controlled the Fertile
Crescent from Egypt to Mesopotamia. Nomadic unity
came from the ideological base of a new religion. Muhammad, a young merchant from Mecca, began to preach the
new message early in the seventh century, drawing on
Christian and Jewish roots but also incorporating some
of the cultural traditions of Arabia itself. By the time of
Muhammad's death in A.D. 632, his followers controlled
the key cities of Mecca and Medina and much of Arabia.
By 635, they had united the desert nomads into a mobile
force capable of moving north. By 651, they had conquered the whole of the Sassanian Empire and the Byzantine provinces of Syria and Egypt.

Thus, in hardly more than a decade and a half, culturally marginal leaders from the Arabian cities had set themselves up as a new dynasty controlling parts of the former
Roman and Sassanian empires. They moved the capital
to Damascus and soon lost control of most of Arabia.
They took the Arabic language with them, but the Islamic
civilization that emerged owed far more to Persian and

Roman traditions than it did to Arabian. The new dynasty took over Byzantine administrative forms along with some of the Byzantine administrators. The real base for its later conquests eastward into central Asia and westward to Spain was the Fertile Crescent, not Arabia.

Conquest was followed by conversion, but it was more than mere conversion to a new religion. The political unity of the caliphate lasted only a short time, but the religious unity of the Islamic world made for a new region of intercommunication. Islamic civilization became heir to the cultural and technological heritage of the zone stretching from the Atlantic to the frontiers of India and China. With Arabic as the universal language of religion, the Islamic world was in a position to act as mediator and transmitting agent, even between culture areas that had not been conquered or converted to Islam. Greek philosophy, for example, was taught to northwestern Europe through Muslim transmitters, and the "Arabic" system of numbers was diffused from India to Muslim Spain and then to the rest of Europe.

ISLAM IN AFRICA

From the eighth century to the eighteenth, Islamic civilization was to be Africa's chief contact with the intercommunicating zone. Nevertheless, Islam was slow to move into sub-Saharan Africa, as though the very success of the Muslim drive to the north had removed the temptation to move in other directions. The Christian kingdoms of the upper Nile and the Ethiopian highlands were left alone for several centuries. As a result, they found themselves more isolated than they had been in Roman times —cut off from easy contact with their co-religionists in

Egypt by the fact of Muslim rule there.

Much the same was true of the Indian Ocean network of maritime trade. Roman ships had traded as far south as present-day Tanzania, and Sassanian Persia had later dominated the western basin of the Indian Ocean, keeping up communication between the African coast and the civilizations to the north. But the rise of Islam and the Muslim conquest of Persia drew Persia into a new orbit of trade and communication within the Islamic world itself.

In place of the Sassanian Empire, the new Abbasid Caliphate moved its capital from Damascus to Baghdad. From about 750 to 1000, the Abbasid Caliphate dominated trade to the east, not only in the Arabian Sea. For a time, Abbasid ships sailed on past the Bay of Bengal and the South China Sea to Canton itself. They also took up the old Roman routes southward down the African coast.

Contact between the sudanic states of West Africa and the Islamic states of the north was also intensified, though more through the possession of camels than on account of military superiority. The Muslim conquest drove rapidly across North Africa and into Spain, but the nomadic peoples of the Sahara were hardly touched by that conquest. Nomads, from the Beja of the Red Sea coast to the Berbers of the western Sahara, looked on the sedentary civilization as nomads have usually done — that is, as fair game. The "Arabs" who now ruled North Africa found themselves in charge of a sedentary civilization with a frontier to defend. Aside from defensive operations, they left the desert people alone. Most of them became Muslim by voluntary conversion, but rarely before the tenth century and often much later.

Thus, the rise of Islam created a new zone of very intense intercommunication, stretching from Spain to

Persia and beyond. The camel caravans brought the sub-Saharan shore of the desert into the Muslim economic sphere—at least into its fringes. Islamic conquest moved in other directions. Thus, black Africa was in much the same position as northwestern Europe during the Dark Ages—on the fringes, having some commercial contact with the Islamic world, but, through religious difference as well as physical barriers, beyond the frontier of "civilization." But Europe's return to the inner zone was comparatively easy. Northwestern Europe still retained some of the culture and technology of the Roman Empire, and Islamic civilization was also an heir of Rome. Christendom and Islam also faced one another across military frontiers in northern Spain, Italy, and the Mediterranean islands. For sub-Saharan Africa, the barrier of the desert remained in one sense; sedentary states to the north and south still had trouble controlling the nomads between them. But gradually that barrier began to crumble. From the eleventh century onward, Islam began to penetrate south of the desert, bringing knowledge of the alphabet, literacy for some, and at least a distant and tenuous contact with the dominant civilization of the time.

Like earlier influences from the outside, Islam came to sub-Saharan Africa through several different channels. In the far west, the Sanhaja Berbers of the Sahara were converted to Islam shortly before A.D. 1000. Commercial contacts and missionary work then carried the religion to the Senegal Valley, just south of the desert. In about 1030, the rulers of Takrūr became the first sub-Saharan dynasty to embrace Islam. Other states in the western sudan, however, resisted religious change. Ghana, which reached its greatest power in the ninth and tenth centuries, appears to have kept its traditional religion in spite of its commercial contact with the north.

A second route of Islamic penetration was southward from Libya through Fezzan to Lake Chad. Roman penetration of the desert had followed this direction, and the Fezzani had long dominated the Sahara trade. Their conversion to Islam in the ninth century was a step toward the conversion of Kanem, the most important black state in the Lake Chad basin. The first Kanembu ruler to accept Islam came to power in 1085, though religious conversion of the general population undoubtedly took place only gradually in the centuries that followed.

Conversion came less peacefully to the Nile Valley. In the early centuries after the rise of Islam, commercial contacts across the Red Sea and movement of people from Arabia to Africa brought some degree of Islamic influence, but the Christian Nubian kingdoms still held out—along the desert reaches of the river where the Nile provides irrigation water, as well as in the savanna country farther south. In the 1280s and 1290s, however, attacks from Muslim Egypt destroyed Christian Nubia along the Nile. Even though the savanna kingdom of 'Alwa lived on, there was no longer a sedentary state capable of controlling the desert. Partly as a result, Arabs began to move into Africa in greater numbers than ever before. During the fourteenth and fifteenth centuries this migration became so large that the Nilotic sudan was permanently Arabized in language and many aspects of culture, though the Arab immigrants also mixed with Africans to create a present-day population that is only partly of Arab descent. This Arab penetration of the sudan resembles other nomadic attacks on a sedentary state, but in this case the marginal leadership was missing. Rather than seizing or re-creating a new state, these Arab invasions destroyed Christian Nubia without putting anything in its place. About 1500 a Muslim sedentary state, the Funj sultanate, did emerge in the savanna country of the upper Nile, but it was founded by black Africans, not by Arab nomads.

In Ethiopia and the horn of Africa, Islam also entered into competition with existing Christian states. Commercial and cultural contact between Ethiopia and Yemen had always been close, and Islam spread first to the port towns on the African side of the Gulf of Aden. By A.D. 1000, peaceful conversion was already well advanced in the eastern highlands of Ethiopia, while Christianity was spreading in the meanwhile in the western highlands. By about 1300, the Muslim sultanate of Ifat emerged as a military competitor of Christian Abyssinia for the control of Ethiopia, but this time the Christian state won. By 1415, most of the Muslims had been driven out or forcibly converted to Christianity.

Outside influence came to East Africa by sea, and not merely from the Muslim world. Traders came from India, Indonesia, and even China, but commercial ties with Persia and Arabia became dominant from the thirteenth century onward, and the port towns of East Africa began to enter the intercommunicating zone. Mogadishu in present-day Somalia was the principal center for the northern coast. Farther south, Kilwa came to dominate the trade that flowed from the Rhodesian gold fields to the coast at Sofala. Here and elsewhere along the coast, stone-built towns whose remains can be seen today are evidence of African membership in the greater world of Islam. But Islam was engrafted to an African cultural base. Arabic was used for writing and religion, but a Bantu language ancestral to modern Swahili was the language of ordinary speech.

By 1450 or so, on the eve of maritime contact with the Europeans, Islam had penetrated at many points on the fringes of sub-Saharan Africa, but Africa as a whole was still isolated from the main currents of change. In spite of eight centuries in the shadow of Islamic civilization, constraints to communication with the outside world remained impressive. In the Nilotic sudan, for example, Islam came through Arab infiltration and invasion—really another case of nomadic attack on a fragile sedentary state. The region became Muslim, but its communications with the Mediterranean world were no more regular or effective than they had been during Roman times.

The obvious prosperity of the East African port towns is also deceptive. They were African towns, but they looked toward the Indian Ocean. The trade with the interior appears to have been carried by people from the interior, and the immediate hinterland was sparsely populated. Wide belts were infested with tsetse fly, or were semi-arid. It was not, perhaps, such a formidable barrier as the Sahara, but it was barrier enough. One sign of isolation is the geographical knowledge available in the Muslim world. The Arab geographers were avid for any scrap of information they could come by. From the eleventh century to the fourteenth, they were able to give a fair account of the geography and culture of the western sudan, but they knew almost nothing about the interior of East Africa.

Any assessment of African and world development over the period from about A.D. 600 to about 1500 must be one of sharp contrasts. The sweep of Islamic civilization, stretching by the end of this period from Morocco to Malaya, had brought an intensity of intercommunication never reached before in Afro-Eurasian history. One result of this change was the rapid development of northwestern Europe, largely through its ability to borrow and assimilate the technology that was available anywhere— from Greek science to Chinese printing and gunpowder, from Indian positional numbers to Muslim ship's rigging and algebra. But Africa was still largely isolated, and its technological lag behind the intercommunicating world was greater than ever—not because Africa was unchanging, but because the rest of the world was changing more rapidly than ever before. African achievements up until this point had been considerable, in art, music, jurisprudence, and material technology, but they were necessarily based mainly on what Africans could invent for themselves.

Chapter Fourteen

THE END OF ISOLATION

HISTORICAL KNOWLEDGE ABOUT AFRICA HAS A CURIOUS
relationship to African history. Written records are available only for those times and places where literate people
were present—either alien visitors or Africans who kept
records. Since literacy is a crucial technique for human
societies, and it was imported into Africa (as it was into
most of the world) after having been invented elsewhere,
literate reporting from any part of Africa is a rough marker
for the end of African isolation. The timing of the first
written records varied greatly from one part of the continent to another. The introduction of Islam always meant
the introduction of literacy, since Muslims (like Christians and Jews) are "people of the book." A second great
impetus to literate reporting came with the fifteenth-
century maritime revolution and the appearance of European travelers on the coasts. Finally, its spread inland
took place gradually but with increasing rapidity from the
sixteenth century to the twentieth. As each new part of
Africa appeared over the horizon of literate reporting, the
historical record based on oral tradition and archaeology
can be filled out with a third kind of data.

THE WESTERN SUDAN

For the western sudan, Islam brought both local writing
(most of which is now lost) and reports by Arab travel-

263

ers. It is possible to disentangle much of the web of history after about A.D. 1000, at least to the point of picking up broad patterns of change. We are, however, at the mercy of the few sources. Histories of Africa have a good deal to say about Ghana and Mali, and relatively little about Kanem or Takrūr—not because Kanem or Takrūr were less important, but simply because the Arab geographers whose accounts have survived happened to have more information about Ghana and Mali.

Even for Ghana or Mali, history is difficult to reconstruct. They are usually categorized as "great empires," but the phrase can conjure up a whole world of misconceptions—as wrongheaded as those that most educated people carry concerning the "empire" of Charlemagne. At the peak of its power in the ninth century, Ghana was probably not very different from the Carolingian Empire, either in scale or in degree of control over the subordinate territory. That is to say, neither one was really able to keep a constant surveillance over most parts of the empire, even to the extent of knowing in detail what was going on. We often tend to imagine ancient states as though they were run with administrative technology that was only available much later. In fact, both these empires were distant overlordships over virtually self-governing local regions that did what was demanded of them in order to stay out of trouble and otherwise ran their own affairs. Even such an elementary matter as the general enforcement of a single system of law was beyond the power of either Charlemagne or the rulers of Ghana.

Part of Ghana's function as a state is nevertheless clear from the reports of Arab geographers and its position on the edge of the desert. It was the first of a sequence of "empires" in this location. Each in turn grew to power and wealth by controlling the flow of trade across the

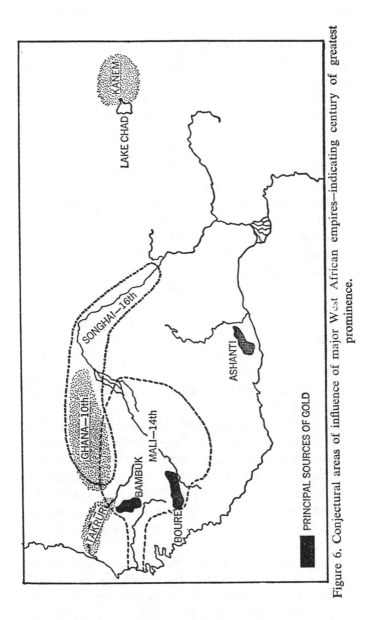

Figure 6. Conjectural areas of influence of major West African empires—indicating century of greatest prominence.

natural frontier between desert and savanna. This trade
was crucial for the western sudan, which lacked a local
source of salt. Rock salt from the desert was exchanged
for gold, mined well back from the desert's edge in Bambuk, Bouré, and later in Ashanti. A state that could dominate the desert-savanna frontier over a considerable distance could tax the passing trade, even though it might
lack direct control over the salt deposits of the Sahara
or the gold deposits of the Sudan.

When Ghana's capital was sacked by a nomadic raid in
A.D. 1076, the empire fell apart. Its place of preeminence
was taken by Mali, not a desert-edge state, but one that
manipulated the gold-salt exchanges by controlling Bambuk and Bouré themselves, and by driving a line of expansion westward down the Gambia Valley to the sea,
where salt was manufactured from sea water. Mali, in
turn, lost some of its power with the fifteenth-century rise
of Songhai on the great northern bend of the Niger. In
the strategy of trade control, Songhai's power marked a
return to the preeminence of the desert edge, and at its
peak Songhai's control reached into the desert to the salt
mines themselves.

But location on the desert edge had disadvantages. Nomadic attack was a constant danger; the climatic pattern
may have been even more telling in the long run. Rainfall
was subject to great annual variation, with the possibility
of no harvest at all in a bad year. This danger was slightly
mitigated by the major rivers that rise farther south in
regions of assured annual rainfall—the Senegal, the Niger,
and the Shari, which flows into Lake Chad. But many of
the people in the northern savanna nevertheless had to
adapt to an uncertain rainfall. In the seventeenth century,
for example, the harvest in the Niger bend country failed
one year out of every seven to ten, and in the eighteenth

century it failed one year in every five. If these failures were well spaced, people could provide for bad years by storing grain, but rain sometimes failed for several years in a row. When this happened, they had to move or die. In recent centuries, at least three periods of general famine and depopulation struck the whole northern savanna belt from the Atlantic to Lake Chad, the first in 1639-43 and the second in 1738-56 and the third was in 1969-73. Oral traditions tell of similar crises in the distant past. The Soninke, the rulers of ancient Ghana, tell of a prolonged dry period that forced them to disperse from a homeland called Wagadu. If Wagadu can be correctly equated with the core area of Ghana, it may be that Ghana fell through famine and depopulation, not merely nomadic attack.

The sequence Ghana-Mali-Songhai was not the only set of states in the western sudan at an early period. Kanem to the east in the Lake Chad basin and Takrūr in the Senegal Valley both have origins at least as far back as the tenth century, and probably earlier still. But the state was not a universal institution in West Africa. The large incorporative empires existed for centuries alongside smaller states and stateless societies. Historians once assumed that the large states must have been created by conquerors who came across the desert (which also explained why they were so prevalent near the desert's edge). In fact, West African political forms are not like those of North Africa; they have far more in common with states elsewhere south of the Sahara. Today, historians believe that African states and stateless societies alike are local developments. They also question the belief that the state is necessarily a sign of human progress. In many respects, such as agricultural technology, the stateless peoples of West Africa were more advanced than those who had the most elaborate political structures. In many circumstances, a minimal political organization lightly unifying a set of virtually independent villages was preferred, even when large states were present in the region and could easily have been copied had there been an inclination to do so.

The large states of the desert fringe nevertheless played an important role in mediating between the Islamic world to the north and the savanna and forest to the south. North African traders stopped at the desert ports, and black Africans from the desert fringe, like the Soninke or the Hausa, carried the trade goods throughout West Africa. They were often among the first to convert to Islam because of their commercial connections with North African Muslims, and their trade networks carried Islam, literacy, and a knowledge of the outside world. By A.D. 1500, these networks had led to the creation of Islamic communities scattered throughout West Africa north of the forest, and the trade routes themselves reached down to the Gulf of Guinea.

THE SOUTHERN SAVANNA

African contact with the outside world, however, decreased in proportion to the distance from the desert ports, and the northern edge of the forest was a breaking point in the pattern of long-distance trade. It is also a breaking point in historical knowledge. It is certain that communication passed through the forest, but none of the surviving records from the northern savannas tell what happened historically in the similar environment to the south of the equatorial forest. It is safe to assume that contact between the northern and southern savannas before 1500 was indirect at best, and the east coast cities were far away.

In this southern setting, African societies developed in isolation; but they did develop, and they were in contact with one another. Innovation could spread widely, though much of it grew from local roots. One important early change in material culture among some of the Bantu-speaking peoples was to adopt a special relationship to cattle. Tsetse fly limited the range of cattle keeping, but those who came to live in fly-free zones added cattle keeping to their traditional hoe agriculture; and they came to value cattle for ritual as well as material reasons.

A second crucial change was the development of regional specialization. Salt was found in some places, but not in others. Local trade in salt therefore began at a very early date. Minerals were also concentrated, and a mining complex grew up in Zimbabwe, Zambia, and Zaire, where iron, copper, and gold were mined as early as the ninth century and probably somewhat earlier. Trade in metals spread from these centers until, by 1400, foreign products imported by way of the Indian Ocean ports were reaching destinations as far inland as present-day Zambia. Glass beads, textiles, and other manufactures were exchanged for African ivory and gold, but the hookup to intercontinental trade came only after the African interior had already developed its own regional commerce.

By the fifteenth century, a series of states began to take shape in the southern savanna, as they had done in the northern savanna about a thousand years earlier. Little is known of the earliest phases of this development, since the states were already established when the Europeans arrived on the coast. It is evident, however, that these kingdoms owed little or nothing to external influence. One of the most powerful was the kingdom of

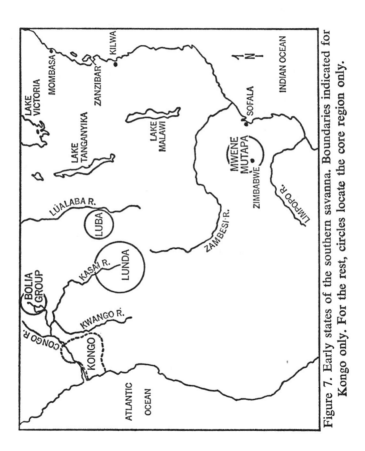

Figure 7. Early states of the southern savanna. Boundaries indicated for Kongo only. For the rest, circles locate the core region only.

Kongo on the Atlantic coast south of the Congo mouth, far from any obvious contact with the rest of the world. It lay mainly in present-day Angola, with a total area midway between the size of Maryland and West Virginia. The basic political unit was the village, as it was in West Africa, with higher administration based on districts and provinces. Traditions recorded in the fifteenth century suggest that the institutions of kingship were borrowed from other peoples to the north, but that is all.

Further inland, other political centers began to develop about the same time. One of these was the Bolia group of states in the dense tropical forest around the northern end of Lake Leopold II. A second in central Katanga was associated at first with the Luba ethnic group, but its institutional forms spread, with modifications, to the Lunda as well, until they finally extended over the whole of the African heartland from Lake Tanganyika a thousand miles west to the Kwango River.

A third center of fifteenth-century state building centered in present-day Zimbabwe. The elaborate stone ruins at Great Zimbabwe were so impressive their name has been used for the ancient kingdom and for the present-day republic, though Great Zimbabwe can be used to distinguish the city from the larger units. This kingdom was founded by the Karanga people, whose power was based on their gold deposits and trade with the Indian Ocean ports, and the most impressive buildings, once dated to the seventeenth or eighteenth centuries, are now thought to have been built late in the fifteenth. That was the period at which the rulers of Great Zimbabwe controlled most of the country between the Limpopo River on the south and the Zambezi on the north, from the Indian Ocean westward to the edges of the Kalahari Desert. The ruler bore the title of Mwenemutapa, which

led the first Portuguese travelers to write about the
"Monomotapa Empire." But the "empire" barely survived the period of their arrival. In the early sixteenth
century, it broke into two parts. The Mwenemutapa still
controlled the north, but a rival dynasty, the Changamire,
took over the southern section.

Far to the north, in the East African highlands, similar
changes were in progress. Since literate aliens did not
visit that part of Africa until the nineteenth century, we
are left with only the record of archaeology and oral
tradition, but that is enough to indicate a similar process
of state-building, beginning perhaps as early as the thirteenth century. A large empire ruled by a dynasty re-
membered as the Bachwezi was roughly contempora-
neous with the height of Great Zimbabwe or the kingdom
of Kongo, but it too appears to have broken down into a
series of small states in about the year 1500.

THE MARITIME REVOLUTION

African societies, whatever their relative degree of isolation, were gradually coming to terms with their environment, borrowing or inventing new techniques for dealing
with the problems of social life and material existence.
Then, quite suddenly. in a few decades before 1500,
Africa's relationship with the intercommunicating zone
shifted dramatically. The cause of this change was a major
breakthrough in the field of maritime technology.

Before the fifteenth century, reasonably safe long-
distance trade by sea was possible only in favorable conditions. The Mediterranean was almost ideal for early
shipping, and the Indian Ocean was favored by a pattern
of monsoonal winds, which blew from the northeast for

about half the year, then turned and blew from the southwest for the other half. Ships were guaranteed a favorable wind from the African coast to the Straits of Melaka and back again, simply by waiting for the appropriate season. This is one reason Chinese ships reached the East African coast in the fifteenth century, and changing styles in Chinese porcelain are still used today by archaeologists to establish the date of many East African ruins.

The whole western coast of Africa was another matter. It was navigable enough, and Africans had some coastwise traffic in large canoes; but the west coast was cut off from other seas by two major barriers. One of these was the stormy coast of South Africa between southern Natal and Cape Town. Even after the Europeans learned to sail around Africa, this coast saw far more shipwrecks than any other. The second barrier was of a different kind. Along the Atlantic coast of the Sahara, it was easy enough to sail southward with the northeast trade winds, which blew all year long and set up an ocean current flowing in the same direction. The problem was to get back to the north against the combination of contrary wind and contrary currents.

The crucial breakthrough, not only for Africa, but for world history, was made off the Saharan coast. The first problem was to develop a ship that could sail to windward efficiently enough to overcome the pull of the current. This was accomplished along the Atlantic coasts of Spain and Portugal through the merging of Mediterranean ship design, new forms of hull construction from northern Europe, and lateen sails borrowed from the Arabs of the Indian Ocean. The result was the caravel—an excellent example of the kind of technological advance that was possible within the intercommunicating world.

The second step was even more important. The Portuguese knew that Muslim traders from North Africa went
across the Sahara for gold. As Christians, they were
barred from the overland route, but they began in the
fifteenth century to experiment with caravels to make the
voyage by sea. Sometime early in the century, they found
that they could return to the northward if they tacked
back and forth so as to take advantage of the fact that the
trade winds blew slightly more onshore in the daylight
hours and slightly more offshore at night. But all this was
merely a prelude to the crucial discovery. Somehow in
the course of voyages down the coast to Senegal, the
Canaries, or Madeira, (probably in the 1440s) Portuguese
mariners discovered that it was not necessary to sail
laboriously north along the coast. A ship that left the
coast altogether and made a long tack to the northwest,
keeping as close as possible to the trade wind, would
sooner or later pass beyond the trade-wind belt. In the
vicinity of the Azores, the current set toward the Portuguese coast, and the winds were variable but mainly
westerly, allowing an easy return home. This discovery
not only unlocked the western coasts of Africa for European shipping, it opened the Atlantic as well. It is significant that Columbus made a voyage to the Gold Coast
before he went to America. He therefore knew that he
could let the trade winds blow his ships to the west, because a zone of prevailing westerlies lay farther north to
blow them back to Europe again. In short, what the Europeans learned on the Sahara coast was not simply a
good sea route to Guinea; it was their first insight into
the worldwide pattern of winds and currents. Within a
few decades, European ships could reach virtually any
part of any ocean.

Simultaneous with the maritime revolution, a second

Elmina Castle, Ghana, construction begun by Portuguese, in 1481.

technological change took place in the intercommunicating world. Gunpowder, invented in China, was joined to improving metallurgy to produce the first effective artillery. By the sixteenth century, cannon were being used not only in Europe but also across the whole belt of countries stretching from Morocco to Japan. The coasts of Africa therefore emerged from isolation confronted by intruders who were both mobile and well armed. As the use of firearms spread rapidly through the Muslim world, a similar confrontation emerged along the fringes of the desert, from the Senegal River to the Red Sea. Africans thus faced better-armed neighbors on all sides.

TIME OF TROUBLES IN THE SIXTEENTH CENTURY

But it would be a mistake to exaggerate the suddenness of Africa's emergence from isolation, or the effectiveness of early firearms. Most African societies, other than the East African port towns, were quite untouched by the first results of the maritime revolution. New currents of trade grew up only gradually. Maize, manioc, and other crops from the Americas diffused inland over decades and even centuries. Some African states, however, felt the direct influence of European power, and faced a crisis of forced and rapid readjustment to the new situation. For most of sub-Saharan Africa, however, it is more accurate to think of a time of troubles, of slow readjustment as the European presence on the coast impinged piecemeal and sporadically on a particular African society.

Portuguese activity in Africa was itself irregular. It was intense for two or three decades after about 1480. In these years, the greater possibility of a trading-post empire dominating the Indian Ocean sea lanes was not yet recognized. Portuguese resources for overseas activity could therefore concentrate on Africa, and the earliest strategy was to enter the African gold trade. In 1481 the Portuguese built an elaborate stone castle at Elmina on the Gold Coast to tap the Ashanti gold fields. They were not interested in conquest or colonization, only in bases to defend their trade against other Europeans. They also hoped to convert some of the more important African states to Christianity, using a program of Christian missions and technical assistance to create dependence on Portugal. The target states in West Africa were the three largest and strongest states lying near the coast—Jollof, which then controlled most of present-day western Senegal, Benin in southern Nigeria, and Kongo in central Africa. In the first two, the plan miscarried. An attempt to install a pro-Portuguese pretender as ruler of Jollof failed in 1488. Trade and diplomatic relations with Benin brought a few missionaries from Europe, but they soon died and nothing substantial came of the effort.

The Portuguese effort in Kongo came nearer to success. In 1487 the ruler, Manikongo Mzinga Kuwu, appealed for missionaries and technicians, and the Portuguese obliged. His son and successor was converted to Christianity, had himself baptized Affonso I, and founded a line of Christian kings. At first, the Kongolese drive for modernization brought some success, though it failed in the long run. The missionaries and technicians were too few, and they died too rapidly to be really useful. In addition, the Portuguese seized the offshore island of São Thomé and turned it into a plantation colony in the decades after 1500. The São Thomé planters needed slaves from the nearby shores of Africa, and their interests predominated over the good intentions of the distant government in Lisbon. The growth of the slave

trade was disastrous for the whole region, but the Portuguese were not the only problem. In the final third of the
sixteenth century, the rains failed more frequently than
usual, and a number of different refugee groups turned
to marauding. The most notorious of these were the
Imbangala, whom the Portuguese called Jaga. At one
point they destroyed the capital of Kongo, though later
on they became allies of the Portuguese, who were
powerless against direct attack. Draught continued into
the early seventeenth century, and the Portuguese
gradually withdrew their principal center from Kongo to
the island of Luanda on the Angola coast just to the
south.

In the western Sudan the time of troubles took a different form. The most important states of the sixteenth
century were Songhai on the Niger bend and Bornu, successor to Kanem in the Lake Chad basin. Their outside
contacts were with North Africa, where important changes
were taking place in the second half of the century. The
Ottoman Turks became a major naval power in the Mediterranean and began to gain control of a series of North
African port towns as far west as Algeria—among others,
Tripoli, which served as the northern terminus of the
trans-Saharan route northward from Bornu. Rather than
posing a threat to Bornu, the presence of a strong power
to the north at a time when Bornu was gaining power in
the south worked in the interests of both. Bornu and
Istanbul established diplomatic relations and cooperated
in keeping trade routes open, and Bornu was able to import firearms and hire Turkish mercenaries. All of this
gave a new impetus to the spread of Islamic learning
south of the desert.

The fate of Songhai was almost the reverse. After
reaching a peak of power and influence during the first

decades of the sixteenth century, Songhai's power began to decline. Religious controversies led to a series of disputed successions and brief civil wars. Portuguese trade with the gold fields cut into Songhai's commercial advantage as a desert-edge state. Meanwhile, Morocco was growing in power north of the desert. In the 1590s a Moroccan army crossed the desert and defeated Songhai. Morocco was not strong enough to maintain control over a large section of the western sudan, but it was strong enough to prevent the rise of a new sudanic state on the desert fringe—one that could again exploit the advantages that had once brought wealth and power to Ghana, Mali, and Songhai. Even without the sporadic Moroccan intervention that continued through the seventeenth and into the eighteenth century, European entry into the gold trade from the coast ruined the possibility of a sudanic state ever again monopolizing that trade as Mali had once done.

The sixteenth-century troubles in East Africa were similar; the Europeans there were strong enough to ruin the older patterns of commerce, but too weak to create a viable alternative. The Portuguese effort in the Indian Ocean region was marked by grand designs and too little power to carry them out. The Portuguese hoped to monopolize the spice trade from Indonesia to the west, but their maritime dominance was sporadic at best. By mid-century Muslim "smugglers" had recaptured much of their former trade.

A standoff between Portugal and the Ottoman Turks at the mouth of the Red Sea was especially damaging. Neither the Turks moving south from Egypt nor the Portuguese moving north from Mozambique were able to control the Red Sea route from the Mediterranean to the Indian Ocean. As a result, trade simply went elsewhere— to the Persian Gulf for the Muslims, or to the round-

Africa route for the Portuguese. In addition, both Turks and Portuguese intervened in the political affairs of the Ethiopian highlands. Early in the fifteenth century, the Turks furnished firearms to local Muslim powers, who attacked Christian Abyssinia and almost destroyed it in the 1540s. Portugal then intervened on the other side, saving Abyssinia from extinction but not from a prolonged decline in power and well-being—a decline that lasted into the nineteenth century. But here, as in Kongo, external influences were not alone. The Muslim-Christian struggles opened the way to a long series of invasions by the nomadic Oromo. Originating in southern Ethiopia, the Oromo moved around and into the highlands, seizing whole regions. In time, they settled down and many of them became sedentary themselves, but meanwhile their invasions and migrations during the seventeenth and eighteenth centuries devastated much of the highland country.

The Portuguese impact on the east coast trading cities was again similar. At their arrival, Kilwa was the dominant power, with control over the coastwise trade as far south as Sofala. A Portuguese fleet attacked Kilwa in 1505. The Portuguese then built a new base on Mozambique island, and they took Sofala as an entry point into the gold trade. For a short time, they were successful even in the interior, establishing cordial relations with the Mwenemutapa and converting some of his people to Christianity, but the flow of gold soon dropped from its previous levels. By the seventeenth century, the Changamire dynasty rose in power, gained control of the gold fields, and dispossessed Portugal's allies.

North of Cape Delgado, Portuguese power was still less substantial. They captured and garrisoned some of the coastal cities, but Turkish raids from the sea came as far south as Mombasa in the late sixteenth century. Where the old prosperity had depended on coastal trade to the Red Sea and Persian Gulf, the southern terminus was now securely held by the Portuguese, the northern by the Turks. Again, the weakening of the coastal cities may have contributed to their difficulties in the hinterland— from the Oromo behind the northern sector in present-day Somalia, and war bands of Zimba who moved northward just behind the coast in the 1580s, sacking both Kilwa and Mombasa. These raids bear some resemblance to the Jaga invasion of Kongo on the opposite side of Africa, and both may have been connected with major political changes in the Lunda empire of the interior. After 1598 the Portuguese built a major fortress at Mombasa to anchor their power on the northern coast, but it remained insecure. By the eighteenth century, even Mombasa was lost, and Portugal was too weak to prevent a trade revival under the general patronage and protection of Oman, in Arabia at the entrance of the Persian Gulf.

For the east coast, then, the coming of the Portuguese was not so much a new link with the intercommunicating world as a breach in the well-established pattern of contact that already existed with the world of Islam. In spite of their partial dominance over some of the coastal cities for almost two centuries, the Portuguese cultural contribution was slight. The cities remained Islamic in religion, grafted onto an African base. It may be that Portugal's most important contribution to East African culture history was to increase the Africanization of coastal culture by reducing contact with Arabia.

Chapter Fifteen

THE ERA OF THE SLAVE TRADE

IT IS ONE OF THE IRONIES OF AFRICAN HISTORY THAT the end of isolation, made possible through the maritime revolution, should have led in hardly more than two centuries to a new commerce in which Africa's chief export was its own people. Historians have long disputed the causes and consequences of the slave trade — both for Africa and for the world — and the debates are far from finished.

Recent research nevertheless makes it possible to dismiss some of the older myths about the slave trade, myths that originated in the eighteenth- and nineteenth-century European image of Africa with all its racist overtones. Where the slave trade was once explained by the "primitive" condition of African societies and the "natural docility" of the Africans, it is now clear that Africa was not primitive and African slaves were far from docile. Slave revolts were a standard feature in the American tropics. Not only were the Afro-Americans of Saint Domingue (now the republic of Haiti) the first non-Europeans to overthrow colonial rule; other, less known, revolts were also successful. Communities of runaways and rebels were scattered through the back country of South America and in the tangled mountains of the larger Caribbean islands. Several such communities maintained their independence of European control until the end of slavery itself ended their need for isolation.

THE ORIGINS OF NEGRO SLAVERY

Other research helps to explain why Africans came
to make up the majority of slaves in the Western world.
In southern Europe—unlike northern Europe, where the
slavery of the Roman period changed gradually into various forms of inequality generally categorized as serfdom
—slavery continued throughout the Middle Ages and
down to the eighteenth century in some places. Mediterranean slavery had nothing to do with the race of the
slaves. It was a matter of religion; Christians enslaved
Muslims, and Muslims enslaved Christians. Black Africans
were present among the Mediterranean slaves, but not
in large numbers until the fourteenth century. Before that
time, the principal external source of slaves for Christian
Europe was the northern and eastern coasts of the Black
Sea.

In the fourteenth and fifteenth centuries, slavery in
southern Europe served three purposes—to furnish domestic service, to provide oarsmen for the galleys that were
the principal naval craft, and to concentrate people for
new enterprises. Wherever mines or plantations were established in places with an insufficient supply of labor,
the institution of slavery was a convenient way of mobiliz-
ing labor, especially for sugar plantations on the Mediterranean islands, southern Spain, or Portugal.

Even before the discovery of America, Europeans began to set up similar plantations on Atlantic islands like
the Canaries or Madeira. By the early sixteenth century,
they had moved as far as São Thomé in the Gulf of
Guinea, and these moves were followed later in the
century by similar establishments in the Caribbean and
Brazil. At each step, the existing population was too

small to provide enough workers for a labor-intensive crop like sugar, and the previously isolated populations lived in disease environments that lacked many of the common diseases of Africa and Europe. This meant that the people had no immunities derived from childhood infection or inheritance. With the introduction of Afro-European diseases, they passed through a series of devastating epidemics of diseases like measles, smallpox, typhus, malaria, or yellow fever. The result was a population disaster, sometimes ending in the effective extinction of the original population, especially in the tropical lowlands of the Americas—the region best suited for plantation agriculture. Europeans already had the institution of slavery as a way of forcing labor mobility; they used it in the Atlantic just as they had done in the Mediterranean.

Some form of slavery or forced labor was useful for other reasons as well. The natural conditions of a frontier region, with plenty of land and few people, made for high wage rates, and high labor costs made for labor-extensive use of the land—often pastoralism or simply hunting wild cattle. It was tempting in these conditions to use force in order to make people work some of the land more intensively. As the Indian populations declined in Mexico and Peru, the Spanish turned increasingly to various forms of peonage. On the eastern frontiers of Europe, the landed class tightened the bonds of serfdom. The solution found for America's tropical lowlands was slavery.

But Africans were not the only enforced immigrants to the New World. Convicts, unsuccessful rebels against the government, and indentured workers who bound themselves more or less voluntarily to serve for a period of years were shipped off to the Americas in large numbers. Indians were also enslaved and used for plantation agriculture, especially in Brazil. Of the three sources of labor—Africa, America, and Europe—it was soon clear that the Africans survived best in the tropical American environment. At the time, African superiority in this respect was attributed to some special quality of the Negro race, but modern knowledge of epidemiology shows that early environment rather than race is the true explanation. Europeans died in large numbers in the American tropics, just as they died in even larger numbers in the African tropics. Indians also died on contact with Afro-European diseases, but Africans were comparatively immune both to tropical diseases and to the ordinary range of diseases common on the Afro-Eurasian land mass. Migration from Africa to the Americas brought higher death rates for the first generation, but lower rates than those of Europeans who made the equivalent move.

Given the choice of slavery as a labor system and the fact that Africans were the most efficient workers, the problem of supply remained. A large-scale slave trade would have been impossible if Africa had been truly primitive; European death rates on the coast guaranteed as much. But Africa was not primitive. Developed commercial networks were already in existence before the discovery of America, both in West Africa and the southern savanna. African rulers often enslaved war prisoners, and the prisoners were sold into the slave trade—often for shipment to distant places where escape was less likely. Some were exported across the Sahara to North Africa, and the Portuguese were briefly in the business of buying slaves in one part of Africa and selling them in another, even before the demand from American plantations drew the focus of the slave trade across the Atlantic.

But slavery in Africa was different from slavery on an

American plantation. A slave was without rights at the moment of his capture; he could be killed or sold. He continued without rights until he was sold to an ultimate master in Africa—or else to the Europeans for transportation overseas. If he ended up on an American plantation, his rights would be few and he was treated as a mere labor unit. But in Africa, slavery was not mainly an economic institution. The object in buying a slave was to increase the size of one's own group, more often for prestige or military power than for the sake of wealth. Women were therefore more desirable than men, but men and women alike were assimilated into the master's social group. They had rights as well as obligations. In many cases, a second-generation slave could no longer be sold. And slaves belonging to important people could often rise to positions of command over free men.

THE SLAVE TRADE IN AFRICA

The Atlantic slave trade thus tapped an existing African slave trade, but in doing so it sent people into a very different kind of slavery. Over the centuries, it diverted increasing numbers to the coast for sale to Europeans. The organization of this trade varied greatly from one part of Africa to the next. In some regions, Europeans built trade forts; twenty-seven were constructed on the Gold Coast over a distance of only about 220 miles. African authorities allowed the Europeans to exercise sovereignty within the forts themselves, but they often charged rent for the land the fort stood on. Other trading posts were nothing more than a few unfortified houses onshore for the storage of trade goods and a tightly fenced yard for slaves awaiting shipment. In that case, the Europeans who stayed onshore between ships' visits did so with the permission of the African ruler, and under his protection. Another form of trade was the "ship trade," in which Europeans sailed down the coast, calling at likely ports, but without leaving European agents permanently stationed onshore.

Whatever the point of trade, elaborate customary procedures had come into existence by the end of the sixteenth century. Trade normally began with a payment to the local authorities, partly a gift to demonstrate good will and partly a tax. Each section of the coast had its own trade currency of account—the "bar" (originally an iron bar), the "ounce" (originally an ounce of gold dust), a form of brass currency called manillas, or cowrie shells from the Indian Ocean. Various European commodities were customarily valued at so many bars or ounces. Bargains were struck in terms of the number of bars or ounces to be paid for a slave and then once more in terms of the "sorting" of different European goods that would be used to make up that value.

The internal trade to the coast was more diverse. In some African kingdoms, such as late-eighteenth-century Dahomey, the slave trade was a royal monopoly, tightly controlled for the profit of the state. Other states, such as Futa Toro on the Senegal River, sold few slaves themselves but charged heavy tolls for the privilege of shipping slaves through the country on the way to the coast. Still other states expanded by conquest in order to be able to control the passage of slaves. The kingdom of Akwamu followed a pattern of expansion in the late seventeenth century, moving to the east and west of the Volta River in present-day Ghana, but some distance back from the coast. After a period of growing strength based on revenue from the flow of trade across the kingdom, Akwamu was able to reach down to the coast itself in the 1680s and dictate terms to the coastal trading states and the European garrisons alike.

Other African societies adjusted to the demand for slaves, changing their own social and political institutions. Along the fringes of the Niger delta, the Ijo had been settled for centuries as fishermen and exporters of salt to the interior. Early in the eighteenth century, a series of new city-states like Nembe, Bonny, and Kalabari came into existence, with a commercial and political organization designed expressly to serve the demand for slaves. Each city-state was divided internally into a series of "canoe houses," in effect a commercial firm based on the extended family plus domestic slaves. The houses operated large trading canoes, vessels that might have fifty to a hundred paddlers and mount a small cannon. Trade was highly competitive between houses, and within a house command went to the most successful traders. A slave might rise to become head of the house. The Ijo canoes on the creeks of the delta were supplied, in turn, by other trade networks leading to the waterside. The Aro subgroup among the Ibo, for example, had small colonies of Aro settled in towns throughout Iboland. Slaves were passed from one Aro community to another until they were sold to the Ijo and finally to the Europeans. The Aro enjoyed this special position partly because they also controlled an important religious shrine, and many of the slaves they collected were originally given as sacrifices at the shrine, though in fact they ended in the Americas.

African societies south of the tropical forest also adjusted to the trade in slaves. By the late seventeenth century, the Imbangala, who had first appeared as destructive raiders a century earlier, turned to commerce. Their kingdom, inland from the Portuguese post at Luanda,

drew slaves from a wide range of central Africa. A little
later, the Ovimbundu in the hinterland of Benguela took
the same course. Bihé and Mbailundu in particular among
the Ovimbundu states became wealthy on the basis of
trade routes reaching far into the interior, ultimately as
far as the present Shaba province of Zaire. Like
Imbangala to the north, the Ovimbundu states were far
too strong to be threatened by Portuguese power on the
coast. In time, a rough alliance came into existence, in
which the Portuguese acquiesced to the trade monopoly
of the inland kingdoms for the sake of having a regular
and plentiful supply of slaves delivered to the coast.

East Africa also made a small contribution to the slave
trade, especially the hinterland of Mozambique City. (To
the north of Cape Delgado, slaves from the Swahili coast
were almost all directed toward Arabia and Persia, though
this trade was small until the early nineteenth century.)
The principal African carriers of the trade within southeastern Africa were the Yao from the vicinity of Lake
Malawi. They first went into the long-distance ivory trade
and then shifted to slaves as demand increased in the
course of the eighteenth century. For southeastern Africa,
the most important destination of that period was the
Mascarene Islands in the Indian Ocean, where the French
developed sugar plantations on the pattern of the West
Indies. A few thousand nevertheless found their way
around the Cape of Good Hope into the slave trade of
the Atlantic.

THE GROWTH AND INCIDENCE OF THE SLAVE TRADE

The European demand for slaves grew slowly and steadily; over many decades African institutions adapted to

meet the demand. From an annual average of less than 2000 slaves imported into the Americas each year in the century before 1600, the trade grew to about 55,000 a year for the eighteenth century as a whole. The peak decade for the whole history of the trade was the 1780s, with an annual average of 88,000 slaves arriving in the Americas each year; deliveries reached more than 100,000 in a few individual years. At least for the crucial period from 1701 to 1809, it is possible to estimate the drain of population from various regions of Africa by taking the combined estimates of the exports carried by the three most important carriers—England, France, and Portugal. (See Fig. 8.) While the map represents the origins of the vast majority of all those carried, it also leaves out some important aspects of the trade. During that century, the sources of the trade shifted dramatically from one part of the coast to another. The Gold Coast, for example, supplied 20 percent of exports in the 1740s, but only about 9 percent in the 1790s. Meanwhile, the Bight of Biafra rose with the development of the Ijo-Aro trade network from about 1 percent of the trade in the 1730s to almost a quarter of the whole in the 1790s. Or again, the exports from central Africa doubled between the 1770s and the 1780s. In short, while the demand for slaves was relatively steady, it was met by rapid shifts from one source of supply to another, depending on African political conditions or the development of new trade routes from the interior.

North Americans, with a view of world history that centers on their own country, often think of the slave trade as a flow of people from Africa to the United States. In fact, about one third of all slaves landed in the Americas went to Brazil; about a half went to the Caribbean islands and mainland; no more than a twentieth came to the United States. Yet the Afro-America population of the United States today is one of the largest in the New World. The explanation lies in a sharp and important demographic distinction between North America and the American tropics. While the Negro population of the North American colonies began to grow from natural increase at a very early date, the slave population of the tropical plantations suffered an excess of deaths over births. This meant that the slave trade could not be a one-shot affair, importing a basic population that could then maintain its own numbers. It had to be continuous merely to maintain the existing level of population; any growth of the plantation economy required still more slaves from Africa.

Several factors help to account for this demographic peculiarity. Disease environment was important in the first generation, since both morbidity and mortality rates were higher among slaves raised in Africa than they were among the American-born. Planters also imported about two men for every woman, and they worked the women in the fields along with the men, preferring to have their labor rather than creating the kind of social setting in which they would be willing to have children.

The planters may have been correct, on strictly economic grounds, in believing that it was cheaper to import new labor from Africa than to allow the leisure, additional rations, and other privileges that might have encouraged a high birth rate among the slaves. The real cost of slaves was very small indeed before the middle of the eighteenth century. In 1695, for example, a slave could be bought in Jamaica for about £20 currency, or about the same value as six hundred pounds of raw sugar sold on the Lon-

Figure 8. Approximate sources of the eighteenth-century Atlantic slave trade, 1701-1800. (Dutch, British, French, and Portuguese exports.) Totals in thousands.

Region	Slaves exported	Percent of Total
Senegambia	201	3.6
Sierra Leone	484	8.7
Gold Coast	677	12.3
Bight of Benin	1,279	23.2
Bight of Biafra	814	14.8
West-central Africa	2,058	37.3
TOTAL	**5,513**	**100.0**

Source: Paul E. Lovejoy, *Transformations in Slavery,* p. 50.

don market, or the European cost of sixteen trade guns for sale in Africa. All things being equal, a new slave could be expected to add more than six hundred pounds to the plantation's production in a single year. Yet a prime slave on the coast of Africa cost only about eight guns or a half ton of iron in bars—little enough to allow a handsome profit on the slave trade itself.

But the real price of slaves in Africa rose steadily during the eighteenth century. One result was to make planters think twice about their policy of importing slaves, rather than allowing them to breed naturally. By the 1770s, several Caribbean planters began to readjust by balancing the number of men and women on their estates, granting special privileges to child-rearing mothers and time off for child care. It is uncertain how generally these new polities were applied, but some of the older colonies, such as Barbados, began to achieve a self-perpetuating slave population by about 1800. Even where slaves were still imported, the demand tended to drop as the local birth rate rose, and the total number imported dropped in each decade from 1790 to 1820. When the United States, Great Britain, and Denmark abolished their own part of the slave trade in the first decade of the nineteenth century, the planters complained, but the really serious need for continued slave imports was nearing its end—at least in the older plantation areas.

The slave trade nevertheless reached its peak in the early nineteenth century. In spite of British efforts to halt the trade by a partial blockade of the African coast—and by diplomatic pressure on Portugal, Brazil, and Spain—a sugar boom in Cuba and a coffee boom in southern Brazil brought a new demand for slaves from places where the plantation economy was newly introduced in that century. The slave trade therefore lasted until Brazil decided, in

1850, to enforce its own anti-slave trade laws and Spain made a similar decision for its Cuban colony in the 1860s.

THE IMPACT OF THE SLAVE TRADE ON AFRICA

Leaving aside the unanswerable question of what Africa might have become over these centuries without the slave trade, some evidence for assessing the impact of the trade is available. We know that most of the slaves sent to the Americas were captured in war. Some warfare took place in order to supply slaves to the trade, and all warfare produced captives who could be sold. Thus, the rise and fall of African states, contested successions, or periods of chronic warfare between states attracted slave dealers who followed the armies and purchased the prisoners. Famine was another cause of enslavement in the regions of unreliable rainfall, where a series of bad harvests forced people to sell their domestic servants, or even their kin and themselves. Judicial condemnation for crime or political dissent also sent some people on their way to the Americas.

But the knowledge that warfare was the principal cause of enslavement in Africa is not as useful for assessing the impact of the trade as one might suppose. If a war took place with the specific and sole aim of capturing slaves, then the slave trade can be blamed for the damage to society at large. When, however, people were enslaved in the course of wars that took place for other reasons, the slave trade was a neutral factor. It might even have been beneficial; all wars are destructive, but a war fought so as to maximize the number of prisoners might well be less destructive than most. Our present knowledge is enough to indicate that both types of warfare took place in Africa, but not enough to tell which type was more common. On one side, historians can point to spectacular events like the collapse of the empire of Oyo in present-day Nigeria, a political change which led to a whole series of wars lasting for many decades in the early nineteenth century. It is clear that these wars were fought over real issues, not merely to supply the slave trade—yet they supplied more slaves to the trade than any other source in their time. In other cases, historians have detected what appears to have been a "gun-slave cycle," where an African state armed itself with guns, used them to capture unarmed neighbors, who were sold for still more guns. Once caught in this cycle, it was hard to escape. Sooner or later, the neighboring peoples would have guns as well; at that point, slave raiding to buy guns might be necessary for survival. Cases can be found where African states, like Dahomey in the late eighteenth century, reorganized as a military machine for the supply of slaves. But the gun-slave cycle may have been comparatively rare. The long reloading time of the typical eighteenth-century muzzle-loader limited its advantage against rapid-fire bowmen in the forest or wooded savanna. In the open savanna, cavalry was still the dominant military arm far into the nineteenth century.

Still another problem in assessing the impact of the trade is the obvious variation from one African society to another. Some societies were completely destroyed, others may have become wealthy by selling their neighbors to the Europeans, still others were never seriously involved in the trade at all—either as sellers or as victims. We might be able to arrive at a better assessment if we knew more about the level of African populations during the period of the trade; we could thus make some estimates as to the per capita drain of population. But it could still be argued that the underlying influence of the trade was far more profound than any mere drain of population or change in the incidence of warfare. Having been isolated from the intercommunicating zone, the Africans of the western coasts had, in the arrival of seaborne Europeans, both an opportunity and a challenge. If they had responded by seeking new products to sell in return for the Indian textiles and European hardware offered by the maritime trade, they might well have been led to new economic institutions, technological innovations, and a more rapid rate of economic development than ever before. As it was, the Europeans wanted slaves, and the challenge of meeting this demand diverted African creativity to an essentially unproductive enterprise. When the slave trade finally ended, African societies took up the challenge of supplying products rather than people, but time was already running out; the European invasions came before the adjustment could be completed. It seems clear from this point of view that, at the very least, the slave trade forestalled some of the positive fruits of more intense contact with the outside world.

On the other hand, it is hard to sustain the view that the slave trade destroyed African civilization or set Africa back on its path to progress. African civilization was not destroyed, and Africa made progress during this period in spite of slave trade. Literacy spread in the western sudan with the spread of Islam. Literacy in English and Portuguese spread along the coast, where slave dealers learned to read and write and sometimes sent their children to Europe for education. Recent studies of African states like Ashanti show a continuous development from small-scale, kinship-based political units to the institutions of a large state, capable of assimilating its conquered territories and exercising administrative control that was at

least as effective as that of feudal monarchies in western
Europe before the thirteenth century. Metallurgy and tex-
tile production also improved, and hand-loomed cotton
cloths were sold into world trade during the eighteenth
century, before the cheaper machine-made cloth from Europe drove them from the market. In short, measured by
technology, there is no doubt that African societies advanced during the period of the slave trade, though it is
equally certain that the advance was too slow to close the
gap between African technology and that of the intercommunicating zone.

Chapter Sixteen

THE SECONDARY EMPIRE OF
THE PRE-COLONIAL CENTURY

THE ERA OF THE SLAVE TRADE AND THE ERA OF EURO-
pean conquest are unmistakable periods in the history of
Africa. They also overlap; the earliest of the major European conquests took place before the last cargo of slaves
was shipped to the New World. But the styles of history
represented in these two eras were not merged end to end
like a cinematic "lap dissolve"—the one gradually fading
away while the other simultaneously brightened. About a
century before the European conquests began in earnest—
that is, about the 1780s, even before the slave trade
reached its peak—new influences and tendencies began
to appear. During this "pre-colonial century," Islamic
renovation in West Africa led to the formation of a series
of new empires. Political boundaries altered sharply over
the whole range of eastern Africa as well, from the Nilotic
sudan south to the Cape. Over all these changes hung the
shadow of the European Industrial Revolution, which increased Europe's technological lead and brought more
intense European activity along all fringes of the continent. Many of these new tendencies of the pre-colonial
century were cut off abruptly by the European invasions;
others were diverted into new channels; but the events
and developments of that century are nevertheless important for understanding the direction in which African so-

cieties were headed before they were pulled so abruptly into the orbit of European colonial rule.

In eastern Africa, the dominant theme was military innovation. From the beginning of history, men have fought wars and changed the arts of warfare. These changes have always tended to alter the locus and distribution of power within society. In Europe, the security of the private castle helped to fragment political power in the feudal age, just as the better artillery of the fifteenth and sixteenth centuries helped build the centralized monarchies of countries like England and France. In nineteenth-century Africa a similar change took place, but with an added twist. Major changes in the technology of war came so suddenly, they were seized and used by one state or segment of society before opponents had a chance either to imitate or to counter with new defenses. The result was a total disruption of the old power relations, as some groups were able to win easily and cheaply over others who had been more isolated.

The military changes of nineteenth-century Africa came from two sources. One of these was industrial Europe. Guns and tactics had been improving steadily in Europe itself. By the middle of the eighteenth century, the chief disadvantage of the musket—its long reloading time—had been corrected to some extent by the tactic of volley firing by disciplined infantry units. As early as the 1750s, this new tactic made European-trained armies dominant in distant parts of the world, such as India. Later, in the nineteenth century, the pace of change increased in weaponry itself. First came grapeshot and explosive shells for artillery, then in the 1860s breach-loading guns that could be fired several times a minute. These were followed in the late 1870s by magazine-loading automatic rifles, and in the 1880s by the first effective field machine guns. Each of these changes opened the way to cheap military conquest by whatever African state could arm itself with the newest weapons before its neighbors could do the same. The result was a new political phenomenon known as a "secondary empire"—secondary in the sense that it was based on the military technology of Europe, but not controlled directly by a European power in the manner of the primary colonial empires of the period after 1880.

The second source of military innovation was similar in its consequences, but completely African in origin. This was the development of new tactics, based on a highly trained and disciplined infantry unit, armed with a short stabbing spear in place of the hurled javelin. In this case, it was not the weapon that was crucial, but the discovery (made several times before in other historical circumstances) that infantry trained to act as a body were far more effective, man for man, than a loosely organized mass of part-time soldiers. The result was the famous Zulu age-grade regiment, or impi, which made its appearance in southern Africa toward the end of the eighteenth century. At that time the Nguni peoples of present-day Natal were divided into a number of small chiefdoms, and the new tactic is generally credited to Dingiswayo, chief of the Mthethwa. Dingiswayo took the existing institution of the initiation school and used it in new ways. All young men passed through a process of education and initiation as they reached puberty, and those who passed through these ceremonies together constituted an "age grade," a continuing social unit. The innovation was to take each age grade in turn and organize it as a permanent military unit of young men who lived together, trained together, and fought together. The ruler thus had a stand-

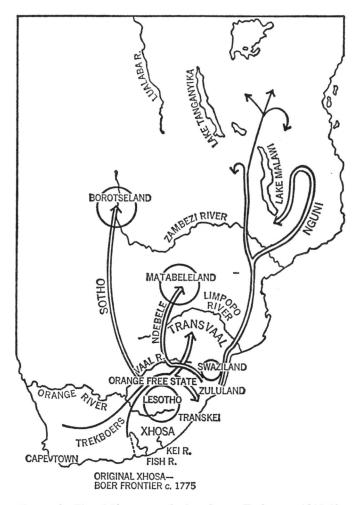

Figure 9. The *Mfecane* and the Great Trek—c. 1815-50.

ing army made up of regimental units that cut across kinship and other social ties. Dingiswayo used this new source of power to conquer and incorporate a number of surrounding chiefdoms until he had built a unified state. At his death in 1818, command passed to Shaka, ruler of the Zulu, who began to use the military strength of the new state far more aggressively than Dingiswayo had ever done.

THE MFECANE IN SOUTHERN AFRICA

Shaka's wars in northern Natal led to a long and complex sequence of conquest, forced migrations, and regroupings that are known as the *Mfecane* in the Nguni languages. While some chiefdoms were incorporated into the Zulu state, others were destroyed and the survivors driven off as refugees. Some of these refugees reorganized and imitated the impi style of social and military organization. Some segments of the Zulu military system broke away and took up their own course of conquest. Some neighbors of the Zulu borrowed the military system and used it to build a state large enough and strong enough to stand off the Zulu attack. The result was a vast movement of political change and migration spreading outward from Zululand, beginning in the early 1820s and lasting into the second half of the nineteenth century.

Neither Shaka's Zulu state nor any of the other new states founded in the course of the *Mfecane* were secondary empires in the ordinary sense of the term. Their military success, however, depended on a similar monopoly over a military innovation. Once the new tactic was well known in the vicinity of Zululand, it was no longer the guaranteed key to success on the battlefield. This in itself

tended to push offshoots of the *Mfecane* farther and farther from the Nguni homeland. As they moved, social
institutions changed and adapted to new situations, but
the incorporative feature of the age-grade regiment, cou-
pled with the practice of rewarding successful warriors
with wives, made it possible for the moving Nguni not
merely to conquer but also to absorb some of the conquered populations. Once embarked on the course of continuous migration and conquest, the emigrant Nguni found
themselves with a built-in dynamic that drove them to still
further conquest and still further movement.

Sooner or later, however, the offshoots of the *Mfecane*
did settle down. The states they founded, and the states
that were founded by others in defense against the
Mfecane, gave a new shape to the political geography of
southern Africa. Several Nguni groups moved across the
Drakensbergs, where they completely disrupted the Sotho
chiefdoms on the high veld, in the present-day Transvaal
and Orange Free State. Some Sotho, however, regrouped
under the leadership of Moshweshwe to found the new
state of Lesotho, which was able to maintain its identity
(if not its original frontiers) right through the colonial
period to ultimate independence. Other Sotho adopted the
Zulu military system and set off on their own conquests;
one such group, the Makololo, ended as rulers of Barot-
seland in present-day western Zambia. To the north of
Zululand, the Swazi also adopted the military innovation
in self-defense and established the state that became
Swaziland, but other Nguni offshoots went still farther
north—one to found the empire of Gaza to the north of
Swaziland, another settling in present-day Zimbabwe,
where they founded Matabeleland, still others north across
the Zambezi Valley, destroying the remnants of Mwenemutapa and the Portuguese sphere of influence in the

process. By the 1840s and 1850s, some of these northern movements had reached into present-day Malawi and Tanzania, where they broke into six separate "Angoni" kingdoms.

THE BOER SECONDARY EMPIRE

During the 1830s and 1840s, the events of the *Mfecane* intersected with those of a true secondary empire based on European weapons. The origins of this confrontation go back to the mid-seventeenth century, when the Dutch East India Company established a way station at the Cape of Good Hope to serve ships passing between the Netherlands and Southeast Asia. The tip of Africa had a Mediterranean climate and a relatively sparse population of Khoikhoi (formerly Hottentots, though the term is avoided today because of pejorative implications in South African usage). It was an easy environment for Europeans, and a small number of actual immigrants from Europe, perhaps no more than two thousand in all, grew into a white population of ten thousand by the 1770s and forty thousand by 1815. By that time, the whole population of the colony was about twice that size, a quarter being slaves imported from East Africa and Indonesia, and the other quarter the descendants of the native Khoikhoi.

Cape society in the eighteenth century was significantly different from the kind of society that later emerged in South Africa. The Khoikhoi had been more isolated than the Bantu-speaking Africans and hence were more susceptible to European diseases. A series of disastrous epidemics reduced their numbers and broke their political organization, with the result that most of the survivors

were assimilated into white society, accepting inferior
status but adopting Western culture. Imported slaves also
took on much of the culture of their masters, and racial
mixture between the whites, the Khoikhoi, and the slaves
produced the racial group that was to be known later in
South African history as the "Cape colored." By the early
nineteenth century, Cape society was multi-racial, but all
races shared a similar Western culture, spoke a kind of
Dutch ancestral to modern Afrikaans, and practiced the
same brand of Calvinist Christianity.

This settler community expanded geographically during
the course of the eighteenth century, as frontiersmen
moved eastward along the relatively well-watered coastal
strip or took up semi-nomadic pastoralism as trekboers in
the more arid interior. About 1775 they met Bantu-
speaking Negroes, who had been settled for several centuries as far south as the Fish River. With that encounter,
the Afrikaaners faced the Xhosa across a frontier line, and
the Xhosa were too numerous to be easily moved aside.
They traded across that frontier for guns and horses,
which made it possible for them to meet the Europeans
on nearly equal terms in a long series of wars beginning
about 1780 and lasting into the 1830s and beyond. Though
the Europeans pushed forward the frontier of European
control in short stages, a relatively dense African population remained on the land. The easy advance of the trekboers came to an end—at least in that direction.

The pastoral trekboers of the frontier districts were already in chronic conflict with Cape authorities. They resented political domination by the city, but they also
needed metropolitan help to push the frontier line forward against African resistance. These tensions became
still more serious when control of the Cape passed from
Holland to Britain during the Napoleonic Wars. The Brit-

ish, like their Dutch predecessors, wanted to restrict frontier expansion. They also established tighter control of the frontier districts under British officials, who were resented on national grounds and because they occasionally acted to protect the rights of Khoikhoi servants.

By the mid-1830s, frontier resentment was nearing the crisis stage. When Britain emancipated the slaves in all parts of the empire in 1834, it seemed to the Afrikaaners that Britain was determined to overthrow the social patterns of Cape society—based as it was on white supremacy. Then came the *Mfecane*. The Xhosa on the frontier were not directly affected, but word came through from the north that the high veld and central Natal were abandoned by their inhabitants and open to white settlement. With that, trekboers from the eastern Cape formed organized parties of migrants and began crossing the colonial boundaries toward the north. This movement, centering on the decade after 1835, is known as the Great Trek. It was partly an act of rebellion or flight from British rule, partly a search for new land to settle, and partly an effort to reestablish the kind of society the trekboers had come to value—a society where Europeans ruled and other races were kept in "proper" subordination.

The Voortrekkers who left Cape Colony were relatively few in number, but they gained a distinct military advantage from bypassing the Xhosa on the old eastern frontier. The Africans on the high veld were disorganized and scattered by the *Mfecane*. Guns were rare both there and in Natal, and the trekkers were skilled in the tactics of mounted infantry that could concentrate, strike a blow, and then retire. It was therefore comparatively easy to defeat the Zulu and lay claim to the temporarily depopulated lands of central Natal. On the high veld, the Ndebele were also defeated and driven off toward the Limpopo.

Since the British declined to push their authority north of
the Orange River, the trekkers were free to set up two republics on the high veld, though the British did move forward and annex Natal to protect the strategic control of
the sea lanes.

The Great Trek not only led to secondary empire, it
also changed the nature of Afro-European relations in
southern Africa. Where the old Cape Colony had been
culturally Western, both Natal and the Boer republics
remained African in culture. The Europeans were strong
enough to assert their over-all dominance and to seize
part of the land, but they were only a small minority within
the territory they claimed. Most African communities remained intact and self-governing in local affairs for many
decades. In the longer run, some Africans took on aspects
of the Western way of life, but whole communities were
not shattered and assimilated as the Khoikhoi had been
in the eighteenth century. South Africa therefore became
a plural society with African and Western culture existing
side by side.

SECONDARY EMPIRE FROM THE NORTH

In these decades of the *Mfecane* and the Great Trek
in southern Africa, another secondary empire was rising
in the Nilotic sudan. Its origins lay in the Ottoman Empire, which had fallen behind the technological progress
of western Europe. After one sultan had tried unsuccess-
fully to modernize the army, Muhammad Ali, a military
leader in the Ottoman province of Egypt, led a successful
revolt, seized control of the province, proclaimed himself
pasha (or provincial governor), and brought in mercenaries to train a new army in the latest techniques of

European warfare. Though he recognized formal Ottoman sovereignty, Muhammad Ali's military modernization made him virtually independent as ruler of Egypt, and at one point he almost gained control of the whole empire.

As a side line to the Egyptian drive for power in the eastern Mediterranean, Muhammad Ali also turned south toward the Nilotic sudan. The most important state on the Nile beyond the Sahara was the sultanate of Funj, founded in the fifteenth century by Negro rulers from the south; to its west lay Kordofan, a province of the larger state of Darfur. Neither Darfur nor Funj was a match for the modernized Egyptian army. Both were easily conquered in 1821. Funj and Kordofan were annexed to become the nucleus of a sub-Saharan secondary empire. Over the next half century, Egyptian forces using Western methods, often under the command of Western mercenaries, gradually extended the size of Egypt's empire. They established a measure of control over the Arab and Beja nomads of the desert, pushed down the Red Sea as far as Massawa in present-day Ethiopia, up the Nile into northern Uganda and a corner of Zaire, and westward into Darfur. They tried and failed in the 1870s to conquer Abyssinia as well, but the Egyptian secondary empire was nevertheless the largest territory under one rule up to this point in African history.

Perhaps because of this vast extent of territory, the administrative structure was always fragile. The Egyptians could profit from borrowed technology to conquer almost anywhere they chose, but they lacked the means to establish effective day-by-day administrative control in the outlying areas. This was especially true in the far south and southwest, where the principal Egyptian interest was the slave trade. Slaves were used in Egypt as domestic servants, occasionally as agricultural workers, but especially as soldiers. Recruitment by purchase was an ancient Turkish military practice which Muhammad Ali retained, even though he turned to Western tactics and weapons. On the fringes of the sudanic empire, therefore, the Egyptian presence was little more than a series of fortified slave-trading posts, and these were often controlled by private merchants who maintained their own armies—in effect, a secondary empire within a secondary empire.

The regime thus suffered from one of the fundamental weaknesses of secondary empires in general—modern weapons gave power, but they gave power indiscriminately. An individual on the fringes, in command of a private army, could easily detach himself from Egyptian power and set out on his own course of empire building. The most spectacular example is that of Rabih Zubayr, who began as a slave trader in the Bahr al-Ghazal region in the 1880s. He then set out with a force armed with modern rifles and marched to the west, fighting and raiding a variety of African states as he moved. By the 1890s he had reached the vicinity of Lake Chad, more than twelve hundred miles from his point of departure. There he destroyed the ancient empire of Bornu and set himself up as ruler of an extensive kingdom until he was finally hunted down and killed by the French in 1900.

By that time the Egyptian empire in the Sudan had itself disappeared—and the process illustrates some of the other peculiarities and weaknesses of secondary empires. Since the ultimate source of their power was in Europe, not in their own technological capacity, the secondary empires were fundamentally unstable—at the mercy of any European state that chose to bring even greater power to bear. In the middle decades of the nineteenth century, however, European states preferred to avoid direct annexation and administration of weaker states overseas. They preferred the kind of indirect control sometimes called "informal empire." The weaker state was allowed to retain its formal sovereignty, but only on condition that it followed certain policies dictated from Europe. Part of the price Egypt paid for its military modernization was an accumulation of debt owed to European bankers. When, in the 1870s, Egypt was unable to repay or meet interest payments, an international commission dominated by France and Britain took control of Egypt, treating the country as though it were a private firm put in receivership. But informal empire was almost as unstable as secondary empire, since the threat of force could easily turn to active intervention. This happened to Egypt in the 1880s, when British troops were called in, and Britain took over effective control of the Egyptian government, even though Egypt continued in theory as an autonomous province of the Ottoman Empire.

When Britain acquired effective control over Egypt in 1882, it also acquired responsibility for Egypt's secondary empire in the sudan, which was just then at the point of collapse. In 1881, only a few months before the British intervention, a religious leader, Sheikh Muhammad 'Ahmad ibn 'Abdallah, declared himself to be the expected Islamic savior, or Mahdi. He rose in revolt against the Egyptian authorities in Khartoum, capitalizing on the unpopular policies of Western officials in Egyptian service and on a variety of other grievances, both secular and religious. By 1885 the revolt had succeeded in capturing Khartoum and the whole core area of the Egyptian sudan. Muhammad 'Ahmad then set up a new Islamic state. For the British in Cairo, this posed a serious problem. It would have been possible to call on enough military power to destroy the new state, but they had come to Egypt to collect old debts, not incur new ones. The caliphate in the sudan was therefore allowed to stand for the time being, and it lasted until 1898, when the British were finally impelled by new considerations to go ahead with the conquest. Meanwhile, the fringe areas of the Egyptian secondary empire fell away into local control.

THE NET OF SECONDARY EMPIRE IN EAST AFRICA

Secondary empire building took a somewhat different form in East Africa. During the eighteenth century, new currents of trade began to move in the East African interior. Direct trade from the coast began to reach inland as far as Lake Victoria in return for ivory and, for the first time, a significant export trade in slaves. The pioneers of these long-distance trade routes were people from the interior, especially the Nyamwezi of central Tanzania, but they were soon joined by Swahili and Arabs from the coast, who pushed their caravans inland after about 1800. The seaborne portion of this growing trade fell more and more under the control of Oman, which had already developed important interests on the East African coast during the eighteenth century. In the early nineteenth century, the Omani were able to take advantage of a British concern to have a strong and friendly maritime power help police the waters of the Persian Gulf and Arabian Sea. Britain was willing to supply financial and technical assistance and to sell modern warships that made Oman the strongest Asian naval power short of Japan. In the 1830s Sultan Seyyid Said moved his capital from Arabia to Zanzibar, and from Zanzibar it was possible to dominate the range of coastal ports from north of Mombasa down to Kilwa.

Zanzibari power was based on exploitation of a commercial system, not merely on British support in becoming a secondary maritime power. The islands of Zanzibar and Pemba were ideally suited for clove plantations, which could be developed with supplies of slave labor drawn from the interior of Africa. Slave caravans could also bring ivory, which found its way into world trade along with the clove crop. Some slaves were also exported to Arabia and the Persian Gulf. To meet increasing demand for ivory and slaves, Zanzibari and Swahili traders from the coast reached further and further into the interior. By 1830 Tabora in west-central Tanzania had become the key Zanzibari trading post in a network that reached on to Ujiji on Lake Tanganyika by 1840, northward into present-day Uganda by the 1850s, and then still farther west across Lake Tanganyika into the whole eastern third of Zaire.

The Zanzibari trade network in the interior of East Africa was a secondary empire, based on their access to the latest European firearms, but it was a special form of secondary empire. Guns were used to protect the trade routes, on occasion to encourage warfare in the interior so as to increase the supply of slaves for sale, but not to establish the rule of Zanzibar over territory or people. Political control was limited to trading-post enclaves. The Zanzibari "empire" was thus a trading-post empire—an economic operation equivalent to the North American or Siberian fur-trade empires of the seventeenth or eighteenth centuries—and it succeeded admirably, from a Zanzibari point of view, until the 1860s.

It was then that Zanzibar began to encounter difficulties with its patron, Great Britain. Having suppressed the slave trade in the Atlantic, the British were anxious to suppress the East African slave trade as well. If Zanzibar acquiesced, it would lose control over the thousands of Zanzibari traders scattered through the interior, since these men

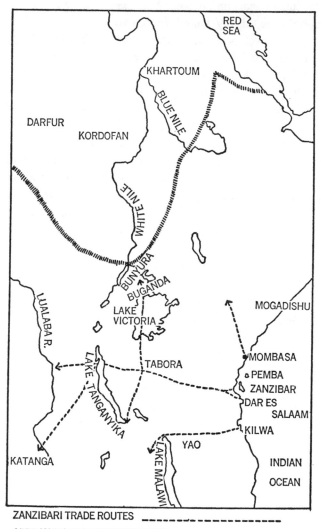

ZANZIBARI TRADE ROUTES   — — — — — — — — —

APPROXIMATE MAXIMUM EXTENT
OF EGYPTIAN PENETRATION

Figure 10. Secondary empires in eastern Africa.

lived by the slave trade and were hardly likely to abandon it until they were forced to do so. But acceptance of British dictates would protect the clove plantations and increase Zanzibari control over the coastal cities. In 1873 Sultan Bargash seized one horn of this dilemma and agreed to an anti-slave-trade treaty. In return, he received British assistance in training a modern army, hence tightening his control over the coastal region.

One result of this decision was to detach the trading-post empire of the interior. The up-country Zanzibari, and any African states that had managed to arm themselves with modern rifles, began to form their own secondary empires over any neighboring territory they could seize. Dozens of new states sprang up in the 1870s and 1880s. To the north of the principal trade route, Buganda and Bunyoro in present-day Uganda began to build secondary empires. (Since Bunyoro had a common frontier with the Egyptian sphere to the north, a nearly continuous band of secondary empires stretched by this time from the Sahara to the Orange River.) In central and western Tanzania two Nyamwezi war lords, Mirambo-ya-Banhu and Myungu-ya-Mawe, each united a large number of previously independent chiefdoms to create two substantial states. Across the mountains, in the upper Congo basin, a Zanzibari trader called Tippu Tib founded a new state in the region west of Lake Tanganyika, while a Nyamwezi trader, Msiri, created still another in Shaba in southern Zaire.

All of these states were short-lived, but they are important examples of the impact of Western technology as it penetrated into Africa well in advance of Western missionaries or Western colonial rulers. It is perhaps futile, but intriguing nonetheless, to speculate on their possible development if they had been left to their own devices for a century or so. Some, like Buganda, had modernizing governments as early as the 1890s and began to adopt elements of Western and Islamic culture and technology. Others might have done the same, and large parts of Africa might possibly have taken a course toward modernization without colonial rule—like Thailand or Japan. As it was, they had no such choice. Within two or at most three decades after many of these states had been founded, the Europeans invaded and annexed east-central Africa to their colonial empires. Even Zanzibar, which chose the road toward modernization under British aegis in 1873, was caught up in the rivalries of the European powers and accepted a British protectorate in 1890.

Chapter Seventeen

COMMERCE AND ISLAM: THE DUAL REVOLUTION IN WEST AFRICA

DURING THE CENTURY FROM ABOUT 1780 TO 1880, West Africa passed through its own period of dramatic change, with a pattern and style that contrast sharply with those of secondary empires to the east. Part of the explanation may be the slave trade itself. Whatever its moral failings, the sale of slaves had introduced firearms on a wide scale—a form of inoculation against the possibility of large-scale secondary-empire building. Instead, West Africa passed through a dual process of very rapid adjustment—readjustment to the end of the slave trade which reached its all-time high and then dropped to nothing during this century, and readjustment to the incomplete introduction of Islam into the savanna belt. As so often in earlier phases of African history, part of the impetus came from the intercommunicating zone outside Africa and part came from the internal change in the special conditions of quasi-isolation.

ISLAMIC REFORM

The introduction of Islam into West Africa was a slow process; one that had already been under way for a thousand years before the revolutionary upheavals of the nineteenth century. The barrier of the Sahara had not

317

prevented the spread of Islam, and it may not have done much to retard its acceptance, but it had a profound influence on the nature and form of Islam in West Africa. In many parts of the world where Islam became the dominant religion, it was introduced by conquest and spread through state influence; but it came to West Africa through the individual efforts of merchants from North Africa who happened to be Muslim and acted as amateur missionaries. For the most part, they were not members of the learned class, the *'ulamā* of the North African cities, and their version of Islam was seldom the Sunni orthodoxy of the urban elite. Instead, they brought in less-accepted doctrines, preserved on the northern fringes of the Sahara.

Over the centuries, these doctrines were modified by new influences, and, in a situation where the institutions of an Islamic state were rarely present to articulate religious life, one of the most important was the religious brotherhoods. The brotherhoods (*turuq,* sing. *tarīqa*) first became important in the eleventh century, with the growing influence of mysticism in Islam. Hundreds of different orders sprang up in the Muslim world, each grouping together followers of a particular religious leader, who accepted his way of achieving a sense of personal communion with God. Only a few *turuq* crossed the Sahara, and the most important was the Qadiriyya, an order founded in eleventh-century Baghdad, and one that was among the most orthodox and broadly tolerant, as well as the largest, in the Islamic world.

The Qadiriyya was especially well suited to the religious condition of West Africa. The mystical element helped to make Islam an effective religion where the state was either unable or unwilling to enforce Muslim law.

In this connection, it is important to remember that Islam is far more secular than Christianity. While both look forward to a life after death, Islam also aims at using the law to improve the moral quality of life on earth. All Muslims have a religious obligation to obey the law and to see that it is properly enforced on others. While some West African states embraced Islam as the official court religion, few if any tried to enforce Islamic law or to insist on the conversion of the whole population. The mass of the people continued to follow one of the traditional religions. Islamic elements could easily creep into traditional religions and commonly did. At the same time, in the absence of a clerical class closely associated with the power of the state, it was equally easy for those who considered themselves good Muslims to incorporate many pre-Islamic practices and beliefs.

This is not to say that well-educated clerics, like the leaders of the Qadiriyya, were always tolerant of unorthodoxy. On the contrary, many were profoundly disturbed by the condition of Islam, but they were rarely able to make their political influence felt. As a minority, even where nominal Muslims might be a majority, they tended to seek safety for themselves within their own community, and orthodoxy through the brotherhoods. At times, it was possible to secure the right of internal self-government for the Muslim community, and Muslim groups with special privileges were to be found up and down the trade routes. The price of encapsulation for self-protection, however, often was to give up the goal of converting the whole world to Islam. But Allah's command to wage holy war, in both a physical and spiritual sense, was not altogether forgotten. It was recalled with ever greater frequency from the seventeenth century on-

ward—not only against genuine pagans, but also against rulers who were only lukewarm in the faith or who tolerated pagan practices.

THE FULBE

These recurrent calls for holy war were more often internal than external. That is, they were a call for revolution, the overthrow of secular rulers, and the substitution of theocratic government. Only after a theocratic state had been created was the call turned outward toward the conquest and forcible conversion of non-Muslim peoples. It may seem surprising, then, that a very high proportion of these *jihads* or holy wars also had contained an ethnic or national element. All of the most prominent leaders of the large revolts were Fulbe (sing. Pulo), a nationality that speaks the Fula language and originated in Futa Toro on the middle Senegal River, though they are found today (as they were in the eighteenth and nineteenth centuries) scattered through the savanna belt of West Africa from Senegal to northern Cameroon.

It is not surprising that the Fulbe were often associated with the cause of Islam. Their homeland is in the far north of the savanna country, where the Senegal River makes a swing to the north near the edge of the desert. The banks of the river have long been capable of supporting an unusually dense population, based on irrigation agriculture. The early Fulbe were therefore among the most northerly of dense black populations in West Africa, and they were among the first to accept Islam. Indeed, one Arabic word for a Negro Muslim is Takrūri, derived from Takrūr, the Arabic word for Futa Toro.

Several theories have been advanced to explain the

Fulbe diaspora which produced their present spread from
one end of West Africa to the other, with descendants of
the emigrant Fulbe far outnumbering those of Futa Toro
itself. The hypothesis that seems most reasonable at the
present state of knowledge is based on the ecological
peculiarities of the Senegal Valley. The people along the
river are sedentary farmers, but the land to the north and
south of the river is well suited to grazing during the rainy
season lasting from June through September. In the distant past, some of the Berber pastoralists of the Sahara
fringe apparently detached themselves from the patterns
of nomadic life and began to return each dry season to
the perennial supply of water along the Senegal. In time,
they intermarried with the sedentary Fulbe, producing an
element in the general Fulbe population that has a partly
European appearance; this physical type is somewhat
more common among the pastoral than among the sedentary Fulbe. All Fulbe nevertheless speak the same language and share most cultural features.

Once the pattern of transhumant pastoralism was established alongside sedentary farming on the riverbanks,
the problem of periodic dry periods remained. If the rains
failed, pastoralists were driven far off to the south in
search of wet-season pastures. At times, they must have
found themselves unable to return for the customary dry
season near the Senegal. As a result, they were forced
to seek a new dry-season base somewhere else, while
continuing the practice of transhumant northward migration each wet season. Given the annual north-south
migration, it was easy to drift eastward as well, over a
period of years. Since the Fulbe were expert cattle keep-
ers, they were usually welcome among sedentary populations, though their semi-nomadic life tended to preserve
much of the original Fulbe language and culture.

A second occupational group among the Fulbe also tended to travel widely. These were the Islamic clerics who had skills as literates, merchants, and makers of charms; these skills made them readily employable elsewhere. They too often settled down away from home to become a permanent community of Muslim teachers living in an alien society. Still other Fulbe of the noble or warrior class also emigrated, perhaps because the pastoralists and clerics had already set the pattern and established emigrant Fulbe communities that might welcome them. By the seventeenth century, political conflict in Futa Toro normally ended in the *fergo* or emigration of the losing faction and its supporters. They often tried to settle somewhere in the vicinity to wait for a change of fortune, but many kept moving and permanently joined other Fulbe communities.

The result was a network of Fulbe scholars in West Africa towns, men who were in touch with one another and shared a common nationality, language, and religion. They were not the only group of wandering scholars, but, unlike the others, they shared the nationality, language, and often the religion of the pastoral Fulbe, who might be a large minority of the rural population almost anywhere in West Africa. Thus, in the event of conflict between the Muslim community and a secular ruler, the Fulbe scholars had the possibility of rallying the Muslim community on religious grounds and their pastoral kinsmen on national grounds to create an alliance that stood some chance of success in battle.

The great religious revolutions of the nineteenth century were based on alliances following this pattern, but the tradition of an Islamic jihad under Fulbe leadership goes back at least as far as the seventeenth century. The first recorded jihad among the Fulbe came in Futa Toro itself in the 1670s, though the leadership in this case was partly Fulbe and partly *zwaya,* clerical nomadic tribes of Berber extraction in southern Mauritania. In this instance, the clerical party managed to hold Futa Toro for only a few years before it was defeated and the secular dynasty returned to office. A second and more successful attempt was made in the 1690s, when a Pulo cleric named Malik Sy founded the almamate of Bundu just beyond Futa's eastern frontier. This was the first of a series of dynasties that proclaimed their theocratic intentions by taking the title of "Almami" in Fula from the Arabic *al-Imam* and denoting religious rather than simply political leadership. The second almamate followed a generation later, when in the 1720s Fulbe in the Futa Jallon highlands started a successful revolution under clerics who were also kinsmen of Malik Sy. In the 1770s the example was followed by a third almamate, this time in Futa Toro.

THE NINETEENTH-CENTURY JIHADS

While the first three almamates set a precedent, they were small kingdoms that were (or soon became) mainly Fulbe. The nineteenth-century jihads, however, led to political structures that rivaled the scale of earlier empires like Mali or Songhai. The earliest in time began in Hausaland of present-day Nigeria, an area that had never before been united as a single state. Between the old centers of political power in Bornu near Lake Chad and Songhai in the Niger Valley lay a region dominated by the Hausa city-states. In each of these, a walled town served as a commercial and political center and ruled over the surrounding countryside. At various times in the

past, either Bornu or Songhai had been able to incorporate some of the Hausa cities and establish its general
hegemony, but neither Bornu nor Songhai was especially
powerful at the beginning of the nineteenth century. The
main centers of power were the Hausa states themselves,
especially Zamfara, Katsina, and Gobir.

Islamic reform was already an issue in several of the
Hausa cities in the last decades of the eighteenth century,
and the spark that set off a general jihad came from Usuman dan Fodio, a Pulo cleric whose activities centered
on Gobir. Many of the clerical class, both Fulbe and non-
Fulbe, shared his distress at the laxity of Hausa rulers,
who claimed to be Muslim but made no effort to enforce
Muslim law; and the clerics were in communication
through the network of Qadiriyya. In 1804 Usuman dan
Fodio called for a holy war against Gobir. Some Hausa
Muslims joined him, but the greater part of his military
strength came from the pastoral Fulbe and the Tuareg
nomads of the desert to the north. By 1808 Usuman dan
Fodio was in command of Gobir.

Even before this success, religious revolt broke out in
other Hausa city-states. In each case, the leadership
tended to be drawn from the clerical Fulbe, though the
rebel alliance differed considerably in different regions.
These additional jihads were not directly controlled by
Usuman dan Fodio, but the leaders recognized his spiritual authority and over-all leadership—largely because of
his immense religious prestige. By the 1830s the rebels
had succeeded in conquering most of what later became
northern Nigeria and northern Cameroon, and the movement spilled over into non-Hausa states like Nupe and
parts of the old Yoruba empire of Oyo. The resultant
empire was organized as a series of emirates, each of

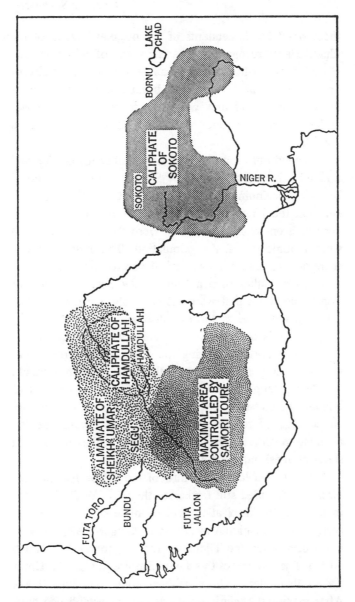

Figure 11. Islamic empires in nineteenth-century West Africa.

them ruled by descendants of the original leaders of the jihad. Each recognized the caliphate of Usuman dan Fodio's heirs, whose capital came to be the new city of Sokoto. Thus the Fulbe clerics became a new ruling class in Hausaland, and they were able to extend their power under British rule and to keep it in the post-colonial period.

A second but separate jihad with similar inspiration and a similar following was led by Sheikh Ahmadu Lobbo of Massina, beginning about 1818. But the region of Massina (in the Niger basin upstream from Timbuktu) was very different from Hausaland. Here the Fulbe herdsmen were a majority of the population. The holy war was therefore an assertion of clerical control over the Fulbe themselves, rather than a Fulbe and clerical conquest of non-Fulbe states that were incompletely Muslim. The result was nevertheless the establishment of a second new caliphate, this one centered on the newly founded city of Hamdullahi and dominating the Niger Valley from Timbuktu on the north to Jenne in the south. Sheikh Ahmadu had less prestige than Usuman dan Fodio in the field of Islamic scholarship, but he achieved more of the declared aims of religious reform, perhaps because he led a single revolt, rather than assuming leadership over a series of quasi-independent revolutions.

A generation later, the third of the major Islamic empires was founded still farther to the west. While it rested in part on the inspiration and example of the predecessors, its organizational base was no longer the Qadiriyya, but a new order, the Tijaniyya, recently founded in North Africa. The founder of this Tijani Empire was Sheikh Umar Tal, a Pulo cleric whose original home was Futa Toro. After making the pilgrimage to Mecca, he established himself in 1839 on the frontier of the old Fulbe and Islamic state of Futa Jallon. From this base he began to recruit followers and import European arms from the coast. By 1848 he was ready to launch his holy war, first pushing northward toward his own homeland in Futa Toro. Though he failed in his effort to seize Futa, he attracted many thousands of followers from among the Futanke, who departed in a great *fergo* or emigration toward the east, thus providing Sheikh Umar with his principal support in the conquest of the pagan states of Kaarta and Segu and the caliphate of Hamdullahi. By the time of Sheikh Umar's death in 1864, he had established the largest of all the new Islamic empires in West Africa.

Like the secondary empires elsewhere on the continent, the Islamic empires were submerged by European conquest at the end of the century. They nevertheless had a profound influence on the history of West Africa. Not only did they remake the political map, they also established Islam more firmly than ever before, setting the stage for its spectacular growth in the twentieth century. In spite of the hiatus of colonial rule, many members of the religious and political elite in West Africa today belong to families which trace their power and position to the place of an ancestor in one of the jihads.

COMMERCIAL REVOLUTION ON THE COAST

In a narrow sense, the commercial revolution was simply the substitution of other products for slaves as Africa's principal export. In the broader context of Atlantic history, however, it was the African manifestation of a much larger and more diverse set of political, economic, and social changes. The American and French revolutions, with an ideology drawn from the rights-of-man philosophy of the Enlightenment, marked the first steps toward the end of slavery in the Americas. The Christian revival in the early nineteenth century brought a new humanitarian concern and a new burst of missionary zeal. The Industrial Revolution produced a stream of new products in search of markets, and at prices that declined steadily. It also brought a new demand for tropical products, especially fats and oils for food, lighting, lubrication, and the manufacture of soap. In military affairs, Europe became more powerful in comparison with non-industrial societies like those of Africa. By 1850 medical discoveries made it safer than ever before for Europeans to visit the African coast; the death rate of Europeans in Africa dropped by 75 percent between the first and second half of the century, even before the true cause of malaria or yellow fever was known. All of these factors were, of course, part of the background for the conquest of Africa after 1880, but Europe had not yet decided to conquer Africa. The dominant European aims in the pre-colonial century were to end the slave trade, to increase "legitimate trade," and to establish European influence through informal empire and conversion to Christianity.

To do any or all of these things required many more Europeans physically present in Africa than the slave trade had ever done. In the French sphere, the old slave-trade posts in Senegal became more substantial bases for the trade in gum from the Sahara and peanuts from the immediate hinterland. In the 1820s the French reestablished an up-river fort at Bakel, reached by the newly invented steamboat. In the 1840s they built new fortified trading posts in Gabon and on the Ivory Coast. The British meanwhile returned to the Gambia, which had been abandoned, and built the new town of Bathurst as a

British commercial enclave at the mouth of the river. Sierra Leone was established in the 1790s as a settlement colony, though the settlers were mainly Negro loyalists displaced by the American Revolution. The Gold Coast trading forts gradually became a center for influence in the hinterland. By mid-century British steamboats were operating on the lower Niger, and British merchants were especially active in the palm oil trade along the coast of present-day Nigeria. Given the disparity of power, a larger European presence meant more frequent European intervention in African affairs, even though actual annexation was limited; and the web of informal influence surrounding the Western enclaves grew broader and tighter as the 1880s approached.

Within Africa, the commercial revolution brought dramatic changes, at least to some regions. The long-distance routes of the slave trade were diverted to internal markets, as the export trade dropped and then disappeared. Since the new "legitimate" exports were harder to transport, their production was concentrated near the coast of the riverside. But in these restricted areas, the peanuts of the Senegambia, timber in Sierra Leone, and palm products from the Gold Coast to Cameroon brought a new level of affluence to the peasantry and to new groups of traders, who had not been in a position to profit from the slave trade. Income from the new commerce also increased progressively through the first two thirds of the century, as the prices paid for European manufactures declined while those of the African exports remained steady or rose slightly. In effect, some of the benefits of European industrialization were passed to African economies through this favorable shift in the terms of trade—even though that shift was to be reversed in the final third of the century.

The new intensity of contact on the African coast brought a conscious effort to change African cultures as well—from the Europeans in the form of Christian missions, and from some Africans who wanted to modernize their societies by borrowing Western technology. Africans near the slave-trade posts had already begun to shift toward some aspects of Western culture, and the pace of change accelerated in the nineteenth century. The "French" traders in the Senegal Valley and southward along the coast of present-day Guinea were actually Africans from Saint-Louis and Gorée, some with one or more European ancestors. The citizens of these Senegalese towns were recognized as French citizens in 1848, and they later sent elected representatives to the National Assembly in Paris. An equivalent group of Anglo-African merchants grew up in Gambia, the Gold Coast ports, Lagos, and Calabar in Nigeria.

Sierra Leone, however, was the principal center of culture change in the British sphere. The colony of black Americans began to receive new settlers after the legal abolition of the slave trade, as British cruisers of the anti-slavery patrol began to unload cargoes of recaptured slaves there. Missionaries paid special attention, because the liberated Africans were associated with their humanitarian campaign against the slave trade. As a result of their proselytizing and educational work, combined with the normal pattern of rapid culture change among those who are uprooted and set down in a strange community, the liberated Africans of many origins rapidly formed a new group known as Creoles, partly African and partly Western in culture.

Since the mountainous peninsula of the original colony was not well suited to agriculture, many Creoles turned to trade with the hinterland, and then to coastal trade by sea as well. Creole merchants from Sierra Leone, especially those of Yoruba origin, began to settle permanently in Lagos and Badagry in Western Nigeria during the 1840s. Others moved into the Yoruba hinterland, and sent for missionaries to join them. By mid-century a Creole Christian clergy had come into existence, and many of the missionaries to Nigeria and elsewhere along the coast were Sierra Leonean. After the British annexation of Lagos in 1861, Creoles served as officials of the British colony.

Other returned slaves from the Americas also brought back Western cultural influences, as they too found it possible to return to Africa. Ex-slaves from the United States began to settle in Liberia in 1822. Ex-slaves from Brazil began to arrive in present-day western Nigeria, Dahomey, and Togo in the 1840s. They were generally less well educated than the Creoles from Sierra Leone, but they became important in commerce and in the skilled trades. By the 1880s they dominated the trade inland from the French post in Dahomey (now the People's Republic of Benin), just as the Creoles dominated that of Lagos. Even today, the older houses in Western Nigeria show the influence of Brazilian architecture, brought back by the returned ex-slaves. Nor was Western influence limited to the European enclaves. Both the Fante states of the Gold Coast and Abeokuta in Nigeria experimented with modernized constitutions under the influence of Western-educated Africans, and other African authorities sometimes sought Western technical assistance.

It is hard to know where this process might have led, if there had been no European conquest. In fact, there *was* a European conquest, and many tendencies of the pre-colonial century were reversed. With the colonial period, Europeans reasserted their authority over the missionary movement. Europeans replaced most of the Africans who had held high posts in government administration, medical services, and the like. The African middle class of traders in Senegal, Sierra Leone, Liberia, and elsewhere found it increasingly hard to compete with large European firms in the export trade to Europe, though Africans continued to fill the role of middlemen between the African producers and the European firms. In the colonial setting, Western impact increased immensely, but with Africans playing a smaller role as responsible participants in the process.

Chapter Eighteen

FORMS AND CONDITIONS OF CONQUEST

IN RETROSPECT, THE EUROPEAN CONQUEST OF AFRICA looks inevitable. It was part of a worldwide pattern of annexation reaching a high-water mark in about 1920. By that time almost the whole world was under the formal or informal control of the European powers, or ruled by overseas Europeans. The non-Western countries that escaped formal annexation did so only by a process of defensive modernization like that of Siam, Turkey, or Japan —or else by the fortuitous circumstance of falling between rival European empires as a buffer zone that was prudently left neutral, though it might be honeycombed by several varieties of "informal empire." Circumstances of this kind preserved the independence of Afghanistan, Iran, China, and Ethiopia. In the perspective of world history, it is hard to imagine a combination of circumstances that would have prevented or delayed the European annexation of Africa.

From an African perspective, however, the final conquest appears both sudden and unexpected. The European powers had been satisfied with slow encroachment here and there during the pre-colonial century. African isolation was coming to an end more rapidly than ever before. In West Africa, modernization within the coastal trading enclaves, and beyond, suggested a satisfactory course and direction of change. Most of the secondary empires in eastern Africa looked substantial enough in the 1870s —substantial enough, that is, to serve Europe's interest in stability and expanding trade, without calling for the expensive commitments to imperial administration. For that matter, Zanzibar, the Boer republics, and the Egyptian sudan were already within the sphere of "informal empire." But then, after 1880, the whole structure came apart, and the Europeans fell into a frenzy of competitive annexation.

THE BACKGROUND

Some causes of the sudden change lay in Europe, others in Africa. Underlying both was the continued progress of European technology. The military hardware that had made possible the earlier secondary empires was replaced by still newer and more effective weapons. By the 1880s machine guns and light artillery capable of firing explosive shells gave the Europeans an incomparable advantage over any African opponent. Medical progress meant that European soldiers and administrators could be sent to tropical Africa without the old constraint of astronomical death rates from disease. Naturally, none of these changes could cause the conquest of Africa, but they slashed the price of any military action a European government might choose to consider; and, in Europe, economic growth made the cost smaller still in terms of available resources.

Other changes in Europe made empire building seem desirable—at least to some. England, with the lion's share of informal empire and African trade, was content with the established pattern of influence. But France, having lost the Franco-Prussian War in 1870–71, had reason

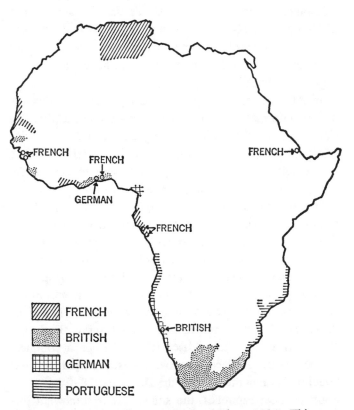

Figure 12. European toeholds in Africa, 1884. This map shows the spheres of influence of the various European powers prior to the Berlin Conference. The dots indicate the footholds or trading stations. With the exception of two French trading stations in Senegal, European influence was entirely restricted to the coastal areas. (Adapted from L. Dudley Stamp, *Africa, A Study in Tropical Development.*)

enough in wounded national pride and the web of international rivalries to seek spectacular victories overseas.
Still other nations, seeing Britain as the economic leader
of Europe and also in possession of the largest overseas
empire, could easily assume that empire brought wealth
—a point that historians now believe to have been true in
some cases, but not in others.

In Africa itself, European advantage lay with the low
cost of informal control over secondary empire. But this
situation could change if secondary empires failed to maintain relatively peaceful control over their territory, hence
the stability Europeans thought necessary to commerce.
Some of the secondary empires began to break up in the
1870s as Zanzibar lost control over the interior. At the
beginning of the 1880s, Egypt became hard to manage,
with the result that Britain took firm control of Cairo,
while Cairo in turn lost its control of Khartoum and the
sub-Saharan secondary empire. In these two instances,
the Europeans found that the wreck of a secondary empire
lay beyond the remedy of informal control. Only recon-
quest and direct administration would serve. Both the
Nilotic sudan and East Africa fell to European conquest
as the pressures of competitive annexation and international rivalry mounted during the 1880s and 1890s.

In the Boer republics, the situation was somewhat different. After an attempted British annexation of Transvaal
in the 1870s, their informal control became very weak,
but that was all they needed until after 1884, when the
gold of the Witwatersrand became known. These deposits
were the largest ever discovered, but to mine ore of this
quality in this location required heavy capital expenditure.
The mining companies that put up the capital were mainly
British, and the companies wanted a more docile govern-

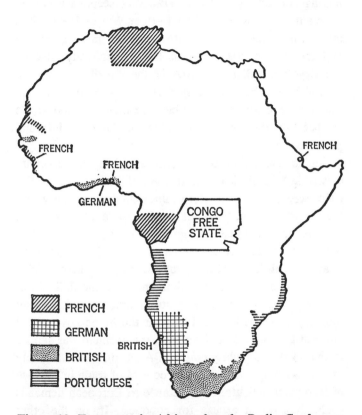

Figure 13. Europeans in Africa after the Berlin Conference, 1885. (Adapted from L. Dudley Stamp, *Africa, A Study in Tropical Development*.)

ment than Transvaal could supply. Tensions between the mining community and the Transvaal secondary empire were a major cause of the Anglo-Boer War of 1899–1902, after which the British finally annexed both Transvaal and the Orange Free State, as they had already annexed the Egyptian sudan and parts of the Zanzibari sphere in East Africa. Thus, the major secondary empires fell to full European control, either because they were too fragile or because they were unwilling to bow to informal pressure.

Similar temptation to change informal to formal empire existed in West Africa as well. Central governments in Europe were often reluctant to annex African territory, but the Europeans on the spot in the trade enclaves were tempted to use force whenever they came into conflict with weak or recalcitrant African states. They saw their relations with local African authorities as so many diplomatic problems. Whenever diplomacy became difficult, as it often did across lines of cultural difference, it was all too easy to shoot first and consult the home government afterward. From the African side, the problem was similar to that of the secondary empires. A strong state was likely to use its strength to protect its control of trade in the face of European pressure; its resistance to European demands could thus be an excuse for conquest. If, on the other hand, it was weak, unable to maintain peace and order or to keep open the flow of trade, that too could be an excuse for European conquest. The line between these two dangers was very thin indeed. A halting encroachment had been spreading outward from the British and French trade enclaves for some decades before 1880, but in the next two decades encroachment turned to conscious conquest sanctioned by the home government.

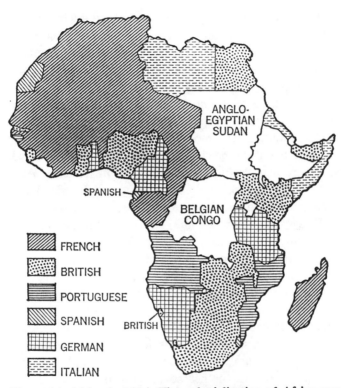

Figure 14. Africa in 1914. The colonialization of Africa was complete—the four South African colonies had united to form the Union; the Congo Free State had been annexed to the Belgian Crown; the Anglo-Egyptian Sudan was well established as a condominium; the French had established themselves in Morocco, the Italians in Libya, and the British protectorate of Egypt was declared. Subsequent changes, until 1957 with Ghana's independence, were in boundaries or in occupying power.

The first round of competitive annexations in western
Africa was touched off by a series of French moves in
1879–82—a projected railroad inland from the upper
Senegal into the empire founded by Sheikh Umar, seizure
of new trading posts along the Gulf of Guinea, and some
territorial annexations north of the lower Congo. Diplomatic historians still dispute among themselves as to which
of these moves was most important in alarming other
powers, but the crucial fact is that they were alarmed.
Germany and Portugal joined France in annexing African territory for fear of being left out, and Britain shifted
from informal to formal control for the same reason.

From that point on, the European annexation took
place on two separate spheres—one in Europe, and one in
Africa. In Europe, competitive annexation led to a series
of diplomatic crises. After each one, the powers bargained
and agreed among themselves, drew lines on maps indicating what territory each should be allowed to conquer,
and then settled down to prepare their bargaining position
for the next crisis a few years later. Looking back, this
whole process has a ring of unreality, as diplomats met
and assigned one another sovereignty over peoples they
had barely heard of, most of whom had never seen a European. But it was nonetheless important for the future
of Africa. The lines drawn on maps in the European capitals became the boundaries of the European colonies, and
these boundaries in turn became the frontiers of modern
African states.

This map work was mainly completed between 1882
and 1902, while the actual conquest took place in Africa
itself. During the first phase, the Europeans marched small

armies here and there to establish their claims. They also fought wars against major African states, and in some cases the conquest was drawn out over a period of years. But military victory was only the first step toward creating a colony. Administrations capable of governing followed later, and their main framework was barely completed on the eve of the First World War. Several of the more isolated African states were not conquered until the 1920s, and a few fringe areas were left until the 1930s.

A NEW GENERATION OF SECONDARY EMPIRES

While most of the first generation of secondary empires collapsed faster than African states with a long-standing tradition of loyalty and support, a new group came into existence during the period of conquest itself. One of these was the Congo Independent State. This was the private creation of King Leopold of Belgium, who began by organizing an "association" which was actually a regular business firm in the European tradition of corporate enterprise. In Africa, the association began by assuming the powers ordinarily held by a sovereign state. It conquered a part of the Congo basin and succeeded in getting the European powers to recognize its sovereignty. This late-blooming secondary empire lasted from 1884 to 1908, when the Belgian government took it over as an ordinary European colony.

Liberia also acquired most of its present territory during the period of the European conquests. The Americo-Liberian settlers had already gained recognition of their independent status in the middle of the nineteenth century. As the Europeans advanced into the interior, they too advanced into their own hinterland, conquering the indigenous peoples. The result was a secondary empire, dominated by settlers from America and their descendants, though often under a measure of informal control by the government of the United States. From the point of view of local Africans, the result was hardly different from conquest by Europeans, but Liberia continued to be marked on the maps as "independent" rather than "colonial."

The only traditional African state to survive the general conquest was Ethiopia. The Christian kingdom of Abyssinia had the good fortune to be located at a strategic intersection of imperial rivalries between Britain, France, and Italy—with the natural protection of mountain barriers as well. It also had an especially able leader in Menelik, who ruled from 1889 to 1913 and was able to manipulate international rivalries in the lower Red Sea and Nile Valley in order to get a supply of modern arms from France. With these, he defeated an Italian invasion in 1896 and went on to conquer the neighboring peoples in the Ethiopian highlands to create the present-day empire of Ethiopia. Like Liberia, this was not merely an African state that kept itself free of European control; it was also a secondary empire built by conquest and maintained by the dominance of the Christian Amhara from the old core area. Though Ethiopia passed through a phase of Italian occupation from 1935 to 1941, that period was too short to be truly comparable to the colonial experience in other parts of Africa.

A final exception to the usual pattern of conquest and colonization is found in southern Africa. The British victory in the Anglo-Boer War was a clear case of a secondary empire defeated by a European power, but the aftermath of the war was different. Within a few years, the British granted the right of self-government to the white minority in the Union of South Africa, which included former Boer republics. This move was partly an effort to conciliate the defeated Boers; the exclusion of non-whites was a concession to the prevalent racism of the times. After the First World War, a similar grant of control over Rhodesian affairs was made to the overseas Europeans in that colony. In 1931 South Africa became independent, though it was still under the firm control of the European minority; and Rhodesian whites declared their own independence from 1965 to 1980, when the country became Zimbabwe.

From one point of view, the triumph of the overseas Europeans in southern Africa could be seen as the final victory of the Boer republics. The Afrikaans-speaking segment of the white population became politically dominant in the Republic of South Africa; and the Republic became the dominant force in southern Africa as a whole. But South Africa of the mid-twentieth century was no longer a secondary empire. As gold mining was followed by industrial development, the power of the overseas Europeans no longer rested simply on their ability to use the output of European industry. With the industrialization of South Africa itself, the dominant minority gained its own source of power to rule over the Africans by force and on a long-term basis, without the fragility that marked the nineteenth-century secondary empires.

FORMS AND CONDITIONS OF CONQUEST

Given the disparity of military power, the Europeans had no great difficulty conquering the areas they had assigned to one another. But conquest was rarely on the basis of "unconditional surrender," giving the victors a free hand to do as they liked. Instead, the pattern of conquest and pacification was enormously complex and variable from one local situation to the next. The form taken by the conquest itself, the implicit or explicit terms of surrender, and fear of rebellion all set limits on the policies the Europeans might follow.

One major determinant was the nature of pre-colonial political structures. Some were as large and powerful as the recently created empire of Sheikh Umar, ruled at the period of the conquest by his son, Ahmadu. It was finally conquered by an African army under French officers, but only after a dozen years of intermittent campaigning. At the other end of the political spectrum were stateless societies, and these too often posed a military problem. With the highest political authority at the level of the village, there was no central army to be defeated once and for all, no central authority to make a surrender agreement. One aspect of this problem is illustrated by the fact that the British ordered no less than five hundred printed treaty forms for use in accepting the surrender of the Ibo in eastern Nigeria. With the Ibo, and with others like the Tiv farther north, the Europeans began by sending punitive expeditions through the country as a way of demonstrating their military power, but this was only a first step. Real "pacification" could come only after they had established a permanent government administration, and this could only be a gradual process. Typically, it was a matter of military patrols and gradually increasing pressure for peaceful submission. In the end, it required some measure of consent on the African side, as individuals and then groups within African society began to see the possibility of using the alien presence for whatever advantage it might offer. The process therefore stretched over a considerable time—at least a decade in most cases, and often two. Chinua Achebe's novel, *Things Fall Apart,* explains the varied Ibo reactions in a single village better than any formal work of history could do.

Other African societies accepted European influence, and then European rule, without the need for military action. In some cases, European rule seemed preferable to other dangers that threatened. The Fante and other peoples on the Gold Coast, for example, were caught between the European forts on the shore and Ashanti power in the hinterland. For them, the first step, as early as the 1820s, was to bring in the British as military allies against Ashanti. This led on to informal influence and a partial protectorate by the 1840s—accepted voluntarily by the African leaders, though always with the threat of Ashanti power in the background. When, in the 1870s, Britain converted the partial protectorate into full control, hardly more than a threat of force was needed to gain acceptance.

Elsewhere, Europeans were sometimes invited in to help an African regime against its internal enemies. In 1858 in the almamate of Bundu (now in eastern Senegal), a certain Bokar Saada Sy was one of a number of contestants in a succession crisis. He entered into a military alliance with the French, on terms that left him as an independent monarch. As a result he won control of Bundu until his death in 1885, and the French made him a *chevalier de la Légion d'honneur* out of gratitude for his cooperative attitude toward their expansion farther to the east. During his long reign, however, he made enemies —some in Bundu itself and even more in the surrounding countries. In 1886–87 a revolt broke out, aimed partly at the almamate and partly at the French on the upper Senegal. It was suppressed by French African troops, but Bundu had now become so dependent on foreign support, it was impossible to avoid a French protectorate on French terms. This meant incorporation in the colony of Senegal, but it was not the end of political power for the ruling family—descended from Malik Sy, who had founded the almamate in the 1690s. They continued to rule Bundu as the appointed local government right through the colonial period and for some years after Senegal had emerged as an independent republic.

Similar cooperation between the Europeans and a particular political faction was an underlying condition of conquest in other African societies as well. One of the best-known examples is Buganda, the African kingdom on the north shore of Lake Victoria, which had turned to secondary-empire building well before the European arrival. In the 1880s and 1890s Buganda was in religious ferment, with competing factions supporting Islam, Protestantism, Catholicism, and the traditional Ganda religion. With British help, the two Christian factions joined together, deposed the king, and seized power for themselves as an oligarchy. In 1900 they made a written agreement with the British, which guaranteed their position within the British colony in return for their support of British rule. Among other things, this agreement turned over more than half of the land in Buganda to less than four thousand of their own followers, and Apolo Kagwa, principal leader of the Protestant faction, received a British knighthood. Buganda was preserved as a semi-autonomous administrative unit within the larger British protectorate of Uganda, and the descendants of the religious revolutionaries of the 1890s became an aristocracy with effective power over local affairs until the end of the colonial period.

Still another African response was the attempt to amalgamate small African states into a unit large enough and powerful enough to stand off the European invaders. Perhaps the most spectacular effort of this kind was that of Samori Ture, a Malinke from what was to become upper French Guinea. He first emerged as a local military and political leader in about 1870. For the first decade or so, he concentrated on building a local power base by conquest. Then, in 1880, he took the title of Almami and proclaimed himself the head of a new religious revolution in the tradition of Sheikh Umar. Some authorities doubt the seriousness of his concern for Islamic reform, but all agree that he was a military genius. His wars against the French invasion began in 1882 and continued with only a few periods of truce until his final defeat and capture in 1898. As he stood off the French to the north and west, gradually giving way as necessary, his armies continued to conquer African territory to the east until, at the end of his career, his empire stretched across the northern Ivory Coast into present-day Ghana.

Unlike most of the earlier West African jihad leaders, Samori Ture mobilized the economic resources of the country in order to buy European weapons from the coast. In this respect, his conquests resembled the pattern of secondary empire, and he also set up his own arms industry on a small scale, gathering together several hundred African smiths for the manufacture of breach-loading rifles and cartridges. Since the guns were all handmade, the total output was low, but the effort itself shows that the European challenge could lead to technological innovation. In this case, however, innovation was not enough to stave off defeat.

But an initial defeat and surrender was not necessarily the end to resistance. Many African societies were caught unprepared for the initial European impact; they had emerged too recently from their previous isolation to put

up more than a brief fight. For that matter, the reality of
the colonial situation was slow to emerge. The initial stage
was often no more than the march of a European-led
force through the country—hardly enough to make ordinary people comprehend the coming trauma of alien rule.
Only when the Europeans began to act, and the reality
of their occupation was brought home, did the Africans
begin to regroup and prepare for a serious fight. In this
case, the "rebellion" that followed was actually the first
serious opposition to conquest.

Organized rebellion in the early stages of colonial rule
could also be interpreted as an attempt at state building,
assembling a larger political unit than any of the pre-
colonial states in the region. In Rhodesia, for example,
the initial conquest was assigned to the British South
Africa Company under a charter that gave it some of
the sovereign powers of the British Crown. The company
first conquered the Shona of eastern Rhodesia in 1890–
91, then turned to the west and defeated the Ndebele of
Matabeleland in 1893-94. The Ndebele themselves were
an offshoot of the *Mfecane*, and they had been chronic
enemies of the Shona up to this time. Nevertheless, in
1896–97, the Ndebele and Shona rose simultaneously
against the whites in a movement that was remarkably
successful in its early stages, and the new unity was based
on religion—just as Samori had used Islam as a unifying
force in West Africa. The Europeans soon brought in
overwhelming force and broke the rebellion, but the
legacy of combined action was passed on to the nationalist
movements that emerged later in the colonial period.

In considering the conditions of conquest in Africa generally, the most obvious point is that Europeans wanted
to gain control as easily and cheaply as possible. It was
therefore in their interest to form alliances with some Afri-

can states, and with some social classes or other grouping within states. When this happened, there had to be a pay-off to those who favored the European occupation. Often, those coopted into the European structure were the local aristocracy, and that aristocracy remained in power to the end of the colonial period—as it did in Zanzibar, Rwanda, Burundi, Buganda, or northern Nigeria. But even where there was no clear and lasting alliance between the Europeans and a local group, the form and conditions of conquest became a key factor in the political and social patterns of the colonial period, and beyond. The legacy of the Rhodesian revolts is a case in point. So too is the carry-over from resistance to nationalism in West Africa, an obvious example being the way Sékou Touré of Guinea made political capital of the fact that he is Samori's grandson.

But the form of conquest made itself felt in ways that were still more subtle and complex—too subtle and too complex to be traced here in detail. Even the indecisive and time-consuming penetration of stateless societies like those of the Tiv or Ibo in Nigeria as reflected in Tiv and Ibo responses during the heyday of colonial rule, and many similar legacies of the conquest period are still important in the social and political patterns of post-colonial Africa.

Chapter Nineteen

THE COLONIAL ERA

IN THE EUROPEANS' RUSH TO ANNEX AS MUCH TERRITORY as possible before some other power beat them to it, they had little opportunity to learn much about Africa—and the cultural arrogance prevalent in the early twentieth century provided little incentive to do so until after they found themselves with the responsibility of running an African empire. Aside from the desire to exploit known mineral deposits, they began with no fixed ideas of what they wanted to do with the colonies, once they had them. This made for an early uncertainty about ultimate objectives, but as the colonial era moved along, a variety of different goals appeared.

Certain aims were universal. First of all, any colonial government had to set up an administration—"to keep the peace," in the phrase of the times. This implied at least a minimal control over the African population—enough to stop local warfare and slave raiding, and to allow free access for missionaries, administrators, and traders. This much was an essential first step, no matter what other policies followed. But administration was expensive, and the first step led automatically to the second—the colonies had to pay their own way. The taxpayers at home were hardly inclined to view empire as a philanthropic enterprise, but making the colonies pay was not an easy

351

matter. The European administration was usually an additional layer of government, above and beyond the existing African authorities, and there was seldom a system of regular taxation that could simply be diverted to the alien government. As a result, some form of economic development had to be fostered, especially a kind that would create taxable income.

THEORIES OF EMPIRE

Beyond this general agreement that they should keep the peace and make the colonies pay their way, Europeans had a wide choice of possible policies. But the choice was limited in practice by the fact that Europe already had a body of theory about the government of non-Western empires. Europeans also had a body of received opinion about the nature of Africa and Africans, largely built up in the nineteenth century and based on pseudo-scientific racism and cultural arrogance. (See Chapter 3 above.) This heritage of ideas helped to confine European attitudes to a limited number of general ways of looking at "the colonial problem."

One tradition carried down from the early nineteenth century can be called "conversionism." It held that the best possible future for Africa, or any other society, was to adopt as much as possible of the European way of life. This implied conversion to Christianity, Western education, Western manners, and in time, a Western political system. Some conversionists had a long-run expectation that a colony sufficiently "advanced" toward "civilization" would become an independent state. Others hoped that it would join the European mother country as a part of "overseas France" or "overseas Portugal." This tradition was weakening in the early decades of the twentieth century, but it still had many followers.

One reason for the weakening of conversionism was the rise of a competing group of ideas that can be labeled "permanent trusteeship" or paternalism. Their point of departure was pseudo-scientific racism, with its view that Africans were permanently inferior to Europeans and could never successfully adopt the "civilization" of Europe. Believers in trusteeship nevertheless regarded Africans as human beings deserving the protection of their "superiors." The best policy for a European empire was therefore to treat them as minors, incapable of running their own affairs, but entitled to the guidance and discipline of those who were wiser than they. The crucial difference between conversionism and this new doctrine was its expectation for the future. Conversionists might advocate guidance and discipline as a step toward full maturity and Westernization, but the new school of trusteeship saw Africans as minors who could never grow up. In this view, it served no purpose to hold out the goal of conversion to "civilization." Racial inferiority placed that goal beyond their reach. Better to let them develop "in their own way," even though one recognized that that way was inferior to the European way.

Conversionism and trusteeship had a certain moral tone in common, and both were used to justify empire as well as directing the course it should follow. A third general category of imperial theory was less concerned with moral principle, and even more rigorous in its insistence on racial inferiority and its attitude of cultural arrogance. This school of thought can be called "racial subordination," though the Afrikaans word, *baasskap* or domination, may be even better in catching the essence. In this view, the best possible future for Africans was neither Westernization nor yet autonomous development, but subordination as servants in a Western society—and permanently so. It began with the underlying belief that anything Africans could develop on their own was not worth having. But as servants of Europeans they would at least enjoy some of the material benefits of industrialization, they would be protected in their weakness, and they would be given the kind of discipline they needed. This view was not very common in government circles, and its greatest following came from the overseas Europeans in South Africa and Rhodesia—to a lesser extent in the Belgian Congo and a still lesser extent in Kenya. It was common enough in Europe, however, though it tended to be muted in public discussion simply because it was open to the charge of self-serving immorality. Even in South Africa, the official defense of racial subordination came to be set in terms of *apartheid* or separate development, which is actually a variant form of permanent trusteeship.

In practice, the clusters of ideas or attitudes identified here as conversionism, trusteeship, and subordination rarely occurred in isolation. An official government policy might be guided by a mixture pulling together separate and even contradictory elements from all three. The administrators who translated policy into practice had their own attitudes, which could easily warp the original intentions beyond recognition. Nevertheless, in tropical Africa the ideas of permanent trusteeship dominated the early colonial period, and they were gradually modified by an increasing element of conversionism, especially in the 1940s and 1950s. In much the same way, racial subordination was dominant at first in southern Africa, changing only gradually to the slightly softer doctrine of permanent trusteeship.

But no colonial system was built on intentions alone; the reality of African experience was bound to be different from European intentions. Administrators went to Africa as adults, already set in the forms of Western culture and prepared to see Africa only in the light of attitudes they brought from home. Africans also saw the colonial situation against a background of African society, culture, and the modes of thought they had learned in childhood. A common humanity and a common experience in the setting of colonial Africa assured that, for some matters, the two evaluations would be complementary; but just as surely historical and cultural differences made them see other matters in quite a different light. Once the first period of conquest and "rebellion" had passed, the great majority of Africans tried to make the best of the situation. But the nature of the colonial experience made it unlikely that they and their rulers could ever see eye to eye on all issues—or even come to a mutual understanding of what the issues were. Communication is likely to be faulty across cultural barriers in any case, and between rulers and ruled, faulty communication is even more common. Major changes took place with a large element of European and African cooperation, but the process was accompanied by a constant suspicion of tyranny, stupidity, and lack of good faith on both sides as things rarely turned out as either group expected. The result was a pattern of "working misunderstanding."

"KEEPING THE PEACE"

One important part of this working misunderstanding was the nature of administration itself. All colonial gov-

ernments had to use some African administrators; there
were simply too few Europeans to do the job by themselves. Whenever possible, they turned to Africans who
were already in authority. Traditional rulers had prestige,
could work through existing habits of obedience, and had
a base in local support. The British in particular made a
virtue of necessity and developed the theory that indirect
rule through the chiefs was the best possible form of
colonial government. The ideal of trusteeship suggested
that it was better to "develop" African institutions than
to import new ones. All the colonial powers therefore
made an effort to promote the study of African societies,
so as to understand their point of departure. They then
tried to modify and reform whenever possible. In some
cases, when the existing political system appeared not
to be suitable, they went so far as to invent new "African"
institutions for local government. Even the French, who
preferred a more direct administration, with authority
from the top and obedience from the bottom, were forced
to depend on African authorities at the village level—and
they often kept the old rulers in office, as they did in
Bundu.

But indirect rule could hardly work as planned. A traditional chief at any level ruled through an intricate balance of political and constitutional forces. The very fact
of his being coopted into the colonial administration upset that balance. If he stuck by the traditional ways, he
might keep his local power base, but he could hardly be
an effective agent for the Europeans. If, on the other
hand, he took the European side, as often happened, he
lost his local following and continued in power only because the Europeans were willing to keep him there.

More important still, the European attitude toward African institutions was highly ambivalent. Few adminis-

trators really believed that the African way was best—
only that it was best for Africans. They therefore sought
to preserve and alter at the same time. While they might
keep African forms of government at the local level, the
colonial governments added new ranges of government
services at the top—veterinary departments, health services, railway departments, labor recruiting bureaus, agricultural services—and these expanded in time to work at
the local level as well. These services had to be staffed
by Africans, at least in part; they needed trained personnel to serve as clerks, typists, medical assistants, and men
to run mimeograph machines. The European commercial firms and mining firms needed similar personnel. As
a result, the alien rulers were forced to introduce at least
some elements of Western education. Missionary societies
were ready to supply it, often with financial support from
the colonial government. Most administrators claimed to
admire "the unspoiled African from the bush" and de-
spised the Western-educated class that began to appear
in the coastal cities. But the "unspoiled African" was
unable to drive a truck or pound a typewriter; he could
therefore find no place in the modernized sector where
the economic and political rewards were greatest.

Africans were also ambivalent in their assessment of
African and Western cultures. They soon learned that
Western education was the gateway to success in colonial
society. One common reaction at the earliest stages of
Western penetration was to reject African culture as much
as possible and imitate the Europeans in everything. But
Africans were rational men, who could see that the West
had not created a perfect society, however useful their
technological advances. Western-educated Africans therefore began to mix their own combinations of traditional
culture and Western learning, varying the combination

according to opportunity and personal preference. One important variable was the amount of education; a man with only a primary education had access to only part of the Western tradition, and thus a limited range of choice. But Africans who took advanced degrees in European universities ended most often with the hope of making Africa modern, yet at the same time preserving the basic traditional values and African identity.

This African ambivalence toward the West was quite different from the Western ambivalence toward Africa. The point of departure was different, and the long-range goals were different, but the "working misunderstanding" contained enough common ground for Africans in the modern and traditional sectors alike to cooperate with the European goal of keeping the peace. As a result, in the realm of politics many of the traditional elite survived the colonial period and emerged with continued power in the era of independence, but always alongside a new elite whose status came from Western education and whose power increased as they took over the administrative positions vacated by the departing Europeans.

"MAKING THE COLONIES PAY"

When colonial rulers thought of economic development, they thought first of government revenue. In the early days of minimal government, revenue came from import duties. Imports in turn depended on having exports that could be sold on the world market. It was only natural for administrators to look for a few commodities that could be sold overseas, rather than considering the general health of the local economy. From their point of view, a general increase in local production and the consumption of locally produced goods was hard to translate into government revenue, while an increase in external trade could be easily taxed. For that matter, external trade might be increased, even if there were no appreciable change in total productivity. Colonial economic thought therefore began with a special emphasis on exports—and all too often it ended there as well.

But economic development rarely went according to plan. The most successful export crops were those the Africans discovered for themselves. That is, African farmers responded on their own initiative to the fact that Europeans were willing to buy at an attractive price. This had happened in the pre-colonial growth of peanut exports from the Senegambia or palm products from the Niger delta. It happened again in the colonial period with the spectacular growth of cocoa farming in the southern Gold Coast. Agriculture departments might push a particular crop for some region of Africa, but African farmers would not respond voluntarily if the economic advantage seemed marginal or uncertain. This fact occasionally led colonial governments to resort to force, laying down quotas for each farmer in cotton or some other crop— quotas with penal sanctions for those who failed to produce. While this system no doubt induced the desired production, the cost of enforcement was often so high that the net return to government was negligible.

Resource endowment was far more important than planning in dictating that some regions would be centers of relative prosperity, while others became economic backwaters. Africa is not a rich continent for agriculture; rainfall is often low and irregular. Production for the market might well be profitable near the easy transportation routes, but a long haul to the coast cut deeply into the price that could be paid to the peasant producer. Export crops therefore tended to be concentrated in the more favored regions. Mineral deposits were even more concentrated, although they were sometimes valuable enough to justify special transportation facilities like the net of railroads that reached to the Witwatersrand at an early date, later to the Zambian copper belt and Katanga.

Another uncontrollable factor was the shifting nature of European demand for particular commodities. The great depression of the 1930s was a special kind of disaster for Africa, since the prices of primary products dropped further and faster than those of manufactured goods. This meant not only a steep drop in production, but also an unfavorable shift in the net barter terms of trade as African producers received less per unit for what they sold and paid more per unit for the imported goods they bought. Other shifts in demand grew out of technological change in Europe. Beginning in the 1890s, the coming of the automobile in the developed world brought a sharp increase in the demand for wild rubber. But high prices also encouraged the development of plantation rubber in Malaya and elsewhere. By the 1920s the price of wild rubber had dropped so low that it was hardly worth gathering except in the most favorable circumstances.

Technological factors were also important in encouraging the economic development of some regions and not others. Africa had a long history as one of the world's main sources of gold, but some forms of gold deposit can be exploited by the new industrial technology, while others cannot. The old gold fields of Bambuk, for example, were widely scattered placer deposits, easily mined by hand. They are still in production, still mined by hand, because modern technology has little or nothing to offer in exploiting deposits of this kind. The South African gold fields, on the other hand, are the largest ever found anywhere, but the ore is poor in terms of gold per ton of rock mined. The mining boom that began in the 1890s and set South Africa on the road to industrialization was therefore made possible by the fortunate coincidence of newly discovered resources at the exact time when techniques for dealing with them became available.

One field in which government policy was crucial in encouraging or discouraging economic growth was railroadization, and later the construction of motor roads. Private capital was available for railroads that led to mineral resources, but not otherwise. Very little private investment of any kind went into tropical Africa during the colonial period, and most railroads were built either with government funds or under government guarantees to the investors. The investors were right in their reluctance. Outside the mining regions, most privately financed railroads failed, and the others ran at a loss. In some cases the planners simply miscalculated. Other lines were built as a form of subsidy to economic development—investment in infrastructure, it would be called today. Still others were built for a variety of political reasons. The Uganda railway from Mombasa to Lake Victoria required a special vote of funds from the British Parliament, justified as a subsidy to "legitimate trade" and also because the cost of holding and administering Uganda without it would have been even greater. The French Congo-Ocean line was even more clearly a political rather than an economic venture. It connected Brazzaville on Stanley Pool with Pointe-Noire on the Atlantic. Since the Belgians had already built a parallel railroad south of the Congo, its only justification was the need felt to keep a vital transportation link entirely within French territory.

Railroad investment, so often political in motivation,

also had political consequences. A railroad bound the hinterland to the coast, and it set up internal lines of circulation for people as well as goods. The Nigerian railroad system, for example, attached the Hausa and Muslim north to the coast by two lines—one through eastern Nigeria and one through the west. These lines helped to bind the country together—in contrast to French West Africa, where each port had a rail line to its own hinterland, but no links to a general rail network. Partly as a result, the internal lines of circulation ran inward from the port towns to the local hinterland, and, in time, each rail terminus became the capital of an independent republic. Even the efforts to join together some of these states, such as in the brief Mali Federation linking Senegal and Mali, were based on the economic and political realities that grew up around the rail line—in this case, the railroad from Dakar east to Bamako on the Niger.

Railroads also multiplied the tendency of other factors (such as resource endowment) to "pile up" economic development in a series of regional centers. These, in turn, drew population from the comparatively undeveloped regions round about. With the railroad finished from Mombasa to Lake Victoria, Uganda farmers became prosperous growing cotton for export, drawing in thousands of migratory workers from Rwanda, which was both overpopulated and hard to reach with cheap transport.

Economic development was not only irregular in spatial distribution, it was also irregular in timing. In spite of the high price some parts of Africa paid in the pain of colonial conquest, the early colonial years, up to the mid-1920s, were a period of economic growth. Growth brought some regions like the cocoa-growing areas of Nigeria and Ghana not only increased gross territorial product, but rising real wages as well. Then, with the beginning of the Great Depression of the 1930s, most of tropical Africa passed into a period of comparative economic stagnation. The colonial powers had all they could do to handle the economic problems at home, and small African entrepreneurs had insufficient resources to do much on their own. Once the post-war crisis had passed, however, sharp recovery set in during the early 1950s and continued well into the 1960s. It was this economic spurt that helped to pave the way for independence and for the great optimism both Africans and foreign observers felt during those years. And it was followed, of course, by the post-independence slump from the mid-1960s to the mid-1980s.

Only South Africa seemed to keep the momentum of the early post-war decades. But South Africa's spectacular growth was only another aspect of lopsided development in sub-Saharan Africa as a whole. It was geographically lopsided, concentrated in the south and elsewhere on favored areas. It was racially lopsided in territories where settlers were present, with incomes very unevenly distributed. It was lopsided in its concentration on production for export, rather than production for local sale. It was technologically lopsided, with some regions and some industries using the most up-to-date processes Western technology could provide, alongside other means of production that were backward and inefficient.

Africa nevertheless altered beyond recognition during the course of the colonial period. Some Africans were better off materially, but the important change was not so much in the size of income; it was the new ways incomes were earned. Migratory labor, or permanent migration into mining towns, river ports, rail junctions, and market centers brought Africans together who had little contact across ethnic lines in pre-colonial Africa. It also

brought them into contact with the fruits of Western technology, Western culture, and Western education. Many
were converted to one of the outside religions—Christianity or Islam. They formed new kinds of associations
in the towns, and new associations linking the new townsmen with their kin who remained in the villages. There
was, in short, a new intensity of intercommunication both
within Africa and between Africans and the West. One
inevitable result was to increase the problems of personal
adjustment to an unfamiliar and rapidly changing world.
Another was an increase in social friction between ethnic
groups caught in new and highly competitive situations.
Still another result was to channel intercommunication
within the boundaries of a colonial territory. As colonial
frontiers created new barriers, colonial transportation and
communication networks erased some of the old ones.
In time, this opened the possibility of colony-wide political organization which could give effective voice to a
new demand for independence.

Chapter Twenty

TOWARD INDEPENDENCE

JUST AS THE CONQUEST OF AFRICA WAS PART OF A worldwide movement of imperial expansion, the coming of independence was part of a worldwide liquidation of European empires. It can be fully understood only in the perspective of world history, which would take account of events as diverse and distant as the modernization of Japan, the success of the Communist revolution in China, and the physical and emotional state of Europe in the aftermath of the Second World War. Whatever the causes, near and remote, most of the non-Western world achieved its independence in the very short period of only two decades, from 1945 to 1965. For Africa, the process reached its climax in 1960, and coming of independence in sub-Saharan Africa was more peaceful and orderly than in any other major region of the world.

But the success story of the independence movement should not obscure the other side of the picture. Southern Africa was not included. Angola and Mozambique continued as Portuguese colonies until 1976. The white-dominated government of Rhodesia refused "decolonization" and remained under white domination until 1980. After that, however, South Africa (with its client state, Namibia) has alone held out as an independent country under the strict control of the white minority.

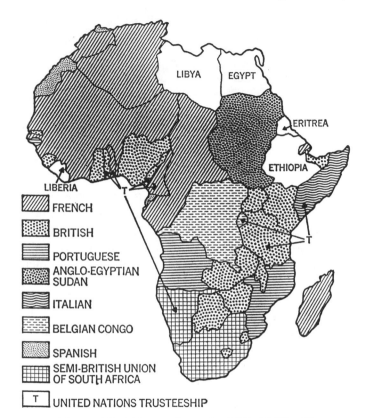

Figure 15. Africa at the end of World War II.

NATIONALISM

Most accounts of the African independence movement deal with the force of nationalism, while far too many accounts of post-independent Africa emphasize the importance of "Tribalism" as a disruptive force. "Nationalism" is ambiguous in itself. "Tribalism" is not only ambiguous but loaded with pejorative overtones drawn by the myth of a savage Africa. (See Chapter 1 above.)

The term "nationalism" applied to African affairs has a similar history. Ever since the late 1940s, political commentators have written about the rise of "nationalism"—meaning resistance and protest movements against colonial rule, and political parties demanding independence for each colony. The term was borrowed from European history, and especially from the nineteenth-century political movements, in which people with a common culture, common territory, language, and historical tradition claimed to be a nation—and claimed for that nation the right of self-determination, the right to join together under an independent state. At times, as with Germany and Italy, the aim was to bring together a group of small states to form a larger unit with borders approximating those of the "nation." With Yugoslavia and Poland, it was a matter of separating out and joining together bits and pieces from larger multi-national states. In any event, the sense of nationhood with its emphasis on a pre-existing unity was the essence of nationalism.

African "nationalism" had no such emphasis. Most pre-colonial African states had long since been swallowed up in the political structures of the European colonies, and there was remarkably little disposition to rejuvenate them. Only a few—such as Swaziland, Lesotho, Rwanda, and Burundi—kept their territorial identity during the colonial period and reemerged as independent states. Elsewhere, the African leaders in the independence movement claimed independence, but not on the basis of national self-determination. In a sense, theirs was the reverse of European nationalism; Europeans began with the nation, which they wanted to become an independent state. The

Africans had states—the existing colonial units through
which the Europeans ruled—and they wanted independence for these units, *so that* they could become nations.

But the goal of nation building was not really central
to their purposes. First and foremost, they were against
alien rule, against European arrogance, against European
racism that branded them as inferior. Insofar as nationhood was a mark of equal status with other nations in
the world, they were for it. Insofar as a feeling of patriotism or nationality could help persuade individuals to
make sacrifices for a common cause, this too was useful.
But these were merely means to other ends—to recognized
equality of status, to independence, to modernization and
economic development. Of these, the keys were equality
and modernity, not nationality. The term "nationalism"
has nevertheless been used to describe the African independence movement far too long to make it worth while
trying to invent a better one. But it remains important
to recognize that nationalism in Africa means something
quite different from nationalism in Europe.

Given the colonial experience, it is remarkable how
little anti-European sentiment there was in African nationalism. The nationalists wanted to get rid of European
rulers, of course, but the ambivalence toward European
culture that first emerged in the "working misunderstanding" of the colonial period still continued. Europe remained a model of some of the things an independent
state might aspire to. Especially those Africans who were
educated abroad wanted the better health services, better
education, and higher incomes for their own people. They
preferred most aspects of African culture, and they
wanted a society that would still be African, but technologically modern.

This is not to say that the European sense of loyalty

to an ancient national identity was absent in Africa. Many African kingdoms had the same kind of loyalties that go with the European type of nationalism—loyalties based on common historical traditions, language, and way of life. Ashanti was certainly a nation in this sense; so was the kingdom of Kongo; so too was Buganda. Yet these nations were incorporated in the new independent states without a serious struggle, and this fact itself seems to call for explanation.

It is clear that a sense of loyalty to pre-colonial nations did not disappear, or even weaken markedly, when faced by new claims of loyalty to the post-colonial African states. The older of these loyalties, often and wrongly called "tribalism," still plays an important role in African politics. But independence was nevertheless claimed for the territory marked off by the boundaries of each colony, not for the territory of a pre-colonial state. (The only exception is Somalia, where a sense of Somali nationality prompted the demand that all Somali people be brought within a single state.) Elsewhere, the colonial territories each received independence as a unit, and they survived as a unit through the first decade of independence. Attempted secessions, of Katanga from the ex-Belgian Congo and of Biafra from Nigeria, were both defeated by force of arms.

Part of the explanation lies in the fact that it is easy psychologically for an individual to have two simultaneous national loyalties, as long as they are not in direct conflict. Americans of Irish descent have no trouble taking pride in their Irishness, while remaining patriotic Americans. It is just as easy to combine a dual loyalty to Ashanti and to Ghana, and the desire for modernization favors the new state against the old nationality. The post-colonial

A.L. Adu, an African administrator toward the end of British rule in the Gold Coast.

states have the advantage of being larger than the pre-
colonial, thus more viable in the modern world. They
have a second advantage of a modern administrative
structure as a legacy from the colonial period.

RESISTANCE AND PROTEST

The movement for African independence began far
back in the colonial period. In a sense, it began with primary resistance to European conquest on the part of African states—or even more clearly in the several attempts
to pull together larger political units in order to oppose
the Europeans. But primary resistance failed, the early
revolts were defeated, and the traditional framework of
government either disappeared from the scene or was
coopted into the lower reaches of the European administration.

Ordinary people then found themselves face to face
with incomprehensible changes. Once physical resistance
had failed, it was only natural to seek supernatural help.
Some found it through a traditional African religion, some
through Islam, which made enormous gains in partly
Muslim areas during the early colonial period, and some
turned to Christianity, the religion of the conquerors
themselves. The search for comprehension and consola-
tion through religion was usually an alternative to protest,
not a form of protest, but resistance to the Europeans
could also be expressed through religious organization.
Part of the popularity of Islam lay in the fact that it offered itself as a modern religion, and thus a useful vehicle
for religious change that was not closely associated with
the colonial governments. Many of those who adopted
Christianity protested against European control over the

churches by breaking away and setting up their own African church. Literally thousands of new churches were formed in this way, more than two thousand in South Africa alone.

Some of these religious movements hoped for supernatural aid in handling earthly problems, while others placed their main hope in a better life after death; but all three religious alternatives—traditional Africa, Muslim, and Christian—might also turn millenarian. The idea of a millennium, a last judgment after a thousand years, is specifically Christian, but present usage classifies any system of religious belief as millennial if it predicts drastic measures of divine intervention in the world, and in the relatively near future. A predicted millennium is usually not a sign of Christian influence, but rather of widespread loss of hope and understanding in the face of cataclysmic change. The reaction of the Xhosa in 1856, after repeated defeats in their frontier wars against the advancing whites from the Cape Colony, is a classic case. It followed the typical pattern of such movements. They usually require two people to get them started—some sort of visionary or prophet, and an impresario or organizer. In this case, the vision was that of a young girl, interpreted by an important religious leader as a command from the gods to kill all the cattle, destroy all grain, and sow none for the coming season. The prophecy held that, if this were done, new cattle and grain would appear, ancient heroes would rise from the dead, and the whites would be swept into the sea. The Xhosa killed more than 100,000 cattle, burned their grain, and waited for "the day"; but the millennium failed to come. Tens of thousands of people died of starvation. Though the Xhosa cattle killing was the most spectacular event of its kind, it was to be repeated again and again on a smaller scale with the same elements—the prophecy, the call for sacrifice in expectation of the millennium, and then disappointment.

Quite different reactions to conquest appeared among the more sophisticated Africans, especially those of the former trade enclaves along the west coast. From Saint-Louis-du-Sénégal to Calabar in eastern Nigeria, many of the old port towns were allowed representative government at the municipal level. Africans also held a few seats on legislative councils in many of the colonies. The port towns of Senegal began sending a representative to the National Assembly in Paris from 1870 onward, and Blaise Diagne was elected in 1914 as the first African representative. These channels of legal representation were also supplemented by organized pressure groups. The Western-educated elite of the Gold Coast joined with some of the traditional chiefs to form the Aborigines Rights Protection Society, and the ARPS could sometimes influence the colonial government. On occasion it bypassed the colonial governor and took its case directly to the Colonial Office in London.

Other protest took the form of spontaneous or nearly spontaneous riots against specific grievances, and these could sometimes spread into open rebellion over a wide region. In 1927–30, protest against forced labor and forced cotton planting among the Gbaya of the present-day Central Africa Republic became a general insurrection. The French lost control of the rebel territory for months or years and were finally forced to repeat the conquest at great expense. Or, again, at the same period in eastern Nigeria, rebellion came as a result of cross-cultural misunderstanding. The British had recently introduced direct taxation in the form of a head tax payable by every adult male. The rumor began to circulate that women were to be taxed as well. This was a serious threat to the Ibo, since many believed that counting people could cause their death. They also took the tax to be a form of tribute, symbolic of servile status. As the rumor spread, bands of women began attacking colonial courts and administrative offices and sacking European-owned shops. The movement spread over a considerable area and was only suppressed by force after several months, with some fifty-five women killed by the military.

Neither appeal to the supernatural, the polite protests of the educated elite, nor sporadic rioting and local rebellion were strictly speaking a "nationalist" movement in either the African or European sense of the term. They could be effective in forcing the Europeans to modify their policies; but the true nationalist movement that emerged after the Second World War was not aimed at influencing policy—it wanted to capture the colonial administration itself. Its most effective weapon was the Western-style political party, organized on a colony-wide basis by members of the Western-educated elite, with mass participation at the local level. No movement of this kind existed in tropical Africa before 1945, in spite of certain forcrunners like the West African National Congress of the 1920s, which was still limited to elite groups.

The first example of a political party with a mass following came instead from South Africa. There young men, some of whom had been abroad for education, had founded the forerunner of the African National Congress in 1912. Though the ANC did not aim immediately for a mass following, it was soon paralleled by the Industrial and Commercial Workers Union of Africa, founded in 1919 by Clements Kadalie as a dock workers' union. In a short time, it spread to other trades and became a mass party, even though Africans had no effective means of representation through an electoral process. By 1928 Kadalie had enrolled about 250,000 members; but the authorities simply disregarded peaceful protest, and the white trade unions refused to cooperate with ICWU in strike action. The alternatives were violent revolution or a general strike by all African workers, but Kadalie held back from these stronger measures. The membership gradually became disillusioned and drifted away during the early years of the Great Depression. The lesson then and since in the South African setting is that mass organization and peaceful protest are not enough where the government has a strong military position and the intention to maintain white domination at any cost.

THE COMING OF INDEPENDENCE

The independence movement in tropical Africa developed in a broader world setting. Demands for independence were especially strong from Asia. The United States had promised independence for the Philippines before the war, and it made good on the promise in 1945. A British plan for Indian independence had been built into the structure of Indian government since 1935. In 1947, Britain came through with independence for India (which soon split into India and Pakistan).

In Southeast Asia, the struggle was tougher. The Dutch set out in 1945 to reconquer Java, where the nationalists had seized control on the surrender of Japan. They won, but the pressure of world opinion led them to grant independence to Indonesia in 1949. The French had also been dispossessed by a Japanese occupation of

Indochina, but they reconquered southern Vietnam. When the Vietnamese forced the surrender of a large French army at Dien Bien Phu in 1954, they gave up and recognized the independence of a puppet ruler in the south and the de facto independence of the north.

The lesson was clear for African nationalists and colonial governors alike; colonies could only be held by force in the face of a resolute local opposition. In Africa as well, an insurrection broke out in Algeria in 1945, modelled on the French resistance to the Nazis in Europe. It failed, but the French counter-measures killed some five to ten thousand Algerians. Another insurrection struck in Madagascar in 1947, and again the French retaliated with wholesale repression that killed an estimated fifty to sixty thousand Malagasy.

The independence movement elsewhere in Africa speeded up immediately after the Second World War. Wartime dislocation and shortages increased people's dissatisfaction. A new generation of Africans had gone overseas for education in the 1930s and now began to return, more militant than the older leadership and determined to build mass parties. The colonial powers also began to change their own policies. France liberalized the forms of colonial government in 1946, and the British began to introduce new constitutions that gave a larger voice to elected African representatives in each colony. Between 1944 and 1948 the first parties with mass support began to emerge—the National Council of Nigeria and the Cameroons, the Convention People's Party in the Gold Coast, the Rassemblement Démocratique Africaine in French West Africa.

As African politicians began to increase their pressure for greater self-government, the colonial powers began to retreat, first in West Africa, then elsewhere. For the

British, the crucial decision was reached before 1951. In that year, Kwame Nkrumah and the CPP won an election, though he was in jail for sedition at the time. The governor freed him and installed him in office as premier under a new constitution that gave broad powers of self-government to an elected legislature. The very act of introducing a constitution of this kind had implied British willingness to move toward self-government and then to independence. The acceptance of Nkrumah's election in 1951 meant that independence would come sooner rather than later. After that, it was only a matter of time and arrangements, so far as the West African colonies were concerned.

In British eastern and central Africa, the situation was different because British settlers were more numerous there. At first, through the 1950s, the British experimented with a constitutional expedient called "multiracialism," the practice of giving so many seats in the legislature to each separate racial group rather than following the rule of one-man-one-vote. African pressure for one-man-one-vote increased through the 1950s, however, and Britain finally agreed in 1958 to grant independence on this basis. The one exception was Rhodesia, where the legislature was controlled by whites and already had powers of self-government. In the face of British reluctance to grant independence without effective African representation, the Rhodesian whites declared their own independence in 1965 and set out down the road toward racial domination of the South African type.

The French decision to decolonize had a different timing and intent, but it produced the same result. The colonial reforms of 1946 increased the number of African representatives in the National Assembly of France itself. By 1956 it looked as though the French African colonies

might be willing to accept self-government without independence. A new constitutional reform, called the *loi-
cadre,* or "framework act," was piloted through the
French Assembly by Félix Houphouët-Boigny, one of the
founders of the RDA. In 1958, however, the French army
revolted, overthrew the Fourth Republic, and recalled
General Charles de Gaulle as president. As one of his
first acts in office, De Gaulle decided to give the African
colonies a choice between immediate independence—and
an end to all French aid—or continuing with France under
the *loi-cadre.* Only Guinea voted to quit at that point, but
the pace of independence elsewhere in Africa was too
strong for the French to resist. They came to realize that
refusal to grant independence, once self-government had
already been granted, would only deprive them of influence in their ex-colonies. By 1960 the remaining French
colonies in sub-Saharan Africa, with the single exception
of the trade enclave of Djibuti on the Red Sea, had opted
for independence; and even Djibuti became independent
in 1977.

The Belgians followed a somewhat different policy toward the Congo in the first years after the war. They
hoped to isolate the colony from the nationalist virus
by rigid controls. About 1955, however, they came to
realize that this policy was not working. The government
therefore reversed itself on racial discrimination, introduced elections and higher education, and began to
prepare for eventual independence. But the rise of nationalism had already caught them off guard. By 1960
it was clear that independence would have to be granted
immediately, or else they would face an expensive and
futile war of liberation. But independence in the summer
of 1960 was followed by a mutiny in the Congolese army
and several years of disorder before the country was

brought back under the control of a stable, if autocratic, government.

By the early 1960s, the wave of independence had advanced east and south across Africa, till it ended at the frontiers of Angola, Rhodesia, and Mozambique. There it stopped, for a decade or more, as the Portuguese and the dominant whites in Rhodesia and South Africa determined to stand firm and fight if necessary. Guerrilla movements began early—from 1961 in Angola and 1964 in Mozambique. They were not strong enough to win immediately, but they were strong enough to demonstrate the high cost of empire. In 1974, the army in Portugal revolted and overthrew the long-standing Portuguese dictatorship. In 1975, Portugal granted independence to its mainland African colonies, Angola, Mozambique, and Guinea-Bissau.

This shift was crucial for Rhodesia as well. It had long frontiers, hard to protect, on three sides. In 1976, two important guerrilla movements began operations against the white government. Britain took a hand in trying to work out a settlement that would provide independence along with security for the whites—who had, after all, been legally in rebellion against Britain itself since 1965. In 1979, the contenders reached an agreement, held an election, and, in 1980, Rhodesia became independent as Zimbabwe under the Presidency of Robert Mugabe.

Once again, the limits of African independence seemed to have been reached. South Africa refused to grant independence to Namibia, as the United Nations ordered. In South Africa, after serious riots in Soweto in 1976, internal resistance to apartheid became steadily stronger, along with external pressures from the world community. South Africa, however, still had the strongest military force in Africa and was willing to use it not only internally but in armed raids against its neighbors. Whatever the outcome, peaceful decolonization, often achieved elsewhere in Africa with good will on both sides, reached its limits in the mid-1960s. What has been won since then has been won by force, and the prospect of a peaceful solution in South Africa is dim indeed.

Part Four

EPILOGUE

Chapter Twenty-one

AFRICA SINCE INDEPENDENCE

THE UNDERLYING PATTERNS OF AFRICAN CULTURE
and the African past are a necessary guide to understanding the African present and future—that has been
the primary premise of this book. We have made no
effort to analyze the contemporary scene—many other
books make that their specific task. In this final chapter,
however, significant tendencies of the past quarter-
century must be brought together if we are to see some of
the ways the present is growing out of the older culture
and history. It is especially important to highlight longer-
run trends that are not obvious in the daily press.

One of the most obvious trends is the shift in attitudes
about Africa's possible future. In the late 1950s and early
1960s, Africans were immensely optimistic about what
they could accomplish once the incubus of colonial rule
had been removed. One of us recalls meeting an
automobile dealer in a provincial Nigerian city in 1955.
After hearing our favorable reactions to Nigeria's recent
achievements, he said, "But you came too soon. If you
had only waited five years, you'd *really* see something!"

Africans were not alone in the optimism. Western
observors, and especially the professional Africanists,
had first-hand evidence of the important economic and
political advance over the past decade or so. By the early
1960s, to be sure, cracks had already began to appear in

both the Francophone republicanism and the Westminster model of national politics, but some slips along the way were to be expected.

A quarter-century later, both Africans and afrophile observers see another set of evidence and another set of recent trends in whatever barometers we have for measuring Africa's general health and well-being. Where we once saw a track-record of recent improvement, in the late 1980s we see a record of economic stagnation. Where we once had high hopes for a democratic future, those hopes now seem to be confined to small countries like the Gambia, or to Mauritius, an offshore island. Réunion is another exception, but it has become a *départment* of France, even though it lies between Mauritius and Madagascar (both members of the Organization of African Unity).

MODERNIZATION AND NATION-BUILDING

One of Africa's fundamental problems has to do with its reaction to "modernization"—a term used here simply to mean getting the benefits of industrialization for African use. African leaders have sought these benefits—though the extent of economic development over the past quarter century is not a true measure of the effort. They use air-conditioned cars, have their offices in skyscrapers, and all too often they keep their spare cash in Swiss bank accounts. Even from the fundamentalist mosques, the call for prayer comes from a public address system in the mosque tower. But the tools of industrial technology can mask the cultural reality, and African leaders do not want to copy everything the West has to offer.

They also appeal to values of an African past. Leopold

Senghor of Senegal wrote about *negritude* as an abstract
quality that permeates African thought, art, and
achievement. But he wrote in superb French, not in Serer,
his home language. Kwame Nkrumah of Ghana also had
a lot to say—in English—about African philosophy and
the "african personality." Julius Nyerere gave himself
the Swahili title of *mwalimu* or teacher and tried to reor-
ganize Tanzania's rural life along lines dictated by
ujamaa, an African sense of community. Joseph Mobutu
changed his name to Mobutu Sese Seko, changed his
country's name from the Congo to Zaire, and insisted
that his fellow countrymen also change their names to
"authentic" African forms and wear a cut of suit not in
the precise fashion of the Western world. Some of this
window-dressing no doubt represents a genuine effort to
get back to values, real or imagined, of Africa as it was
before the conquest, but the myth of the noble African
lurks there as well.

In fact, the living traditions of African culture do not
have to be recovered. They were never lost—modified to
make innovation possible, but not lost. This in the case in
the most modern-looking situation in such matters as
marriage customs, family affairs, treatment of children
and the way children are trained to treat adults. In the
villages, a whole body of custom lives on. It controls
relations between families, control over the land, and
worship of the gods (including the Christian/Muslim
god). Even in adapting some practices for modern life,
some possibilities feel "right" and others feel "wrong"
and are likely to be rejected.

This sense of "rightness" attaches less easily to the new
life of rural migrants in the slums that surround all African
cities. And it never attached very easily to the colonial
state. The post-colonial state inherited that weakness and

added new weakness on its own. The state is rarely perceived as an institution to which every person should owe his ultimate loyalty. It demands taxes and it gives back benefits like schools, roads, medical care (sometimes), and jobs. It is the focus of political life, but it is not the focus of a sentiment that could be called patriotism. Other institutions than the state are the first source of group loyalty. Even urban Africans tend to keep the foci of loyalty they had in the village—loyalty often based on age and kinship, secondly on common language and common standards of behavior. In the competition with others from other rural areas, the play of these loyalties can appear as "tribalism." When an individual acts for his group, in competition with other groups, it can look to outsiders like favoritism, if not corruption.

Yet neither the post-colonial state nor its colonial predecessor provided people with the kind of emotional support that might have been reciprocated by ultimate loyalty—by feelings the West represents with words like "patriotism." This is not to argue that patriotism is a "good thing," in all circumstances, but African loyalties, since independence as before, have gone in other directions. This has had an enormous influence on what the state can and cannot do. Of the various calls for traditional values, Mobutu's call for authenticity in Zaire is a clear case of trying to redirect older loyalties to the state. There is no evidence so far that it worked very well.

THE ECONOMICS OF INDEPENDENCE

One way to see present-day Africa in the world picture is to place Africa's economy in the world economy. Some of the major trends are clear. A quarter-century ago, the contrasts between the economically advanced and the less developed countries was sharp. Since then, India, Latin America, and the Caribbean have all prospered—not uniformly so, but enough countries have pulled ahead to erase the gulf between development and underdevelopment. In its place we have relative degrees of development with some Latin American countries, like Brazil and Mexico, moving toward industrialization. Other former Less Developed Countries (LDC's) in east and southeast Asia have risen to become Newly Industrialized Countries (NIC's)—Singapore, Korea, Hong Kong, and Taiwan. Still others have hardly moved, or have even become poorer.

A second major feature of this quarter-century was the "green revolution"—the new seeds and fertilizers that increased the productive capacity of the tropical world. India went from being a grain-deficit area to become a net exporter. Other parts of the tropical world, especially rice-producing areas, also profited. Africa, unfortunately, lacked the resource endowment in climate and soils to make the appropriation of these new techniques possible.

Finally, some underdeveloped countries were able to introduce government policies aimed at reducing the birth rate, so as to achieve decreasing death rates without enormous population increase. China had been a leader in this field. By the early 1980s, rates of population increase, at least, began to slow down in much of Latin America and in such heavily overpopulated countries as Indonesia.

But this did not happen in Africa. Instead, the economic growth rates for sub-Saharan Africa were the worst of any equivalent area in the world. But growth, or lack of it, was uneven within Africa. Data on gross national product (GNP) are notoriously untrustworthy for measuring differences between countries—they are more use for measuring change through time in a single country—but for poor countries during the past quarter-century, annual growth in GNP per capita of about 2.0 percent would represent a slow but satisfactory performance. In West Africa between 1960 and 1981, only Nigeria, Togo, Cameroon, Ivory Coast, and the Gambia met that standard. In Central Africa, only Burundi and Gabon did as well. In East Africa, only Kenya did. In southern Africa north of the Republic of South Africa, only Malawi; while off-shore, the Seychelles, Mauritius, and Réunion all met the standard and more.

Over these same decades, nine countries actually had negative growth rates. From worse to better they were Chad, Niger, Ghana, Uganda, Madagascar, Sudan, Senegal, Somalia, and Zaïre. Two-thirds of these countries are on the desert-edge just south of the Sahara. That was the zone that experienced the devastating drought of 1968-74, followed by the return of drought in 1977-78. The third episode in 1983-85 was more serious for Sudan and Ethiopia than it was in the west. These drought years alone were enough to turn moderate growth into decline, but Sudan and Chad experienced chronic civil war as well.

Even though general economic stagnation was bad enough, food production was still worse. Only the Ivory Coast produced as much food per capita in the early 1980s as it had done in 1960. Drought no doubt accounted for a part of this failing, but another part goes back to policies from the late colonial period. During the Second World War and sometimes a little earlier, the colonial powers all introduced economic controls that tended to detach the price paid to the producer from the world market. The original justification was either wartime necessity or the need to shield the producers from the wide fluctuations in world commodity prices.

In the British sphere, Marketing Boards had a monopoly on all important export commodities. The Boards collected the world price at the port, paid the farmers somewhat less, and held the balance—in theory against some future time when the world price might drop. In fact, no marketing board ever paid out a significant part of its funds to compensate for low world prices. Governments soon discovered that such funds were a convenient source of revenue for all kinds of economic development. All too often, this meant that the farmers were systematically underpaid for the sake of development projects, frequently not in the rural areas at all.

For food crops, it was also possible to pay farmers less than the free market price for food as a way of securing cheap food in the cities. This could be done by price controls, or even easier by rigging the value of the currency. Most of the formerly French territories stayed with a common currency based on the French franc, but most of the former British colonies established their own currencies. Once done, they could overvalue the currency, thus raising the international price of exports and lowering that of imports. This favored the urban consumers of imports at the expense of the farmers. When oil also entered the picture, as it did in Nigeria from 1974 onward, oil revenue could be used to pay for imported food, and the local farmers could no longer compete. This policy very nearly ruined the Nigerian agricultural sector.

By the early 1980s, however, economists and even governments came to understand that systematic underpayment of the agricultural sector had been a serious error. Pressure from the World Bank helped to push them toward a more realistic valuation of the currency and more equitable farm prices. By the mid-1980s, favorable consequences were already beginning to appear.

AFRICAN SOCIALISM

Whether or not they claim to be socialist, all sub-Saharan African countries exert substantial government control over, or government participation in, the economy. This can take the form of indirect measures like currency manipulation, but it almost always includes substantial government ownership and management of major industrial and commercial enterprises. Even in "capitalist" South Africa, the government owns and operates the important iron and steel industry.

Most African countries also claim to be socialist. Angola and Mozambique began their independent careers after 1976 trying to create a centrally planned economy on the model of Cuba or the Soviet Union. Neither succeeded, and both have moved to allow a greater play of market forces in the face of guerrilla movements and foreign invasion. Other countries, like the People's Republic of Benin in West Africa, claim to be Marxist-Leninist in inspiration, but actual policies are similar to those of other military dictatorships that make no such claim.

Tanzania followed another course it called "African Socialism." Under Julius Nyerere, the leader at independence, Tanzania set out to escape both the capitalism of the colonial economy and the Marxian model. Nyerere hoped to call up ancient African communal traditions of mutual self-help. Among other things, he nationalized the banks and some other foreign firms, and he tried to reduce the country's dependence in international trade. "Dependency theory," popular in the 1960s and 1970s, suggested that, for poor countries, foreign trade meant "unequal exchange" for the profit of the rich.

The center-piece of Nyerere's economic plan was the idea of communal villages, called *ujamaa* villages from the Swahili word for community. Since most Tanzanians had lived in small and scattered hamlets, the "villageization" program had a long- and a short-term aim. In the short run, it was designed to bring people together so they could better enjoy educational, medical, and social services, and where their farming could be regulated by government agents. In the longer run, it aimed at voluntary collectivization of agriculture with genuine communal farming.

The peasants, however, did not respond to the government appeal. In 1974, the movement of the peasantry into villages was enforced, no longer voluntary. The government created some 7,000 new villages, including some 13,500,000 people by the end of the 1970s. But the communal ideal tended to fade with time; peasants worked on their own account. Many observers at the end of the 1970s thought the program might well succeed. By the mid-1980s, few thought so. The attempt to avoid international trade simply did not work, and exchange controls and overvalued currency had the same consequences for agricultural productivity they had elsewhere in Africa.

Where Tanzania is used (too often) as an example of the failures of socialism, the Ivory Coast is used as an example of success for a "free market" system. The success was undoubted. The Ivory Coast maintained a growth rate of 7.2 percent per year over the whole period from 1960 to 1981. The United States did not do as well. But the Ivoirian system was not quite "economic liberalism" in our sense. The government maintained a set of marketing boards to syphon off some of the world price paid for its exports. In 1977, a boom year, small-holders received only about a quarter of the world price for their export crops. Marketing boards used the surplus to pay for as much as two-thirds of the public-sector investment at that time.

But the government nevertheless did encourage cocoa and coffee production, even though the producers were taxed for the sake of the rest of the economy. Prices paid the farmers were allowed to increase in line with inflation. The government made it easy to hire cheap foreign labor, and it guaranteed security of tenure to farmers producing for the market. The main beneficiaries were not the peasants, however, but the government officials and the urban middle class. The investment did lead to the creation of a significant industry in food processing, textiles, automobile assembly, and light manufacturing.

The Ivoirian system worked very well through the 1970s. Then, in the early 1980s, the growth rate dropped and in 1983 even turned negative. Part of the problem was economic recession and lowered demand in Europe and America; another part flowed from government political economic errors. The Ivoirian economists looked at the high export prices of 1975-79 and assumed they were there to stay. The government then borrowed heavily on that expectation, as the governments in Brazil and Mexico did at the same time. When the recession hit, all three had a hard time meeting debt service and repayment schedules.

POLITICAL ORDER AND DISORDER

Many of Africa's economic shortcomings after independence can be traced directly or indirectly to political conditions. These conditions, in turn, depend in large measure on underlying culture and on the history of the colonial period. To say that the colonial powers failed to prepare Africa for independence is to state the obvious. But it is important to remember that they did not intend Africa to become independent in the 1960s. Even the most enlightened administrators of the 1930s would hardly have expected independence before the end of the century; most would have put it later still; and some would have said "never." Independence was a surprise, even when it came peacefully. Even two decades of conscious preparation might well have brought quite different results, but the colonial powers were not allowed that much time.

The lack of preparation shows in a number of important ways. On the British side, the long-term colonial policy for tropical Africa called for Indirect Rule, rule through the chiefs. In the event, the organized groups that demanded an end to European rule demanded an end to chiefly rule as well. Some of the bloodiest struggles during and after decolonization were on precisely this issue. The anti-Arab revolt on Zanzibar and the peasant risings in Rwanda and Burundi come immediately to mind, though they were not alone. The people the British had been grooming to take over— though in the far more distant future—were not, therefore, the ones who actually came to power.

In addition, neither France, Belgium, nor Britain, made a serious effort to prepare Africa for electoral democracy. For the French colonies, the Senegalese communes had a long electoral experience, but the new electoral freedom under the Framework Law brought only one election before independence was declared. For the Belgian Congo, the only national election was the one that led directly to independence. In the British sphere, what electoral politics had existed was limited to the old port towns and a very limited electorate. In tropical Africa generally, some politicians had secured electoral victories before independence, but virtually no one had left office even after an electoral defeat. Politicians were therefore loath to leave office, suspecting (quite correctly) that their successors would never give them another chance.

A third source of non-preparation for independence was the colonial treatment of the military. The conquest of Africa had been carried out largely by African troops under European officers. Africans had fought in two world wars, but almost no public attention was paid to the place of the military under the newly independent governments. It was as though the colonial administrators and the rising African politicians shared a belief that the armies would behave under their new officers just as they had under the old.

The colonial powers made the military problem more serious by the way they recruited their armies. Both the French and British had a theory that certain peoples, whom the British called "martial races" were better soldiers than other colonial people. The so-called martial races tended to be people away from the core area of any colony, often from its poorest sections. These were, after all, the places where soldiers could be recruited for little pay. Sometimes, as with Gurkhas from Nepal, the British even recruited their armies from outside the empire. In East Africa, some of the earliest British forces were from the Sudan, recruited there by purchase well before the British had conquered the Sudan. Later on, in Ghana, Nigeria, and Uganda, the recruits (though not necessarily the local officers) were drawn from the comparatively impoverished northern territories. The importance in the longer run was that such soldiers tended to have ties to others from their home districts, to their fellow soldiers, and to their officers at times, but rarely to the civilians or the people of the core area of the colonial state.

At independence, the initial forms of government were universally democratic, and, almost as universally, they did not stay that way. One of the first steps was to shift power to a strong president, replacing as chief executive officer the prime minister responsible to a parliamentary body. Ghana became independent in 1957. By 1960, President Kwame Nkrumah secured a new constitution which gave the president the right to veto any legislation, to pass laws without calling on parliament for approval, and to control the budget. A common second step was to set up a one-party state. In Ghana in 1964, Nkrumah made his Convention People's Party the sole legal party. In theory, important decisions would be reached by democratic means, but within the single party, not outside it. In 1966, Ghana reached a fourth stage: the military seized control of the country while Nkrumah was overseas. Supreme power then passed to a group of officers that called itself the National Liberation Council.

These stages—from the Westminster model, to a powerful presidency, to a one-party state, to a military dictatorship—were not universal, but they were common enough to represent a process. Some stopped short at the stage of one-party state. Several one-party states were remarkably stable, and some of their leaders remained in office from independence into the 1980s—Kenneth

Kaunda in Zambia, Sékou Touré in Guinea-Conakry, Félix Houphouët Boigny in the Ivory Coast, or Julius Nyerere in Tanzania. In other cases, the party went on in power, though the leader may have died, like Jomo Kenyatta of Kenya in 1978, or resigned, like Léopold Senghor of Senegal in 1980.

The more usual pattern, however, was to move on to military dictatorship. That political form was dominant in sub-Saharan Africa in the mid-1980s. Of the 45 states in Africa and the off-shore islands, more than half were under military rule, though the nature of the military control varied considerably. Ghana and Uganda have become what are sometimes called "praetorian" states — after the military units that determined who ruled in ancient Rome. Governments changed, but only when one military group overthrew its military predecessors. Other military regimes called themselves socialist with more or less Marxist-Leninist trappings, like Madagascar, Benin, and the Congo Republic. Others had built an originally-military source of power into something that resembled a one-party, non-parliamentary state, like Mobutu Sese Seko's Zaïre. Others regarded themselves as interim regimes, ready to pass control over to a new civilian government when circumstances warranted — like Nigeria.

One final category of government went well beyond the usual rules of military take-over. In the late 1960s and into the 1970s, Africa had a few governments whose record for tyranny was among the worst in the post-war world — though less cruel than that of either Stalin's Soviet Union or Hitler's National Socialist Germany. These were Equatorial Guinea under Macias Nguema from 1968; Jean Bedel Bokassa of the Central Africa Republic from 1965, which he renamed the Central

African Empire; and Idi Amin in Uganda from 1971. This phase has apparently passed for tropical Africa. These three worst tyrants were all deposed in 1978, leaving only South Africa as the most systematically repressive government in sub-Saharan Africa.

The most tragic of the three was Uganda, if only because the country had a record of rapid modernization and great expectations at the time of independence. Part of the background was a conflict between the previously dominant Ganda people near the capital, and their neighbors. Milton Obote became the first President, mainly with non-Ganda support. He was not generally popular, and he quickly suspended the constitution and created a one-party state. His lack of support made it all the easier for the army to revolt under Idi Amin, whose followers were mainly badly-educated soldiers from the poverty-stricken north. Most were Muslim, though the majority of Uganda was Christian. They set out to rule Uganda like a conquered country, being credited with killing more than 100,000 people before they were driven from power by a Tanzanian invasion in 1978. But the fall of the tyrant was only the beginning of a process of rebuilding a stable and prosperous country.

FRONTIERS AND SECESSIONS

At the time of independence, many people expected old, "tribal" loyalties to re-emerge and to dominate African international affairs as one "tribe" after another tried to bring all its members within a single state. In fact, no such thing happened. Africans created an international organization, the Organization for African Unity (OAU), on the model of the Pan American Union. It has not been very effective in advancing Pan-African claims or in forging a genuine African unity; but it has helped to arbitrate certain international differences within Africa, and it served as a regional body within the broader framework of the United Nations.

The newly independent states did stand firm, however, on one issue—international boundaries. The OAU declared that, however accidentally boundaries may have been set, they should stand as they were. For the most part, African leadership has accepted this position. The only important international wars over frontier issues were Somalia's attempt to conquer the Ethiopian province of Ogaden in 1977-78 and Libya's apparent attempt to annex part of northern Chad in the mid-1980s.

Secession movements were another matter. The past quarter-century has seen four different and sustained efforts by one part of an ex-colony to break away. The first of these was a rather ephemeral attempt by the Belgians to organize the secession of Katanga province (now Shaba) from the ex-Belgian Congo in 1960-63. It ended with UN intervention on the side of Congo.

A far longer lasting struggle involved the effort of the former Italian colony of Eritrea to break away from Ethiopia. Culturally, Eritrea had more in common with the dominant Amhara of Ethiopia than most other parts of the Ethiopian empire had, but the Eritreans resented Amharic rule and wanted self-determination for the unit created by Italian imperialism less than a century earlier. Guerrilla resistance began in the 1970s and was still active at the time of writing in 1987.

The long civil war in the southern Sudan is still another long-standing, "non-tribal" struggle. When the British took over the old Egyptian secondary empire, it included the Muslim northern Sudan just to the south of the desert, plus the non-Islamic far south. There, the British had brought missionary education in English, not Arabic. The result was a linguistic and religious split, added to animosities that went back to the northerners' pre-colonial slave raids into the south. Even after independence, the south was comparatively poor and backward and regarded itself as oppressed by the mainly-Muslim government in Khartoum. The first guerrilla war broke out in 1962 and ended in 1972 with a truce granting a measure of local autonomy; but the truce did not last and the south went into rebellion again in the early 1980s in a new war that had not yet ended in 1987.

The Nigeria civil war of 1967-1970 came closer to the European pattern of a war for "national" independence. It began in southeastern Nigeria, where the Igbo-speaking people had a poor and overpopulated home-land. Igbo-speakers were unusually quick, however, to take advantage of missionary education, which made it possible for them to emigrate to cities all over Nigeria looking for work or business opportunities. By the 1960s, more than a million Igbo-speakers were scattered through other parts of Nigeria, where they were known as Ibo. Other Nigerians disliked Ibo pushiness and envied Ibo success.

In Northern Nigeria in 1966, anti-Ibo sentiment turned to violence following a military coup led by Ibo army officers against a civilian government dominated by northern Muslims. Riotous crowds roamed the strangers' quarters of northern cities, beating or killing whatever Ibos they could find. Estimates of the dead run from 5 to 30 thousand. Many Ibo emigrants to other parts of Nigeria fled back to Iboland. In 1967, the Igbo-speaking region declared its independence as Biafra, setting off a civil war that lasted to 1970. The federal government won — and the victors went out of their way to welcome the defeated Biafrans back into the Nigerian federation. Ibos gradually worked their way back into government posts and into businesses, and they enjoyed more security after the war than they had before the riots.

So far, no movement of this kind has succeeded in upsetting the permanence of the "independence" boundaries, though these wars and other sources of instability have bred an enormous flow of refugees from the fighting. Over the decade of the 1970s alone, the estimated number of political refugees in Africa rose from about 750,000 to five million—becoming about half the world total of refugees. It is still too early to know whether or not these politically motivated population movements will join the economically motivated movements to create a new distribution of people, or whether the refugees will drift back home as opportunity permits.

EPILOGUE

To return to the alternation of optimism and pessimism about Africa, outlined at the beginning of this chapter, we must admit that our unguarded optimism of the 1960s was mistaken, even though it had been based on the undeniable trends of the recent past. Although the trends of the past quarter-century give little room for optimism today, those of the past five years promise more hope. The economy appears to be improving in scattered places, like Zimbabwe and the Ivory Coast. Policies that did the most to discourage food production are being reversed. Democracy has shown no tendency to return, but the worst of the tyrannies have been ended.

A number of "if's" remain. The biggest is the continuing crisis in South Africa and the possible role of the powers. The United States in the Reagan years followed a barely-disguised policy in support of white supremacy. American foreign policy threatens to polarize southern African issues in terms of a "cold-war" rivalry between the super-powers. If disaster from this source can be averted, the problem remains of persuading the white South Africans to give up their monopoly of political power.

Yet we remain convinced that the underlying resilience of African culture will help African societies to pull still further out of the two-decade post-independence crisis. The open question is how much more culture change is possible or desirable?

African leadership today is unanimous in wanting to "modernize," and whatever else is included in modernization, this means creating a society that is capable of high per capita productivity and consumption. The question is no longer whether modernization is possible or desirable, but how to implement it. Modernization is impossible without culture change. How can it be achieved without destroying the values of African life? Many advantages flowed from the security of the extended-family household, but in many parts of Africa the monogamous family is becoming more and more prevalent—the nuclear family of parents and children, living in an isolated household, takes precedence over the old network of strong ties to more distant kin. Some Africans see the change as undesirable but inevitable. Others want to keep the vital kinship systems that have played such an important part in avoiding the cold isolation they see in Western family life. Similar conflicts of values and choices between cultural forms are found at every level of African life today, affecting the economy, religion, child rearing, and formal education. Africans will meet these problems, not at the political level of decision-making, but in millions of discrete adjustments to a changing world. While some specific forms of society and culture will be laid aside, other forms will grow out of them. This is why the cultural patterns of recent Africa and the historical patterns of the African past are a necessary introduction to the Africa of today and tomorrow. People must and will make choices—and necessarily make them on the basis of the historical experience and all the culture available to them, whatever its origin.

FURTHER READING

A FLOOD OF NEW WRITING ABOUT AFRICA HAS appeared in the past thirty years. The vast majority of the best work on Africa has, indeed, appeared since the first edition of this work came out in 1964. The books and articles listed below are little more than a sample of where to begin on particular topics.

Bibliographies

Hector Blackhurst, (ed.), *Africa Bibliography 1984* (Manchester: Manchester University Press, 1985) is the first volume of a recent annual series which replaces an earlier annual series published by the International African Institute in London. More up-to-date references can be found in the principal periodicals listed below, and in the bibliographies of recent books on several of these topics.

Bibliographical Guidance

In the early 1980s, the Social Science Research Council/ American Council of Learned Societies, Joint-Committee on African Studies supported a series of reviews of the literature in various fields of African Studies. These were presented at the African Studies Association meetings and later published in *African*

Studies Review (cited hereafter as ASR). The articles not only listed recent work in their particular fields, they also discussed the development of knowledge in these fields in recent decades. They are listed below under the appropriate subject headings. Each is marked JCAS to indicate its sponsorship.

Periodicals

Newswatch and *African Development* are news magazines dealing with Africa, following the same general format as *Time* or *Newsweek*. *The Economist* (London) also prints an American edition, and it has good coverage of African news. *The Journal of Modern African Studies* (Cambridge Press) is somewhat more technical and covers the special fields of international relations, political science, and economics. *Cahiers d'etudes africaines* (Paris) is also multidisciplinary, dealing with literature, politics, anthropology, and history. It is published in both English and French. *Africa,* published by the International Africa Institute in London is more concerned with social anthropology, including linguistics. *African Studies* (London) is somewhat broader and published a good deal on history. The principal historical journals, however, are *Journal of African History* (Cambridge Press) and *International Journal of African Historical Studies* (Boston). For archaeological developments, the relevant journal is *African Archaeological Review.*

General Books

The best of the recent general books on all aspects of African studies is Phyllis M. Martin and Patrick O'Meara, *Africa* (Bloomington: Indiana University

Press, 1977), with a new edition expected. In addition, two recent atlases are far more than collections of maps. These are Jocelyn Murray, *Cultural Atlas of Africa* (New York: Facts on File, 1982) and J.F. Ade Ajayi and Michael Crowder (eds.), *Historical Atlas of Africa* (Cambridge: Cambridge Press, 1985).

Specialized Books

GEOGRAPHY

William A. Hance, *The Geography of Modern Africa,* 2nd ed. (New York: Columbia Press, 1975) is a useful summary for the entire continent. A regional geography of prime quality is R.J. Harrison Church, *West Africa,* 7th ed. (London: Longmans, 1974), while David Dalby, R.J. Harrison Church, and Fatima Bezzazz (eds.), *Drought in Africa* (London: IAI, 1975) is a useful collection of articles on the causes and consequences of the sahelian droughts.

PREHISTORY

For the earliest evidence of man in Africa see Toth, Nicholas, and Kathy D. Schick, "The First Million Years: The Archaeology of Protohuman Culture," *Advances in Archaeological Method and Theory,* 9:1-96 (1986) and John W.K. Harris, "Cultural Beginnings: Plio-Pleistocene Archaeological Occurrences from the Afar, Ethiopia," *African Archaeological Review, 1:3-31* (1983).

David Phillipson, *African Archaeology* (Cambridge: Cambridge Press, 1985) is the most recent general survey of the later archaeology of Africa. J. Desmond Clark, and Sven A. Brandt (eds.), *From Hunters to Farmers* (Berkeley and London, Cal Press, 1984), is an important collection of recent papers on the transition to agriculture, while Christopher Ehret and Merrick Posnansky (eds.), *The Archaeological and Linguistic Reconstruction of African History* (Berkeley: University of California Press, 1982) correlate linguistic with archaeological evidence.

GENERAL HISTORY

Two recent landmarks in the historiography of Africa are the eight-volume sets dealing with African history from the beginning to the post-colonial world. These are *The Cambridge History of Africa,* 8 vols. (Cambridge: Cambridge Press, completed in 1986) and UNESCO, *General History of Africa,* 8 vols. (Paris: UNESCO, to be completed by 1989). The Cambridge volume is principally the work of British historians of Africa, while each of the UNESCO volumes is edited by an African scholar, though the contributors are drawn from the international community of Africanists.

In briefer form, Philip D. Curtin, Steven Feierman, Leonard Thompson, and Jan Vansina, *African History* (London, Longmans, 1978) deals with the history of the whole continent in a single volume. It's treatment of the colonial period, however, is shorter than desirable, and it has little to say about the post-colonial. Here it should be supplemented by David K. Fieldhouse, *Black Africa 1945-80: Economic Decolonization & Arrested Development* (London: Allen & Unwin, 1986), which has an economic slant, or by Ali A. Mazuri and Michael Tidy, *Nationalism and New States in Africa* (London: Heinemann, 1984), which has a political slant. For the colonial period, Adu Boahen, *African Perspectives on Colonialism* (Baltimore: Johns Hopkins University Press, 1987) is the reflections of one African historian on the period. Lewis H. Gann and Peter Duignan (eds.),

Colonialism in Africa, 1870-1960, 5 vols. (Cambridge: Cambridge Press, 1969-75) is a series under different editors for various aspects of the history of the times.

At the regional level of synthesis, each major region has had a multi-volume work of synthesis devoted to it. In some respects, these have been superceded by the UNESCO and Cambridge histories, but David Birmingham and Phyllis M. Martin, *History of Central Africa,* 2 vols. (London: Longman, 1983) is recent and of unusually high quality. Central Africa in this case means the whole region from Chad on the north, southward through Zaïre and Angola and east to Mozambique on the Indian Ocean. J.F. Ade Ajayi and Michael Crowder, *History of West Africa,* 2 vols, (London: Longman, 1971-76, third edition of volume 1, 1985). This edition does much the same kind of job for West Africa and the first volume has been recently revised.

For South Africa, the recent crisis has encouraged a stream of books, many of high quality. Perhaps the best recent treatment by a journalist is Joseph Lelyveld, *Move Your Shadow: South Africa, Black and White* (New York: Viking Penguin, 1985). For more distant background, Leonard Thompson, *The Political Mythology of Apartheid* (New Haven: Yale Press, 1985) traces the justification for the doctrine. For a broader framework of social history see the individual contributions to Shula Marks and Anthony Atmore (eds.) *Economy and Society of Pre-Industrial South Africa* (London: Longman, 1980) and Shula Marks and Richard Rathbone (eds.), *Industrialization and Social Change in South Africa: African Class Formation, Culture, and Consciousness 1870-1930* (London: Longman, 1982).

On particular themes, Paul H. Lovejoy, *Transforma-*

tions in Slavery: A History of Slavery in Africa (Cambridge: Cambridge Press, 1983) deals with both slavery and the slave trade. Many different books deal with the histories of individual countries. Of these, John Iliffe, *A Modern History of Tanganyika* (Cambridge: Cambridge Press, 1979) is especially recommended.

POLITY

Two classic accounts of "traditional" African policy are Meyer Fortes and E.E. Evans-Pritchard, *African Political Systems* (London: Oxford Press, 1940) and John Middleton and David Tait, *Tribes Without Rulers* (London: Routledge and Kegan Paul, 1958). For more recent studies of the interaction of culture and politics, see Crawford Young, *The Politics of Cultural Pluralism* (Madison: Wisconsin Press, 1976) and Igor Kopytoff (ed.), *The African Frontier: The Reproduction of Traditional African Societies* (Bloomington: Indiana University Press, 1987).

For a survey of contemporary politics see Gwendolen Carter and Patrick O'Meara (eds.), *African Independence: The First Twenty-Five Years* (Bloomington: Indiana University Press, 1985). John Lonsdale has written a perceptive survey of the post-colonial African state in "States and Social Processes in Africa," ASR, 24:139-226 (1981), JCAS.

For political instability and military regimes, several works are available, but one of the most recent and comprehensive is Staffan Wilking, *Military Coups in Sub-Saharan Africa: How to Justify Illegal Assumptions of Power* (Uppsala: Scandanavian Institute of African Studies, 1983).

For recent international relations see Peter

Calvocoressi, *Independent Africa and the World* (London: Longman, 1985).

ECONOMY

For the pre-colonial economy some of the older works are again useful. See, in particular, S.F. Nadel, *A Black Byzantium* (London: Oxford Press, 1942) and Paul and Laura Bohannan, *Tiv Economy* (Evanston, Illinois: Northwestern University Press, 1968). Among more recent theoretical works see Claude Meillassoux, *Maidens, Meal, and Money: Capitalism and the Domestic Community* (Cambridge: Cambridge Press, 1981). Sara S. Berry, *Fathers Work for their Sons: Accumulation, Mobility, and Class Formation in an Extended Yoruba Community* (Berkeley: University of California Press, 1985) is an exemplary study of the ways in which present material life responds to the on-going traditions of an African society. See also her "The Food Crisis and Agrarian Charge in Africa: A Review Essay," ASR, 27:59-112 (1984), JCAS, along with Frederick Cooper, "Africa in the World Economy," ARS, 24:1-86 (1981), JCAS.

For recent problems, see The World Bank, *Accelerated Development in Sub-Saharan Africa: An Agenda for Action* (Washington: World Bank, 1981); Paul Richards, "Ecological Change and Politics in African Land Use," ASR, 26:10-72 (1983), JCAS.

And for particular themes see Francis Wilson, *Labour in the South African Gold Mines 1911-1960* (Cambridge: Cambridge Press, 1972), John Iliffe, *The Emergence of African Capitalism* (London: Macmillan, 1983), and Bill Freund, "Labor and Labor History in Africa," ASR, 27:1-58 (1984), JCAS.

DISEASE

For the role of disease in Africa, Gerald W. Hartwig and K. Davis Patterson, *Disease in African History* (Durham, North Carolina: Duke University Press, 1978) is a good introduction. For traditional African medical practices, John M. Janzen, *The Quest for Therapy: Medical Pluralism in Lower Zaire* (Berkeley: University of California Press, 1978) is an excellent introduction to African medical practices in a single region. Feierman, Steven, "Struggles for the Control of Disease in Africa," ASR, 218:73-148 (1985), JCAS, surveys the development of the field.

WOMEN IN AFRICA

The growth of women's studies in recent decades has brought a flood of new publications. Kenneth L. Little, *African Women in Towns: An Aspect of Africa's Social Revolution* (Cambridge: Cambridge Press, 1973) and Edna G. Bay and Nancy J. Hafkin (eds.), *Women in Africa: Studies in Social and Economic Change* (Stanford: Stanford University Press, 1976) can serve as samples.

Jane I. Guyer, "Household and Community in African Studies," ASR, 24:87-138 (1981), JCAS, surveys a slightly broader field that includes women's studies.

ART

Many attractive books deal with African art. Frank Willett, *African Art* (London: Thames and Huston, 1960) is especially valuable because Willett is both art historian and anthropologist; his book contains a well-chosen selection of plates, good descriptions of techniques, a thorough and interesting review of the literature from the 1860s through the 1960s. Among the older picture books, William Fagg and Eliot Elisofon, *The Sculpture of Africa* (New York: Praeger, 1958) is a beautiful match between the art historian and the photographer.

Jan Vansina, *Art History in Africa* (London: Longman, 1984) is quite a different approach, concerned not simply with styles and style changes and aesthetic factors, but even more with the way art interacts with society, history, and other aspects of culture.

LANGUAGE

The accepted language classification for Africa is Joseph H. Greenberg, *The Languages of Africa,* 3rd ed. (Bloomington: Indiana University Research Center, 1970). For social aspects of language use and literacy see also John R. Goody (ed.), *Literacy in Traditional Societies* (Cambridge: Cambridge Press, 1968) and Joseph A. Greenberg, *Language, Culture, and Communication* (Stanford: Stanford University Press, 1971).

African literature in English is now represented by a wide variety of works by different authors from the plays of Wole Soyinka to the novels of Amos Tutuola and Nadine Gordimer.

Harold Scheub, "A Review of African Oral Traditions and Literature," ASR, 28:1: 1-72 (1985) is the relevant JCAS-sponsored survey of oral literature.

RELIGION AND PHILOSOPHY

E. Bolaji Idowu, *African Traditional Religions: A Definition* (Maryknoll, Orbis Books, 1973) and John S. Mbiti, *African Religions and Philosophy* (New York: Praeger, 1970) provide an introduction to African traditional religion. Terrence O. Ranger and Isaria Kimambo (eds.), *The Historical Study of African Religion* (Berkeley: University of California Press, 1972) deals with some of the historical problems. The JCAS sponsored three separate studies in this increasingly important field of knowledge. They are: Wyatt MacGaffey, "African Ideology and Belief," ASR, 24:227-274 (1981); V.Y. Mudimbe, "African Gnosis: Philosophy and Orders of Knowledge," ASR, 28:149-223 (1985); and Terrence O. Ranger, "Religious Movements and Politics in Sub-Saharan Africa," ASR, 29:1-69 (1986).

INDEX

technological development of
Western Europe influenced
by, 260-61; as a vehicle for
religious change under
Christian conquest, 371
Islamic empires, 323-27; West
African history influenced
by, 327
Issa. *See* Djibouti
Ivory Coast, 31, 104; Atutu artists
of, 105-106; economic problems since independence,
391-92; increase in gross national product since independence, 388
Ivory sculpture, 93

Jaga, 278, 281
Jihads: called for by Islam, 319;
Fulbe as leaders of, 320, 322-
23, 324-27; in the nineteenth
century, 323-27

Kadalie, Clements, 374-75
Kalahari Desert, 21, 23, 24
Kanem: conversion to Islam, 258
Katsina, 324
Kaunda, Kenneth, 396
Kenya: increase in gross national
product since independence,
388; Swahili as official lan-
guage, 73; uneven population
distribution in, 62
Kenyatta, Jomo, 396
Khoikhoi people, 49; decimated
by European diseases, 305-
306; mixing with whites and
slaves to produce "Cape
colored," 306; protected by
British administrators, 307
Khoisan languages, 70, 71; and
physical appearance, 71
Khoisan people, 49; first appearance of, 222
Kikuyu, 13
Kilwa: dominating east coast
trade, 280
Kingship: as a sacred office, 153;
nature of, 151; rotating, 151

Kinship groups: becoming legal
entities, 135-38; as production units, 140
Kinship relationships: as basis for
stateless societies, 150; descent and sex based, 112; determining behavior, 125;
roles within, 112-13, 115;
types of, 112. *See also* Lineage systems; Non-familial
kinship groups
Klemm, Gustav, 59
Knox, Robert, 59
Kongo, kingdom of, 369; basic
political unit in, 271; Jaga invasion of, 281; Portuguese
in, 277-78
Kuba state court system, 164
Kush, Kingdom of, 248

Labor: European views of Africans as, 142; forced migration of, 143-44; low wages
for Africans, 142, 144; oscillating, 143-145; rarely offered in traditional African
markets, 173-74; stabilized,
142; traditional forms of,
139-40
Labor migration, 74, 75; consequences of, 363-64; forced,
143
Lake Chad, 21
Land: African perceptions of,
129-38; association with society, 131-32; communal ownership of, 134-135, 137-138;
rarely offered in traditional
African markets, 171, 173-
74; rights to farm, 133-34,
136; social maps of, 131-34;
Western style mapping of,
130-31. *See also* Community
lands
Land systems and property systems, 134-38
Land usage: and lineage grouping, 132-33; Western and
African approaches to, 134

Social organization: connected to space by community lands, 131-32; tied to territorial grouping of lineages, 132-33

Soils in Africa: alluvial, 28; humus deficiency in, 26-27; minerals leaching from, 27, 29; shifting cultivation used to farm, 27-28

Somali peoples: sense of nationality of, 369

Somalia: attempt to conquer Ogaden, 398; negative growth rate in, since independence, 388; political changes in, 15; variable rainfall in, 26

Songhai: controlling desert trade, 266; declining power of, 278-79

Soninke: drought affecting, 267; trade diasporas, 175; as traders, 268

Soninke culture, 248

Sotho people, 304

South Africa, 49; *apartheid* policy in, 145, 354, 379; Caucasians in, 49; ceasing to be a secondary empire, 343; continuing crisis in, 400-401; copper production, 33; as dominant force in southern Africa, 343; economic growth in, 363; forced migratory labor in, 143-44; gold fields, 360-61; gold production from, 32; Indians in, 50; Khoisan people in, 49; Lands Act of 1912, 143; mass organization and peaceful protest, 374-75; military force used by, 379-80; Namibian independence refused by, 379; Native Reserves in, 143-44; orientals in, 50; Soweto riots, 379; trade unions in, 374-75; white minority control continuing, 365; whites supported by American policy, 401

Southeast Asia: independence movements in, 375-76

Southern savanna: history of, 268-72, 277-82

Southwest Africa. *See* Namibia

Soyinka, Wole, 72, 91

Spanish Guinea. *See* Equatorial Guinea

Spengler, 57

Spice trade, 279

Stabilized labor, 142

State: concept of, 148-49; 150-51; as focus of political life, 386

State formation, 248-49

State-building periods in African history, 269, 271-72

Stateless societies, 149-50; agricultural economy more advanced in, 267-68; authority and power in, 158; bands as a form of, 155, 156; bureaucracy absent in, 158; European reaction to, 158-60; extended family as, 155, 156; forms of, 155-58; law in, 162-65; lineage system as basis of, 155-58; lineage systems providing control of conflict, 156-58; posing military problem for Europeans, 344; self-help used in settlement of disputes in, 166-67

States: formation of, on desert-savanna frontier, 249; groupings within, 151-52; in preconquest Africa, 151-54; role of secret societies within, 152. *See also* African kingdoms

States and stateless societies: coexisting in African history, 267-68

Stone age cultures in Africa, 218-21

Subsistence activity: and working habits, 76, 81, 82

Subsistence areas, 76-83; correlating with other aspects of culture, 76; correspondence with cultural patterns, 76